'*Warrior Guards the Mountain* is a wonderf
become a classic reference for anyone inter
practices of any of the internal martial tra
does it cast a wide net, it brings back some very big fish. Another thing
that impressed me about this book was the consistent focus in the
lives of these masters and their traditions on the importance of the
spiritual core around which everything turns. This book is a rare and
hard-won gift that I would recommend to anyone travelling the path
that has no name.'

– *Red Pine/Bill Porter, author of* Road to Heaven –
Encounters with Chinese Hermits *and* Zen Baggage

'This book is very interesting. It presents the subject of martial arts,
Kungfu, Taiji, Qigong and Silat in a very accessible way, which, even if
one is not a martial artist, like myself, makes the subject very interesting
and simple. The descriptions by Alex, of his own experiences, and
those of his teachers, make fascinating reading, and made me feel some
regret that I had not spent a number of years of my life studying and
practising the arts. I did study meditation and yoga for some time, but
I am, however, a musician, and spend a large part of my life practising
and performing my art, treating my music as a form of meditation, and
hope that I am able to spread a little peace, love, health and harmony
amongst people in a similar way to that which Alex does with his art.
I have always felt that the arts of Kungfu, Taiji and Qigong and Silat
are very peaceful, creative, spiritual forms, and have a lot in common
with all creative arts, music, dance, poetry, painting, sculpture, and
all forms of creative expression; things connected with the soul, and
transmission of the emotion, imagination and communication. Alex
brings it all into focus. It's a great read, I highly recommend it.'

– *Nik Turner, singer/songwriter and founder member of groups*
Hawkwind, Sphynx *and* Inner City Unit, *among many others*

Alex Kozma began his training in a traditional family system of Chinese martial arts at the age of thirteen, and has devoted his life to the practice and study of the martial, meditative and healing aspects of the Eastern arts. He spent eight years practising in Asia under Master Chen Yuen San (Taijiquan), Master He Jing Han (Baguaquan) and other experts. In 1997 he qualified as a teacher of the Neijia arts under his teacher, Daoist Master Serge Augier. For many years he has studied traditional Oriental medicine as a private student of Master Eiichi Tanaka (inheritor of the Daiwa ryu healing system of Shitennogi Temple) and Master Paul Whitrod (Chow Gar family system). Alex now runs a healing clinic in Cambridge, UK, and continues his daily practice and study.

of related interest

Daoist Nei Gong
The Philosophical Art of Change
Damo Mitchell
Foreword by Dr Cindy Engel
ISBN 978 1 84819 065 8
eISBN 978 0 85701 033 9

Bagua Quan Foundation Training
He Jinghan
Translated by David Alexander
ISBN 978 1 84819 015 3
eISBN 978 0 85701 004 9

Bagua Daoyin
A Unique Branch of Daoist Learning, A Secret Skill of the Palace
He Jinghan
Translated by David Alexander
ISBN 978 1 84819 009 2
eISBN 978 1 84642 820 3

Seeking the Spirit of The Book of Change
8 Days to Mastering a Shamanic Yijing (I Ching) Prediction System
Master Zhongxian Wu
Foreword by Daniel Reid
ISBN 978 1 84819 020 7
eISBN 978 0 85701 007 0

Chinese Shamanic Cosmic Orbit Qigong
Esoteric Talismans, Mantras, and Mudras in Healing and Inner Cultivation
Master Zhongxian Wu
ISBN 978 1 84819 056 6
eISBN 978 0 85701 059 9

Creativity and Taoism
A Study of Chinese Philosophy, Art and Poetry
Chung-yuan Chang
ISBN 978 1 84819 050 4
eISBN 978 0 85701 047 6

Warrior Guards the Mountain

The Internal Martial Traditions of China,
Japan and South East Asia

ALEX KOZMA

SINGING
DRAGON

LONDON AND PHILADELPHIA

This edition published in 2013
by Singing Dragon
an imprint of Jessica Kingsley Publishers
116 Pentonville Road
London N1 9JB, UK
and
400 Market Street, Suite 400
Philadelphia, PA 19106, USA

www.singingdragon.com

First published in 2011 by Line of Intent, Inc. Publishing

Copyright © Alex Kozma 2011, 2013

Front cover image depicts Serge Augier practising Ziranmen. Photograph © Alex Kozma.

All rights reserved. No part of this publication may be reproduced in any material form
(including photocopying or storing it in any medium by electronic means and whether or
not transiently or incidentally to some other use of this publication) without the written
permission of the copyright owner except in accordance with the provisions of the
Copyright, Designs and Patents Act 1988 or under the terms of a licence issued by the
Copyright Licensing Agency Ltd, Saffron House, 6–10 Kirby Street, London EC1N 8TS.
Applications for the copyright owner's written permission to reproduce any part of this
publication should be addressed to the publisher.

Warning: The doing of an unauthorised act in relation to a copyright work may result in
both a civil claim for damages and criminal prosecution.

Library of Congress Cataloging in Publication Data
Kozma, Alex.
  Warrior guards the mountain : the internal martial traditions of China, Japan, and South
East Asia / Alex
Kozma.
    p. cm.
  ISBN 978-1-84819-124-2 (alk. paper)
  1. Martial arts--Philosophy. 2. Martial arts--Religious aspects. 3. Martial arts--China. 4.
Martial arts--
Japan. 5. Martial arts--Southeast Asia. I. Title.
  GV1101.K69 2013
  796.815--dc23
                            2012028859

British Library Cataloguing in Publication Data
A CIP catalogue record for this book is available from the British Library

ISBN 978 1 84819 124 2
eISBN 978 0 85701 101 5

Printed and bound in Great Britain

This book is dedicated
to all the masters
who pass on the flame
of the old traditions.

Caution

Do not attempt any of the training or practices described herein without a qualified teacher present.

Contents

The Martial Traditions of Japan

The Martial Traditions of India and South East Asia

Acknowledgements

Many individuals contributed to make this book, and my heartfelt appreciation for all the time and generosity goes to all of you. Sitting through long interviews and countless discussions, answering questions and sharing photos and memories, you all made this book what it is – Dr Serge Augier of Paris, Master Paul Whitrod of London, Grandmaster Cheong Cheng Leong of Penang, Master He Jinghan of Taipei, Drdha Shivanath of Wales, Gordon Tso of Hong Kong, Lindsey Wei and Li Shi Fu of Wudang Shan, Kruu Pedro Villalobos of Thailand, Rudy Ibarra and Lu Yaoqin of southern China, Shihan Tanaka in England, John Evans Sensei of London, Pendekar Steve Benitez and Laarni Benitez of Kefalonia, Greece, Master Gerry Tan of London, Guru Simon Das of England, Pak Muhammad Ariffin of Java and England, Professor Ji Jien Cheng of Hangzhou University.

Special thanks to my friend John Walker for generously sharing background information on the 1928 tournament, Mike Kaniewski for being a sincere student and friend whose generosity has given me space to write my books, Jon Wall for sharing much about the Wudang tradition, Jan for taking Shihan Tanaka pictures.

A deep bow of thanks to everyone who helped as attackers in the photos – with Serge Augier were his students Mark Baker, Yusuf, Bevan, Darren and Philipe, and assisting Sifu Gerry Tan was Jose.

My love and thanks to my family for helping me through a period of ill health while writing this book – to my mother who showed great courage and is always there through it all, to my sister

Helena for kindness and to my brother Arjuna Das for always being there when most needed.

Also a sincere thank you and much love to my teachers, close friends and students who have been there for myself and my family so many times and proved to still be there after the years had passed. This brotherhood and friendship along the path of waking up is for me the fruit of our practice.

Picture credits: all pictures are by and copyright of the author or the subjects of each chapter, except the photo of John Evans Sensei on page 236, which was taken by Coneyl Jay.

Introduction

It has been thirty years since I began my journey through the world of martial arts, healing and meditation. These subjects have taken much of my time and energy, and enabled me to become the student or friend of some very special individuals. Each of my teachers was a lineage holder in his respective fighting system, meaning that they had received transmission from their own master and embodied the complete wealth of knowledge passed down through generations, and each of them was also a healer and a practitioner of the spiritual aspects of the art. None of them were simply fighters, although all had a level of skill which would have made them dangerous people to engage in combat. It is the stories and teachings of these men and other masters that I wish to share with you in this book, with the hope that something of their wisdom and ability may inspire you on your own journey.

Most of this book is entirely new material. Some parts – namely the material of Wan Lai Sheng and some of Serge Augier's and Rudy Ibarra's interview – are taken from my book titled *Ziranmen*, of which a very small run of a hundred copies was published a few years ago. Also included is a translation from Grandmaster Wan's famous 1928 book *The Common Basis of Martial Arts*, a rare copy of which Serge gave to me in 1997.

The rest of this book is from research done over the past decades and recent interviews, often revisiting the masters ten years on from my talks with them in books such as *Esoteric Warriors* or *Beyond the Mysterious Gate*, and equally herein are a number of unique individuals whom I am introducing for the first time. The arts which they practise and teach can impart tremendous benefits to those of us struggling with the complexity and speed of modern society, giving us at the very least a still point from which to view the world with some degree of wisdom and peace.

We have divided the book into three sections, covering the arts of China; Japan; and India and South East Asia, and featuring the teachers in alphabetical order for ease of reference. One of my greatest joys has been to see these masters and their students from such distant countries become friends and share the arts in a spirit of openness.

I hope you enjoy the journey with these wonderful characters and that their teaching helps your practice. To those who gave their time to this book, to my beloved teachers and friends, a deep bow of appreciation. So many of you gave a lot of time and effort to contribute for which I am very grateful. As usual I am simply putting down in writing the accomplishments of men far deeper than myself, and it was a joy to be able to do so.

Wishing you all great happiness and freedom.

The Ancient Martial Traditions of China

Introducing the Ancient Martial Traditions of China

China's thousands of years of rich history and vast size has given rise to an incredibly deep and complex culture. One aspect of this are the martial art systems born out of countless wars and conflicts, systems which over the millennia have been highly influenced by the mystical and medical practices of Daoism and Buddhism. Although the two major martial streams of Wudang and Shaolin are often said to be the source of internal and external Gongfu respectively, this is far from a definitive truth; indeed, many Shaolin systems have very well defined Qigong and medical practices and develop a high degree of softness in the body.

There are also many other streams to be taken into account, such as the martial arts coming from farming folk, from Kun Lun or Emei Mountains, from the hidden arts kept within the walls of the Imperial Palace, and from countless other villages or clans who over generations developed special methods and skills. Weapons skills were developed to a very high degree in China, as such knowledge was literally a matter of life and death for many warriors and common folk. With the coming of firearms many martial arts have changed emphasis to empty-hand methods, keeping weapon forms which, often divorced from an environment in which they can be tested and used, now seem like relics of the past.

In this book we will focus on systems traditionally said to belong to Wudang – Baguazhang (also called Baguaquan),

Taijiquan, Xingyiquan and Ziranmen – as well as those which belong to the Shaolin school such as Chuka and Chow Gar. We present some background information on the basic principles of these systems, alongside interviews with the lineage holders of these schools covering many topics relating to practice and the skills of the masters. In the Ziranmen section a very old text by Grandmaster Wan Lai Sheng has been presented, which details many rare practices from that system as well as describing Wan's special teachers.

Bagua, Taiji and Xingyi

An introduction to Bagua, Taiji and Xingyi

The three northern Chinese martial arts of Baguazhang, Taijiquan and Xingyiquan share many qualities, for example the integration of Shen (spirit) into the Xing (form) and the Shi (force), but the way that each art deals with the critical issues of perceiving and making use of incoming forces is quite distinct. This short introduction to the subject offers a few ideas about the 'why' and 'how' of these distinctions. If you know why an art reacts as it does, it becomes clear that its special techniques developed from that point to overcome the perceived problem.

Baguazhang

Tradition relates that Dong Hai Chuan was the man responsible for bringing Baguazhang out of the mountains and into the public domain in Beijing around the middle of the nineteenth century. Dong had apparently learned a traditional Shaolin martial art style as a child, and then later learned various methods of Qigong and circle walking (the defining feature of the art) from Daoist monks. Fusing these things together he made a reputation for himself as a fighter with superlative, almost mystical skills, and produced many students and grand-students who became famous fighters in their own right and developed their own unique styles of Bagua: Yin Fu, Cheng Ting Hua, Zhang Zao Dong and Gong Bao Tien, to name but a few. Dong taught extensively inside the Imperial Palace and was thus deemed to be amongst the greatest boxers of his era, and he has left a legacy which continues to flourish and grow as Bagua gains more and more followers across China and the world.

Bagua works very well as a combative method to deal with the biggest problem for a man facing a violent enemy, that is, the utter randomness of the event. We know force is heading our way but what shape or direction, and in what combination, is very hard to predict outside of a few obvious factors. The trained fighter knows that the way to overcome this problem begins with perception – that is, his mindset and state of being must 'merge' with the enemy in some way such that he is no longer reacting to an attack but actually a part of it. In other words the gap between the two has to be bridged *before* physical contact takes place, or in a worst-case scenario where attack was unexpected and sudden the same merging of minds must be instantly 'on tap' at the first touch.

Eighty-year-old Bagua practitioner in the dawn mist
of Tientai Park, Beijing, Winter 2001

The Bagua fighter trains his mind/body in such a way that he *allows* force to act on him as it wishes, offering it just enough resistance that he can be safe in the moment plus, in a manner not unlike a powerful spring, use the force to move him to the next quadrant of the theoretical circle which is his constant companion. In the same moment of being moved he will use the concept of 'changing centres' to instantly strike the enemy along a different (and thus quite unexpected) plane. The enemy may feel as if he has been hit with his own power or even his own strike. If this first exchange is not a finishing strike then at every moment onwards the enemy will be faced with a boxer who changes in such a way that it feels he is always half a beat ahead of the attack.

That is the theory, but how can the Bagua man really pull this off against random attack? Two big things – first, he must train in such a way that all of his basics, all his circling forms, stepping, everything, reflect and are infused with this principle of using force to change in a spiralling manner whilst the body is like a huge spring filled with many smaller springs (the joints). Or, in other words, integrity of principle and form. And second, he must develop the knack of knowing exactly how much pressure to bring to bear on the incoming force. How? Well, there are many partner exercises in Bagua which do exactly this, some done whilst one man walks the circle and others attack him, some done on straight lines which repetitively work single changes of line before progressing to using every possible combination of body and limbs. In the same way that a revolving door knows which way to turn against your push so too the trained Bagua man will have made the theory alive and real through plenty of hard work with a partner. The theory holds true for groundwork, against gang attack and with weapons.

Master Li Chao Fu teaches a Bagua kicking technique in a training session on Wudang Mountain, China, 1997

Where other arts seek to hold their ground, Bagua allows the ground to vanish beneath one's feet and thus changes something crucial in the enemy's perception – the feeling of solidity. Whilst this is a simple concept it depends on the practitioner remaining completely centred in the midst of chaos, the eye at the centre of the hurricane.

Taijiquan

Taijiquan – the Great Ultimate Boxing – is certainly one of the most misunderstood martial arts, despite being practised by more people in the world than any other system. The exact history of the art is often a topic for dispute, but what seems clear is that the Chen Clan of Hebei Province in northern China developed a boxing method in the eighteenth century which eventually became the Chen style of Taijiquan. It combined the Pao Chui (Cannon Fist) system of martial arts with certain inner practices (Qigong and Neigong) learned from Daoists, and became codified in a series of barehand and weapons forms which are still practised widely today. Yang Lu Chan learned from the Chen Clan in the nineteenth century and developed his own style, now known as Yang Shr (Yang family) Taijiquan. The Yang style has less obvious external spiralling movements than the Chen style, and exists now in several branches which descend from members of the Yang family – the most famous being Yang Ban Hou (known as a great fighter with a terrible temper) and Yang Cheng Fu (the grandson of Yang Lu Chan, who popularised a much less strenuous form of the art which was taken up by millions of ordinary folk across China). Other styles such as Wu, Hao and Sun now exist, all with their unique characteristics and training methods.

Yang Lu Chan and Chen Fa Ke, two of the greatest Taiji boxers

Archive photos from the author's first stay in Hong Kong, 1983

Taijiquan is the quintessential internal boxing style, but its very softness and fluidity often confuse the student of martial arts who seeks a pragmatic fighting method. To make this art alive and practical there is no way to escape the need for deeply infusing the postures with a very fine and subtle kind of awareness, as only from such a state can one begin to work on 'one part moves, every part moves', 'merging of inner and outer' and 'constant awareness of the substantial and insubstantial'. These principles give a hint as to the mindset developed by the Taijiquan expert – the ability to unite oneself with an attacker and allow his motion to dictate the dynamic much as a fine little cog inside of a Swiss watch (let's not talk of poor imitations…) is acted upon by another cog. This relies on a skill which is taken to a very high level in this art, the Ting Jin or skill of listening.

A Taiji boxer's whole body develops acute sensitivity whilst keeping a very Yin or passive state of being, and a physical state characterised by extreme softness – whereas the hard battering ram of Xingyi and the flexible steel spring of Bagua also require acute mental and physical sensitivity to apply, in Taiji the emphasis is on leading the enemy into emptiness such that his ability to issue force is entirely negated using the barest minimum of effort. This is the 'steel hidden in the cotton', for at the very moment of the enemy being led into an energetic hole which has seemingly appeared out of nowhere (somewhat like a matador leads a charging bull to a place where its power is spent) the Taiji boxer manifests the Yang energy held in reserve deep inside his centre and defeats the attacker in what may seem to be a 'mysterious way'. This is sometimes seen in push hands matches with an old master, where decades of working this listening skill allow him to defeat stronger, bigger men with what seems ridiculous ease. This ease, mental and postural, characterises Taijiquan much as explosive power and constant spiral change could be said to characterise Xingyi and Bagua respectively. Each of the three arts uses a blend of Yin and Yang forces in varying degrees.

Master Zhang Baosheng, last disciple of the great internal boxer
Wang Pei Sheng, practises Wu Taijiquan, Beijing, 2006

This brings us to the topic of Tui-Shou or push hands – what we see of this two-person exercise in the parks and classes of today tends to resemble a kind of social/sportive/wrestling event (not to decry wrestling, for in its form of Sumo it displays very high levels of Ting Jin and explosive power...however, it is not Taiji). You will even see people chatting as they practise! (Actually we have practices for singing and talking whilst training, but this is another thing...) My teachers never talked about 'push hands' but rather did with me a wide range of contact drills which began slow and set and worked up to very fast and spontaneous – the principles which rang in my ears during those years of learning were 'Don't think, feel', 'Not useful, look – Whack!', 'You are stuck, look – Whack!', 'What? It's only a bruise!' and 'OK – how to change well from here?' and such things – in this way you can develop over time the knack of intuitively yielding and redirecting force.

Technically the heart of Taijiquan strategy is found in the 'thirteen postures' – Peng, Lu, Ji, An, Tsai, Lieh, Jo, Kao and five ways of stepping. One teacher I know insisted that the first motion, commonly called Peng, should in fact be termed Bing, which refers to the way the lid of the box worn by horse-riding archers to carry their arrows opened and then suddenly closed again. So this action opens up and then covers in an oblique fashion. His 'Grasp Sparrow's Tail' (Lan Chu Wei in Chinese), which is made up of Bing, Lu, Ji and An – or cover, pull, squeeze and push down

– had the quality of a bird or crane, whereas the Tsai, Lieh, Jio and Kao – or pluck, split, elbow and bump – was reflective of the snake. Other postures in his form, such as 'Step Back and Repulse Monkey', were aspects of the monkey type movement, so in total the movements covered creatures which fly, jump in trees and crawl on the earth. Lan Chu Wei is, he said, made up of five bows, each one producing a different kind of energy. The motions needed an elastic type of quality which meant they could spring out from a position of tension and then immediately contract back to their original place, and the kind of force he could produce using this theory was extremely penetrating and rather dangerous to be on the end of. This same teacher also taught that the real meaning behind the names of the Taijiquan Long Form was related to the teachings and life of Lord Buddha. Thus the sequence of Lan Chu Wei – Grasp Sparrow's Tail – referred to a story in the Buddhist scriptures where many birds joined their heads to tails and flew in that way to greet Buddha at his Enlightenment. He said that the whole meaning of the Long Form was full of such esoteric correlations.

This teacher had four special and very subtle skills in using Taijiquan for fighting, and they were very strange to be on the end of. When he applied them on students no one could stop him, and also no one could work out how he did it.

1. Tun – he absorbed your energy so you felt tired.

2. Tu – he emitted power onto you at will.

3. Fu – no matter which way you went he recovered so you could not move freely.

4. Gai – he prevented you from exhaling so you panicked.

Xingyiquan

Moving now to the art of Xingyi, we find a boxing which is derived from an ancient method of military spear – move forward with a penetrating strike, if blocked change to a ferocious horizontal whipping attack, and have up your sleeve the ability to spiral the weapon in and out to lead the enemy's weapon to a position of comparative weakness. Xingyi empty hand skill shows exactly this. The boxer manifests an intent – steady and unwavering due to absolute focus of mental force, rather than emotion-led raving – to completely destroy the physical centre of the enemy; in other words his troops are on a one-way mission to enter the enemy's castle. This mindset brings forth attacking methods of exquisite simplicity and effectiveness, for the only thing to do is keep progressing against the opposing force, giving way only when overwhelming pressure demands it and even then only changing by a few degrees of body motion until yet another clear route to the castle is opened up.

Xingyiquan is about the search for perfect structure. Its core principle is to adhere to the Liu He (Six Harmonies). The three external harmonies involve the co-ordination of the shoulder and hip, elbow and knee, and hand and foot. The three internal harmonies develop co-ordination of the Xin (heart mind), Qi (energy), Yi (intent) and Li (strength), all of it infused with Shen (spirit or awareness).

The Xingyi boxer has developed a mind-body which perceives incoming force as something to be destroyed, hence he hones his five main tools (the five fists) such that each one is a potent weapon whose job is to split open, crush, drill through, explode into and grind to pieces the attacker. That he may be hit on the way in is par for the course, mitigated in part by the rubber-like quality of the torso and steel-likeness of the limbs which comes from the Neigong inner force work of the art. Where the Bagua boxer waits calmly for an attack, treating it as a chance to be changed to another space, the Xingyi man aggressively pre-empts any motion towards him and takes change into his own hands. I am sure all of you who have trained hard in one of these arts would have noticed in yourself, or perhaps your seniors, how much these types of qualities tend to manifest not only in fighting, but in daily life. The Xingyi man demands a refund for his badly made shoes, giving little ground for compromise until the money is in his hand, whereas the Bagua man uses tact in his dealings with the shopkeeper such that the ground for refusal is taken from beneath his feet and he has no option but to change their way of dealing with the situation – and if refusal persists then the Bagua man may simply walk (barefoot) out of the shop and change brands. Yes, it's a sweeping statement, but I think you get the point. This also shows why Wude (martial ethics) are a necessary sheath to guard against misuse of such power.

Master Ji Jiancheng and the author in Hangzhou, at the grave of the legendary warrior Yueh Fei, who is said to be the founder of the original principles of Xingyiquan

Master Ji Jiancheng and the author practise dragon shape of Xingyiquan at Yueh Fei's memorial, Hangzhou, 1999

Another insight may have already dawned in your mind by this point, before we even begin talking about Taijiquan, and that is that it would be very difficult to truly *become* more than one method. It would be akin to a giraffe taking up a zebra suit – he could get away with it for a while but he would be sticking his neck out. I studied with one Bagua expert who could perform Taijiquan beautifully, but just when you were admiring the black and whiteness of it all here came the deep spiral and those funny little ears. You can only be one thing, although you may be able to explain, perform and understand two or three arts to a high level. And only in the being, the becoming, of your chosen system, comes the mastery, that is, the non-separation between you and the art.

The Bagua Master Mike Gillespie[1] moving through a swooping down technique from the Bagua form

This is not to say that Xingyi is only Yang or hard. It has many practices where a certain kind of softness and acute sensitivity to force is developed, such as Tui-Shou or feeling hands exercises coming directly from the five fists methods and their two-man forms. The question of speed, both how to react to fast attack and how to send out one's own lightning fast strikes, is soon understood to be answered with deep relaxation, such a body state being the most conducive to development of this quality. As soon as contact is made the mind-body of the Xingyi man moves in close to strike, keeping enough pressure on the bridging limb of the attacker that he is mentally put on the back foot – even if his superior weight and strength prevail the Xingyi man will change using as small and subtle a circle as possible and immediately again seek the centre. It is this continual crushing mental ploy which wears down an enemy, often in a matter of a second or two.

The development of this fascinating fusion of Yin and Yang forces in the mind and body is an ongoing challenge for the Xingyi boxer, and he can be experiencing intense efforts to balance such forces and the accompanying joy that success in such matters brings, when all the while an onlooker sees a man holding a simple looking stance. Really a mindboxing!

With the study of the twelve animals a whole new and vast horizon of physical and mental dynamics is opened up. To conclude let us sum up the art of Xingyiquan – it is the search for perfect structure.

Note

1. I met Master Gillespie in 1988 and studied Baguazhang and Xingyiquan with him for five years. Training was intense, three hours physical practice at both dawn and dusk and an equal time spent in meditation and other studies. Mr Gillespie was highly skilled at the Bagua of the Sun Lu Tang style, especially the Bien Bu or changing step practice which was intimately tied in with meditation work. He had three main teachers, two in mainland China and one, Master He Shen Ting, in Taiwan. Mr Gillespie had lived in China since his childhood, was fluent in classical Mandarin and was recognised as an adept by a Buddhist order in mainland China; he was probably the first Westerner with real skill in Baguazhang to teach the art in Britain and his four live-in students are all still practising the internal arts. Since returning from Hong Kong where I first studied Bagua, I searched high and low for Neijia practitioners, but the few people teaching at that time only knew forms and stylised techniques; by a strange turn of fate I met Mr Gillespie in a temple and immediately felt the man had something special.

Ziranmen

Peppered with eccentric and colourful characters, and flavoured with martial heroism and nobility, the history of Ziranmen centres on the famous warrior Du Xing Wu. Born in 1869 in a mountainous part of Hunan Province, he began studying Wushu skills at the age of six. This was a time where official corruption and banditry were widespread, and the possession of martial ability was somewhat of a necessity for survival. The young Du had several teachers as a boy, including a Daoist priest who lived in a nearby mountaintop temple. This was a most unusual temple, for a high moss-covered wall that seemed to have no door or gateway surrounded it. The priest was equally unusual – he entered and exited the place by leaping effortlessly over the wall with the grace and lightness of a swallow. He also had the habit of taking with him wherever he went two spiral cones of iron, each weighing twenty kilograms, which he continuously rubbed and pressed. The young Du was to witness the result of such training when one day the Daoist was challenged and attacked by a bandit, a mean-spirited adept of the Shaolin Gongfu system. After trying unsuccessfully to avoid the challenge, he met the vicious attacks of the challenger with swift defences, culminating in a palm strike to the face that ripped off the man's nose. The man fled, and the Daoist priest decided to leave the mountaintop to avoid the inevitable repercussions of the bandit. A wise choice as it turned out, for shortly afterwards the now empty temple was burned down by the vengeful Shaolin adept and his cohorts.

At the age of thirteen Du Xing Wu was introduced to 'an eccentric and somewhat short wanderer' named Xu Ai Zhai, who moved into the boy's home and proceeded to test him for the next six months by lounging around silently and doing nothing more exciting than smoking his pipe. Eventually, however, 'Little Xu' began to teach him, beginning with Inner Circle Walking. This most fundamental practice of Ziranmen involves sinking the Qi to the lower abdomen whilst rotating the hands in a vertical loop, and Du was required to do this atop wooden stakes fixed in the ground in the pattern of a plum flower, whilst wearing five-kilogram sandbags on each leg. After some months the weights were doubled, and Du was soon able to lead his inner energy to produce force in the exercise.

When no new teaching was forthcoming from Little Xu, Du expressed his desire to learn more. His teacher admonished him that he didn't yet appreciate how much skill could be gained from his practice of the Inner Circle Walking, which was designed to build a solid foundation, and that if he didn't believe him he could try his best to attack the older man. But despite his best attempts, his full speed attacks failed to touch Little Xu, who seemed able to dodge with almost supernatural ability and sensitivity. Appreciating the lesson the youth humbly continued his training, which entailed wearing very heavy sandbags on all of his limbs as he jumped on and off of several tables stacked one upon the other. In this way he was able to develop the 'Qing Gong' or Light Body skill.

In 1885, when Du was sixteen, his teacher decided that he was ready to see the world, and so he led him on an arduous journey through the sharp mountains and treacherous ravines of nearby Guizhou and Sichuan provinces. At one point, whilst crossing a deep chasm spanned by an iron-chain suspension bridge, the youth impetuously decided to attack his teacher from behind. Launching a kick to the buttocks, he was shocked when Little Xu span around and caught his leg before it hit the intended target. Severely admonishing the youth for both his lack of martial etiquette and his foolishness in risking life and limb on the precarious bridge, he went on to explain how he had sensed the attack. It was, he said, a result of years of training and cultivation of the Yi and Qi, which developed highly tuned reflexes and lightning speed. This was something the youth did not yet possess, and which he now had to work towards achieving.

Eventually Little Xu bade farewell to his student, deeming Du Xing Wu sufficiently skilled to meet the challenges of the world but advising him to seek out other teachers so that he could further polish his skills. In 1887, at the age of eighteen, Du took his first job as a bodyguard, a post he was to hold for some years and which would lead him through many life or death encounters with bandits and villains. Further exploits awaited him during the years of the Revolution when he served as a bodyguard for Sun Yut Sen, and also during his academic studies in Japan where he was forced to defend the honour of the Chinese against challenges and attacks from skilled Japanese martial artists. Through all of these adventures he continued to cultivate himself through the practice of Ziranmen and Daoist and Chan meditation, and eventually retired to his hometown in Hunan where he died a peaceful death in 1955, aged eighty-four. It seems certain that Grandmaster Du taught several people during the course of his long life, but by far the most famous and influential of his students was Wan Lai Sheng, who completed a gruelling seven-year apprenticeship under his guidance.

Wan Lai Sheng

Few figures shine as brightly in the recent history of martial arts as Wan Lai Sheng. Born in 1902 in Hubei Province, his first teacher was Zhou Xin Zou, a Master of Northern Shaolin Liu Her (Six Harmonies) style. Zhou had formerly held the position of the emperor's bodyguard and taught the young Wan 'day and night' for ten years. This training gave him a strong foundation, and when he met Grandmaster Du Xing Wu he was able to complete the arduous course of training required to learn the Ziranmen system. He also learned other systems of boxing and Qigong with further masters, including the Shaolin Luohan system under the renowned Lio Bai Chuan.

Wan was also a scholar, graduating from the National Beijing Agricultural University, and a healer, becoming equally renowned in his later years for his ability in Chinese medicine. But it was his ability as a boxer that brought him fame, and one episode in particular gave him notoriety within the martial arts community of China. In 1928 a National Martial Arts Competition was held in Nanjing to determine who were the greatest experts of the day in both barehand fighting and weapons. Grandmaster Wan was at that time aged twenty-six, and already renowned for his superlative skill in Gongfu. Organised by three generals who were also great martial artists – Fung Zu Ziang, Li Jing Lin and Zhang Zi Jiang – the tournament was bloody and brutal. No protection was worn and as the rounds went on more and more injuries were accrued by the fighters. The government officials present eventually stopped the contest, claiming that if the event continued there were sure to be deaths due to the high skill level of the remaining experts.

Wan Lai Sheng dazzled the onlookers with his skills. One Western reporter commented, 'His hands moved like ropes and his fingers were like iron hooks. He rushes forward like a hurricane and backs away like torrential waters!'

But in the semi-final against a White Crane boxer Wan cut his hand on his opponent's teeth and was forced to withdraw. Officially he was posted as forty-eighth on the list of winners, but he was so convinced that he was more skilled than virtually all the other boxers present that he tracked down each one of them and issued a challenge to fight. The exception to this was his good friend and Northern Shaolin expert Ku Yu Zhang, the famous Iron Palm (the ability to strike with one's palm with devastating power) and Iron Shirt (the ability to take blows to the torso without being hurt) master, who was one of the official 'winners' determined by a vote. The full list of champions went as follows:

1. Chu Kuo Fu – Bagua and Xingyiquan

2. Chu Kuo Lu – Bagua and Xingyiquan

3. Chu Kuo Chen – Bagua and Xingyiquan

4. Fu Chen Sung – Bagua

5. Liu Hung Chieh – Bagua and Xingyiquan

6. Chu Gui Ting – Xingyiquan

7. Ku Yu Zhang – Northern Shaolin

8. Wang Shao Chou – Northern Shaolin and Cha Quan

9.   Li Hsin Wu – Northern Shaolin, Tan Tui, Ziranmen

10. Keng Te Hai – Tai Sheng Pek Kwar Monkey style

11. Ma Cheng Hsin – Seven Star Praying Mantis

The event was divided into a combat division and a forms performance division, and it seems that the above list of champions was somehow drawn from a combination of the two. One of the functions of the whole event seemed to be to select boxers worthy of taking official postings, such as heading martial arts academies in various locations throughout China, but the final postings had a somewhat random element to them. The winner of the weapons division was Keng Te Hai, the famous Monkey boxer. Fu Chen Sung, at the admirable age of fifty, was matched against the champion of Sichaun Province, 'Charging Fists' Wong Tak Yuen, a man who had already beaten twenty opponents and who was said to be able to smash rocks and dent iron with his bare hands. Fu Chen Sung eventually defeated Wong after ninety gruelling rounds. Fu then demonstrated his Bagua form, which emphasised multiple spins and lighting fast palm striking, but he moved so fast that he tripped over an uneven plank and fell off the stage. He was uninjured if slightly abashed, but his stunning performances had been enough to convince the judges, and he was later given the post of one of the 'Five Tigers of the North', as was Wan Lai Sheng, and sent to the south of China to disseminate his boxing method.

The 'Five Tigers Go South' were:

1.   Wan Lai Sheng – Ziranmen

2.   Fu Zhengsong – Bagua

3.   Gu Yu Zhang – Northern Shaolin

4.   Li Hsin Wu – Ziranmen

5.   Wang Xiao – Dian

In addition three other northern masters were sent south, these being the monkey boxer Keng Te Hai, Taijiquan Master Tung Yin Chieh, and Sun Yu Fung.

After Wan Lai Sheng challenged and defeated the 'champions' of the 1928 tournament, his ability was rewarded by the Guomingtang

Government, who appointed him Director of Kwangsi Province Martial Arts Academy and titled him Major General. For such a young man to be given this acclaim was rare honour indeed, but whilst he attracted countless followers and admirers wherever he travelled in China he also attracted jealousy and hostility from the students of the vanquished boxers. Being a central figure in the Jiang Hu martial arts society of the early and mid-twentieth century meant that Wan was forced to accept challenges, which by all accounts he seemed more than willing to do. He also wanted to try his hand against the boxers of the older generation, whose reputations at that time must have been truly formidable. One story relates how Wan Lai Sheng went to the Yang family to challenge the famous Taijiquan system of that clan. Yang Ban Hou was one of the sons of Yang Lu Ch'an, founder of Yang Style Tai Chi. Chang Ch'ing Ling, who was a close student of Yang Ban Hou, stepped out to take the challenge. Chang could root his feet so well that they 'sank into the ground' and he was a formidable fighter. Wan Lai Sheng and Chang began fighting but both men injured their hands at the very opening exchange and so the match was declared a draw.

Wan Lai Sheng then challenged Yang Cheng Fu, who was at that time the most senior of the Yang family. They both agreed to use Taijiquan's pushing hand techniques. Yang, a huge man weighing in at three hundred pounds, was startled when Wan Lai Sheng uprooted him and pushed him up into the air. Not only was this the first time that someone had uprooted Yang Cheng Fu, but Wan Lai Sheng had beaten a famous master using the opponent's own special technique. Another story, however, has Wan surprising Yang Cheng Fu as the older master was brushing his teeth, and sending him off balance with a pushing technique! Which of these two stories is more factual is not possible to know after so long has passed.

Eventually Wan Lai Sheng settled in Fujien Province, and became acclaimed by the locals for his skill and kindness in applying traditional Chinese medicine. He also attracted a sizeable following of martial arts students, and developed an integrated system based upon his vast learning of many boxing systems.

What we will hear in the following pages is Grandmaster Wan's memories of his own teachers, written in his own words.

Zhou Shin Jou

My teacher's name is Chuen, he was born in Shuen-Ee where there were many generations of skilled martial artists. He received the heritage at Chang-Zhou with Liu De Kuan's grandmaster. He practised spear and boxing there for more than ten years, learning the Six Harmonies system. Then he studied sword for nine years with Kong Ji Tai. Master Kong was a Fourth Level bodyguard of the emperor, a specialist in the sword and in attacking skills. Since Master Kong's son didn't want to continue his father's way, the master transmitted his skills to student Zhou, who he observed trained very sincerely. After Master Kong died his position as a bodyguard was taken by Zhou, and he kept the position until the death of the emperor.

Thus Master Kong transmitted all of his knowledge only to Zhou, treating him like a son and seeing in him great potential for developing excellent skill. Since the twenty-fifth year of the emperor, Zhou was the teacher for some bodyguards in Beijing. In the twenty-eighth year he opened his own school, called 'Eternal Prosperity Protection Service', which ran for ten years. He travelled and his footprints and fame spread north and south, his reputation enabling him to be welcomed as a brother wherever he went. His fame and prosperity spread to half of the country.

In his free time he often talked about his life story. Later he retired to his hometown. His friends felt it a shame that he hid his skills, but he did not lose all of his life's efforts in the arts as someone hired him as a teacher. I stayed with Master Zhou for ten years, training morning and evening, and he never saw me as his student but rather as an inner-door disciple. He told me that if I had any glimmer of hope in my practice it was because of the foundation of the Shaolin method which he taught me. His personality was righteous, he was not one to flatter people. If anyone flattered him he would quickly leave. Master Zhou loved to collect antiques as a hobby, and in his old age he retired from the martial arts world and opened an antiques shop. He is now fifty-two years old and has three daughters.

Zhou Shin Jou

Master Du Xing Wu – Internal Neigong and Dao-Gong

His birth name is Shun-Hwai, and his hometown is Shang-Jr in Si-Li. He is from a Confucian family and when he was only fifteen years old his father renounced the world and went to the mountains. Du Xing Wu matured very fast as he had to look after his mother, and all the local people praised him for being a filial son. At a very young age he studied martial skills with more than ten well-known teachers. At the age of thirteen he met Grandmaster Xu and followed him to practise martial arts and become a bodyguard, and his skill improved a lot. Some years later Du studied in Japan at the Tokyo Agricultural University, and upon returning to China he passed the government exams and took a literary position in the department of Industry, Agriculture and Business. In the Ching Dynasty he was involved in the revolution and passed through many dangerous times in which he used his skill to save himself. Master Du's appearance is very gentle and scholarly, and looks to be very weak and thin. Even his old friends don't know that he is a skilled martial artist. After Independence he took a job as an agricultural officer in the government.

He never asks for much and even today he is very poor, so everyone who knows him feels much pity. However, Master Du regards his situation very lightly. Except for his responsibilities at work he refuses to see visitors, spending his time meditating and studying Buddhism and shunning society. His house is very silent. Since returning from Japan he has transmitted his knowledge to only one disciple. In thirty years he could not find anyone suitable. I had studied with Master Zhou for six years at the time when I first heard of Master Du. I went to see him and observed that he had deep skill, and sincerely and humbly requested him to teach me. Master Du generously taught me and by following him I learned the structure of the internal martial arts and also became immersed in the way of Chan. Master Du's nature is detached and he doesn't work for strangers or indulge in fame and money. His friends all say he is mad but he just keeps silent. He loves to read Chuang-Tze and is skilled at face-reading and calligraphy. In daily life he neither talks nor smiles much, and only when you talk about Chan or martial arts will he become animated and talk to no end! This is natural, as he loves the arts so much.

Master Du Xing Wu

Yang Wei-Jr – Medical and Gongfu Master

This master hails from Hei-Li in western Szechuan. He first began practising martial arts to avenge the death of his uncle at the hands of the authorities. By the age of fifteen he was accepting disciples and began doing heroic deeds. He is excellent at leaping and piercing attacks, and skilled in both internal and external methods. Whenever he saw bullies hurting civilians he would leap over the wall at night and chop off their heads and pierce their bodies before fleeing. Everyone knew who had done it, but because he was killing bad people they all helped him to escape when the authorities tried to arrest him. Because of his love of heroic deeds all the people loved and respected him. His reputation spread far and wide but some people hated him and wanted revenge against him. Master Yang loved to have friends and hundreds or thousands of brothers followed him. Some of these brothers imitated his deeds and thus the government officers blamed him. His enemies tried to influence the officers to catch him, so there was danger everywhere he went. His surroundings and life got worse. He decided that since he was a hero, he might as well become a government officer and serve his country in the army.

In 'Gwon-Shi eleventh Year' he and forty brothers surrendered to General Bao Chao and joined his army. They fought against the French in Yunnan and beat everyone. The general was very happy with his skill so he was promoted to Vice-General, and eventually became head of the army. Master Yang was very responsible in his post and knew how to protect the citizens, all of whom welcomed him and his sense of morality and good deeds. However, all of this work left his body and mind very tired and in 'Gwon-Shi twentieth Year' he retired.

Master Yang's family had for many generations been experts at Chinese medicine, so he inherited the family medical system and was talented at this. In his old age he had an insight about this and treated people without charge, saving many lives. He knew internal and external medicine and was especially skilled at acupuncture, being without peer in this. After Ming-Guo, [the historical period between the Qing Dynasty and the People's Republic of China], he retreated from the capital and refused to see anyone. He studied

Buddhism. I heard about Master Yang and often went to visit him, each time feeling like I was seeing an old friend. For some years we have been like family and he has transmitted to me both medicine and Gongfu.

Master Yang's personality is very righteous, like 'a thousand clouds in the sky'. Ever since being a hero and an officer he has kept the same way. Unless you are an intimate friend he is not easy to talk to, but he was very happy to tell me his stories, which I have written about here.

Yang Wei-Jr

Master Deng Jr Lin – Master of Dao-Gong

This master's nature is very harmonious and benevolent. Since childhood he studied his family's academic heritage. As a teenager he loved to visit many places, and besides studying Confucianism he also made great efforts in Buddhism and Daoism. No one can understand just how much I have benefited from his guidance. In his free time he taught me the philosophy of Confucius and Mong-Tze. He has wisdom and insight which modern people don't possess. He wrote a book and seriously studied philosophy. In the late Ching Dynasty he studied in the School of Law and Politics and was very well known in the circles of officers and generals. In the first year of Ming-Guo the people asked him to be Commander of the local county. President Yuen hired him as a policy consultant in the third year of Ming-Guo. Three years later he became a senator and in the tenth year he became Financial Commissioner.

Because the political situation became more and more confused, he knew there was no hope and retired. He purchased a million scrolls of books and spent every day reading, ignoring the political situation. When he was born his mother dreamed of an old temple above which hung a wooden board inscribed with the words 'Consistent Heart'. His father interpreted this to be related to the Confucian philosophy of 'As one'. That is why he has a sage's name. At around twenty years of age he read the I-Ching and then wrote a book and painted twenty scrolls based on that book. This was a first, as no one had done that before, and he is really very gifted and talented.

Master Deng often said you can follow Confucius, Buddhism, or Daoism; each one has its true meaning. There is no need to make the three all the same; whilst they have their differences the essence is the same. The ethos is to learn that which can benefit our life.

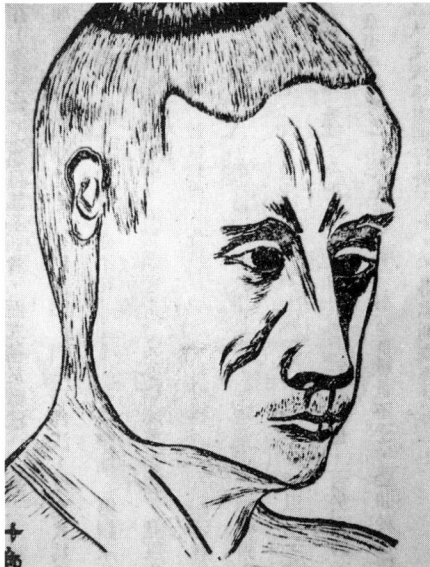

Master Deng Jr Lin

Master Wang – Master of Dao-Gong

For more than ten years this master has lived like a hermit in the capital and he is known about by everyone. He knows the tradition, and he has a gift that everything he sees he can remember and can become skilled at, even the smallest details. He specialised in mathematics and knows geography and astronomy. He knows all philosophy as well as his own palm. Many seekers eager to learn visited him. Master Wang surrendered to the Buddha Dharma and he took it as his mission to save people from Samsara [the painful cycle between birth and death in which all unenlightened beings are continuously revolving]. Even though I have been his friend for many years I still don't know the source of his teaching. It is said that he hailed from Gansu, and people think he is mysterious and see him as a recluse. All his life he has been well known for his knowledge and some even consider him as half-immortal.

Master Wang was very generous in his dealings with people but he gave himself a simple life – he wears rough clothes and eats simple food. He never thinks this is a poor life, and if people offer gifts he thanks them but refuses. He never keeps enough food for the next day but feels easy about this, and his face never shows anger. He buys iron or stone utensils, so I say that he has the nature of metal or stone. I take this as an inspiration for me to improve. Ever since meeting him, be it summer or winter, we talked until midnight before going home.

On the night he bade me farewell he said to me, 'You are a man for practising the Big Dao, and today I will give you some power to help this. In the future you will meet some other teachers. I am in Beijing. How will I know what you will do in the future? Please don't forget!'

Even now I still recall that Master Wang had the talent to do things but was too idealistic to become an officer, so he just spent his life hidden away in an old temple. Often he would sigh and say, 'If I can follow my ideal then I will serve, if I cannot do that then I will simply cultivate myself.'

Dao-Gong Master Wang

Master Wang Long-Biao – Fall-Hit Bone Doctor

Master Wang hails from An-Sze and is Master Jow's adopted brother. He is very skilled at soft skill [a kind of practice which makes the body very soft and supple and cultivates internal energy, as opposed to hard skill, which toughens the body] and specialises in reconnecting the bones and fall-hit medicine [Dit Da]. His surgical methods are fascinating. From a very early age he learned this and is now a bone-doctor in Beijing. Everyone he treats is cured. I hurt my heel bone and was cured by Master Wang, and thus I was not handicapped. Due to this I am very grateful to the master. As I knew martial arts practitioners need to know how to heal, I studied with Master Wang and he generously taught me for free.

He has absolutely no 'Jiang Hu' energy. He is righteous and very humorous, and people are very happy to be close to him. Since he cured me he always said that my bones were different from other people. Thus he is willing to teach me. Maybe it is our destiny. Now he is fifty-four, and has one son and four daughters.

Master Wang Long-Biao

Grandmaster Lio – Master of Wu-Gong, Dao-Gong, Yau-Gong

I don't know where Master Lio is from or his age. He has white hair and a face full of energy. He looks like a man of eighty or ninety but full of vitality and spirit, and the shape of his body is like an infant. He knows about all the martial arts but will rarely discuss them. He has no fixed home. In terms of his mystical side, I don't want to talk about it too much. His medical knowledge is very deep. He can bring the dead back to life and grow flesh back onto white bones! He can look at the present and know the future. People think he is an immortal God.

Master Du, Master Yang, Master Deng – all of them are his students and respect him a lot.

Grandmaster Lio was very happy to be with me, but because I was too young to ask much instruction from him he just corrected the Gongfu which I had already been learning. His personality is not confined by form and although he associates with people he is not attached to them.

When I asked his age he often said, 'Fifty!'

When the country was in chaos he was practising meditation, but he also was well aware of the situation. One family with the surname of Chen had seen Grandmaster as he looks today for several generations.

Grandmaster is very benevolent and forgiving, and dislikes discussing his background. This is a very brief description. Maybe I also see him as an immortal!

Grandmaster Lio

Teachings of Grandmaster Wan Lai Sheng
The Hardship of Ziranmen Qigong

Wan Lai Sheng wields the Jian straight sword

Learning Ziranmen Qigong is not easy if you have never learned external Qigong, in which case it will take you eighteen years of hard work to achieve something. If you study five or six years external Qigong then you may achieve something after ten years' hard work. A good way to go is to make the external strong first and then make the internal strong. Going from external to internal Qigong, in two and half years you can stop the fire attributes. During this period you will feel suffocation in the chest, the Qi up and down, but in the long term down. If you do hard practice it will go up again. Your eyes will become clear. When you sleep or after awakening sometimes you may feel shocked. This is because the route of the Qi is not yet stable. Once your will and mind are stable then the five organs above the abdomen feel very cool and joyful. You will feel in another world!

The eyelids will also suddenly curl up like a fierce tiger. The eyes show the light and they won't need to blink. After all this has happened then whenever you fight your eyes will get sharp and fearsome. Then you enter the gate of Qigong, and thus begins a long slow practice which will make your body light.

Light but rooted
Soft but hard
Move as you will
This is the phenomenon
Of Nature

During this period, if you don't have perseverance then the sharp will may vanish. In that case not only will you not achieve any Gongfu, but your eyes may get some problem due to the energy. This is a key point of the practice.

When you practise the iron rings the tendons of the hands will often hurt, the elbows feel as if they are going to fall off, all kinds of hard sufferings…just put it aside and don't talk of it, practise every day as usual and after some time it will all be cured. When walking, the Kua (the area of the hip joints and inguinal region) and knees also have a big change, but don't stop when you feel the change or else you will get stuck. As long as you practise internal Neigong, follow the idea that in the old time Shaolin followed the idea of moderation. Just keep this in mind and don't overdo things because the Qi is not yet rooted. When you move, the Qi will go up and down as it is unstable, moving suddenly up then down, thus it is easy to get an illness.

After you have completed the achievement then you can do hard practice of the Waigong. Generally after four years' practice of Ziranmen the tendons, flesh, bones and joints of the entire body will have changed. Before that the Waigong seemed very heroic externally, now it will become very benevolent in mood, the body becoming thin and light. Unlike before, when the chest and hips became bigger, now you won't even appear to be like a fighter but instead look like a weak scholar. If you achieve this it means you have completed the Gongfu of our school; if not then you are still in the stage of hard practice.

So we can tell the Neijia or Waijia not only by their body movements but also by their eyes. Generally speaking, Waijia is sharp and fierce, but Neijia people's eyes are clear like a gem and they look noble and righteous. This is a way to classify Neijia and Waijia and is also the most difficult point to break through in order to manifest Neijia.

Ziranmen Roots and Foundation

Ziranmen training and fighting skills have a different foundation to other Gongfu schools. If readers wish to study the details then they must understand what the differences are. Like an architect who builds a house will first take care of every brick and beam and every segment, you too should make the segments and then later combine them. There is no principle that says that if you have wood then you can build a house. Also, even if the architect has completed the individual segments but doesn't combine them, still you will not have a house. So in our system first we practise to make the tendons smooth, since this is the material we need. Then we study every kind of basic method and weapon to complete the roof. Then finally we practise the Light Body skills to combine everything. Thus you have completed a house and have achieved this school's Gongfu. After you have practised this for six years and have completed the first stage, then the following four years will be much easier.

The most fundamental roots are:

- Sink the Qi to Dantien.

- Don't leave alone, don't help.

- Seems you have, but seems you have nothing.

- One side strong and steel like Shaolin, other side gentle and supple like Neijia.

- There is suppleness in steel and steel in suppleness.

The Gongfu that has both steel and suppleness, if applied to the attacking skills, can be applied as you like. It is also the basis for spiritual practice, so the skill is very close to the Dao.

I know the Liu Her of Shaolin and the Ziranmen of Neijia, but other schools I dare not talk about since my skill is very shallow and my knowledge is limited. What I know is like this. When I finished my training my Master Du Xing Wu wrote a proverb for me [additional written teaching given to Wan is included in brackets below]:

> Moving and stillness,
> Changing, no beginnings.
> Manifest, un-manifest
> Natural, as it is.

(Wan Lai Sheng is this system's best student. I have kept these teachings for decades and hope that he will keep these words to guide him.)

Ziranmen Training Methods

Body-balancing stake – this Gongfu is to practise Neigong and can only be achieved very slowly. If you really accomplish this Gongfu you can even put your chest on the stake and balance. Other people lift your two legs and spin you around four or five times. If your Gongfu is even deeper you can even put a hundred-kilogram stone on your back and simultaneously enjoy eating a sweet whilst talking and laughing easily! It is OK to put a piece of cloth on top of the stake. The height of the stake is two feet five inches (42 cm), and buried three feet (90 cm) under the ground (see the illustration below).

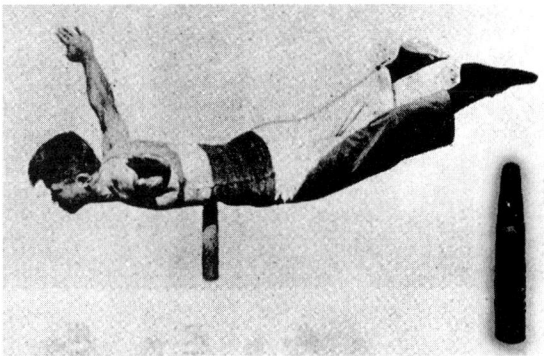

Body-balancing stake

Triangle stakes – these are three foot two inch (95 cm) stakes. They are planted six inches (15 cm) under the ground. Wrap hemp rope around them and practise striking with your legs (see the illustration below).

Triangle stakes

Tiger Mouth stake – it is four inches (10 cm) long and the end is one inch (2.4 cm) in diameter. You practise the Tiger Mouth Jin by using your two hands to pinch it (see the illustration below left).

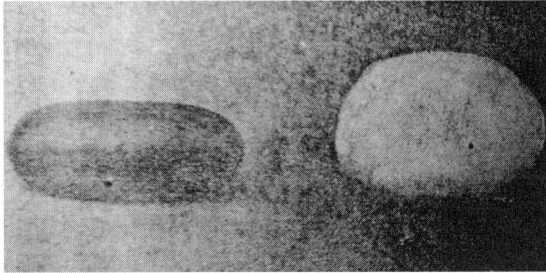

Tiger Mouth stake and sand sack

Sand sack – there are four stages of this, and iron sand as big as green beans is wrapped in cloth. The size of it is five inches by three inches (12 cm by 7.5 cm), and it used to practise the Jin of grab and hook (see the illustration above right).

Paired rings – these are made of lead, each weighing one kilogram (2.2 lb). If your Gongfu is mediocre, first use rings each weighing half a kilogram (1.1 lb), with a total of four pairs, but this doesn't apply to those with good basics. You put the rings on your two arms but not over the elbows, and then push out with the ghost head hands. Some other special skills cannot be taught by illustrations but must be learned directly from a teacher. The inner diameter is 2.6 inches (6.5 cm). The diameter of the lead is 0.4 inches (1 cm) (see the illustration below).

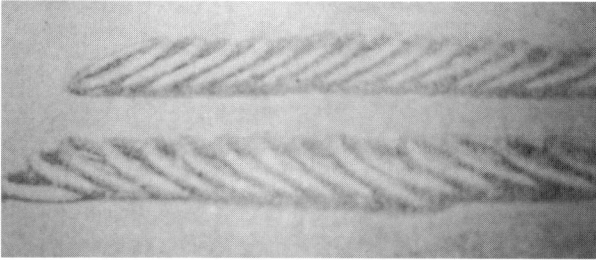

Paired rings

Mother and Son Balls – the right one is the son, the left one is the mother (see the illustration below). Practise the Son Ball first and then the Mother Ball. There are certain skills – grab, chop, cut, prick, throw, brush, point, take and so on, and all of these skills are practised in the morning and evening whilst holding a horse stance. It is taboo to use power, so don't use power! Practise very slowly, and after some time you will achieve something. These Mother and Son Balls are sixteen kilograms (35 lb) and twenty kilograms (44 lb) in weight.

Mother and Son Balls

Then there are paired rings made of lead, sixteen pairs in total, each weighing one kilogram (2.2 lb) to make a total weight of thirty-two kilograms (70.5 lb). When you have trained for three years and nine days then you can have two sleeping rings to train with, but you cannot practise that until the time is right.

Walking on the bamboo basket – the basket is made of bamboo, its weight is eight or nine kilograms (17.5 or 20 lb) and there are about two hundred kilograms (440 lb) of little stones in the basket. Every forty-nine days you pick out three to five kilograms (6.5–11 lb) of stones, keeping up this process until you have removed thirty kilograms (66 lb). After this it is not easy to pick out more stones and still be able to walk. Don't be in a rush to practise this, be patient and ten years later you will start to achieve something. This training is to train the Light Jin in the legs. The two hands can hold the edge of the basket so that you don't fall down when you practise (see the illustration below).

Walking on the bamboo basket

The rest of the tools like Tiger Mouth stake, sand sack, board, bamboo skills, triangle stake, Dao stake, pierce through sand, pierce bricks, running through boards – all of these should be trained for ten years without resting for a single day. Additionally there are many other small skills, but these are the general tools that we use.

These photos are the basic Gongfu of our school; I won't describe the details of the rest.

SONGS OF ZIRANMEN

1. Song for Circle Walking

This is the initial Gongfu for walking circles, so you must understand this song.

> The body is a bow
> Hands as an arrow
> Eyes like shooting stars
> Legs like a drill.

2. Song for Fighting

> Catch the enemy alive
> Escape by slithering smoothly
> Spit and swallow, float and sink,
> Soft like cotton
> Skilfully crisp.
> Then the movements will achieve the Superb upper level.

3. Song of the Hands

> Hook like steel claws
> Pierce like a blade
> Body like iron stone
> Stick like glue
> Relate to the enemy like a baby
> He cannot escape by moving his hand.

4. Poem for Short Hand Skill

> Wave, Split,
> Strike, Chop
> Soar, Hug,
> Dodge, Open

5. Poem for Dodging

The skill is as if you are the breeze
Escaping as if drawing a sword

6. Poem for Body Skills

Hands, eyes, body, step,
Shoulders, elbows, wrists,
Hips, knees, head, neck,
Chest, waist, back.

(Each item should be trained well. You must practise this skill until your palm can break stone, hand can pierce the board, toe-tips break the bamboo, hand like a steel hook, body like iron stone, hard as steel, soft as glue, heavy as if rooted into the ground, light as if walking on ice, hand emerges on one line, hand goes out cannot be stopped – you won't achieve the real skill until you can do all of this.)

This school separates the methods of stillness and movement.

- Stillness – Ling Pai Shr (high officer posture)

- Movement – Eight Methods

- Change – Wave Steps

7. The Skill and Change of Hand

(The skill of the hand is the 'embrace back hand', the change of the hand is the 'ghost head hand'.)

Unlimited ways to fight come naturally
Hand goes out as soft as cotton
Upper body as hard as iron
There is Obvious Force and Hidden Force
Two kinds of method – stick or dodge.

8. The Proverbs

Before you practise Ziranmen Gongfu you have to realise and understand this school's Proverbs. If you follow them you can achieve the higher levels.

> Shrink the body like a crane
> Spit the hand like a slithering snake
> Be agile like a monkey
> Both feet like the centre of a millstone.

If you really want to acquire the secret then you must look at the Qi cavities [points like little wells relating to each of the twelve acupuncture meridians, where the energy can be accessed from the skin].

This is an outline of Ziranmen fighting skills. Train well for ten years, but after six years you can train every morning and you will still keep the skill your whole life. After ten years you will definitely achieve the essence of all the martial arts schools. Although it looks like any practice I really don't know how it was transmitted to Grandmaster Xu [Little Xu, the teacher of Du Xing Wu]. All the skills of this school should be practised.

You can practise on tiptoes, put down nine saucers and stand on them. This is really difficult!

WEAPONS

There are long and short weapons, as well as hidden weapons, and each has its special skill. Long weapons include long staff and the Eight Immortals single head staff. Short weapons include the single sabre. Long range hidden weapons include the continuous round balls. Close range hidden weapons include throwing balls.

ZIRANMEN FIGHTING SKILLS

Since the name of this school is Natural Boxing you should base your practice on naturalness. All readers should understand that before you can obtain the complete skill you will go from unnatural to natural. So if you don't follow the description and don't train hard, how will the day of understanding come?

This school's Gongfu has certain postures, but when you train don't be confined by the form. Follow the natural way but still follow a certain principle or method. A long time afterwards you will become truly natural in training. Actually, the basis of the boxing is very simple, but the keys for each level are complicated to break through. The initial skill is rooted in Inner Circling Hand, Low Posture Circle Walking, Pushing Ghost Head Hand, Study of Yang Palm then Yin Palm, Yang Palm comes out from the wrist and forms a Tiger Claw Palm, Yin Palm comes from under the other Palm, Kicking Legs, Walk Clockwise and Counter-Clockwise, first walking one hundred steps then two hundred, then four hundred and so on. If you continuously practise this then after two years the Qi will gradually sink down and your eyes will become bright. If you practise external to internal for two and a half years you will stop the element of fire outside [violent energy]. After that you start to practise the other methods of Spit and Swallow, Float and Sink, and other hand and leg skills.

When you practise Shaolin skills in the morning you don't go to the toilet because you are afraid that the Qi will be blocked, but in Ziranmen it is the opposite. We have many methods for stretching the tendons in the morning which belong to Ziranmen Jibengong [foundation work]. Ziranmen Gongfu doesn't look graceful but it is very effective for strengthening the body and ridding oneself of disease. This is the Gongfu of Circle Walking. If you can just do Circle Walking every morning it is sure to benefit your body and mind.

Additionally we have Stake Methods to train internal substance, and you can complete this in three years. However, Walking Around the Bamboo Basket will take ten years to complete.

MEDITATION

Meditation posture

I talk about meditation because it is the Gongfu of internal martial arts and is related to martial skills, illuminating disease, lengthening one's life and greatly benefiting the body. People who are too old and weak to practise Gongfu can meditate in order to preserve health. Here I give just one or two examples for your reference.

What is the meaning of so-called meditation? It is to settle your mind and cultivate your energy. People are always busy, from morning to evening, so if there is a free moment use it for meditation so that you can recover from fatigue. If you talk about enlightenment, meditation, Chan or finding higher consciousness, then the journey is not as easy as modern people say. If it only took practitioners several decades to meditate and gain enlightenment then the whole world would be full of immortal beings! And even if some people can do this, they all follow the dark side.

In terms of discussing meditation for health, it is very natural that you can make the thoughts clear, the mind settled and cultivate the energy. Of course in the long term you can have good health.

Some people say that if you regulate the breathing you will have a sound in your belly, but I have never experienced this. I have only heard that practitioners should follow the Law of the Higher

Nature and not be attached to form. If you are attached to form you will go astray.

Today the method I discuss is a common method of meditation for cultivation of energy.

Methods of Meditation

It is best to have a meditation room or, if not, then a simple place is fine. It is best that the floor is firm so the body can be held erect. Every day in the morning and evening sit for a while. Don't worry how long or how short the time, just slowly and gradually do it. Don't focus on the form or breathing, just naturally sit. Close the teeth, tongue touching the palate, the spine is upright and the two hands are put slightly under the Dantien (4 cm beneath and inside navel). You can fold the hands in the Taiji Mudra (left thumb lightly touches the middle finger, right thumb inserts through the Tiger's Mouth of left hand, lightly hold the left hand's ring finger root with the right thumb), or the San-Mei Mudra (two palms face up, right thumb above and crossing left thumb).

When you sit first prepare the posture. Put your two hands on your knees and adjust the body by swaying left and right, front and back, and then become upright. In this way the spine and hip will find the correct position. Single crossed leg or double crossed leg are both fine (single crossed legs is left leg under and right foot above, and is for people who cannot manage double crossed legs). In the morning it is best to sit after emptying the bowels. Before all of this open the window to let air circulate, or in winter close it.

Concentrate your mind when you sit. Breathe out bad energy from the mouth, inhale fresh energy through the nose and swallow the energy to Dantien to make up for the energy exhaled. Exhale fast, inhale slowly. Do this thoroughly rather than half-breathing! Make three rounds of inhale and exhale, exhaling all the bad energy from the belly. Then you can start to meditate. But it is not necessary to do all this in the evening session.

At the start of learning meditation, if you cannot fix your mind you may chant 'AmitaFor' or one-two-three. This is fine for women who have many thoughts. Once you are fixed in deep practice you can leave this method behind, as it is just a temporary practice to settle the mind.

When you meditate to clear the spirit and to lessen desire, introspect into your body and mind until you feel the whole body is clear and light. This is the unity of stillness and motion. In the evening you can meditate to find stillness in your daily movement.

Single or double crossed legs are both fine. For men the left heel touches the right testicle, the right foot placed on the left foot and reaches the left testicle. Females do the opposite, but this is not vital. These points are for double leg crossing. This is the Buddhist way of sitting. If you can use double crossed legs then all the meridians become tensile and the whole body can sit upright. This is the best way to sit for deep meditation.

The Daoist sitting method is 'Five Hearts Towards Heaven'. There is also Kwan Yin sitting, Diamond sitting and many other types. It is best to sit for five to thirty minutes without forcing yourself, and gradually you will improve. It's not good to force yourself or be rushed.

Daily Life Practices

This is for the practitioner to make a regular practice during leisure time, like a game. It may seem unimportant but in fact it contains great benefit for the body. This is a very rare transmission from Grandmaster Lio [Lio Sheng Xian, one of the teachers of Wan]. Please don't neglect these examples, for when you practise them you will find it can cure any disease.

1. Rub the two palms until they are hot. Absorb Qi from the left palm and inhale, then each day swallow twice and do four rounds of each posture. This is to strengthen the Qi and blood.

2. The left hand index and middle finger close your nostrils and count to ten. Then for males, take off the index finger, for females take off the middle finger. Change the breath and then repeat (alternate inhale and exhale). After three times, once you have removed one finger, swallow Qi once and repeat three times. Then stop. After this the breathing will be very smooth and the lungs very clear.

3. Put the left hand on the left waist. Make a bow and arrow stance with hips forming a circle, rotate to right side, then to the opposite way. Do this three or four times. This is to circulate the Qi and blood.

4. For both internal or external Gongfu, after exercising massage all the joints with both palms. Do the right side by the left palm and vice versa. Do this several times and the blood will circulate and flow smoothly. In the long term the joints will be soft, and will not become hard and painful when you get older.

5. Right hand holds the left hand in front of the chest. Stand upright. Raise one leg for five minutes and take turns on each side. This enhances the Qi and blood, improves the circulation to tendons and bones and is good for weak and old people.

6. This is the way for meditators to awaken. Wriggle the finger slightly and walk slowly. Take each step only after the previous one is stable, and in this way you keep the mind fixed.

7. In everyday life you can sit or lay down, the fingers and toes slightly bent. Close the eyes and abandon thoughts. Put intention in the Dantien. Breath naturally. This cultivates the energy and gives you longevity.

How to Meditate

Thoughts – make an intent that you want to do meditation, empty your thinking and contemplate your mind. Let the Qi sink from the shoulders. Close your teeth, purse your lips, exhale from the nose, naturally the shoulders will relax and the Qi will sink down.

Cross the legs – follow the previous methods which I described concerning single and double crossed legs. Pay attention to the spine being straight, sink the Qi downwards.

Once you have left the meditation, still keep your intent in Dantien. No matter whether you are walking, sitting or sleeping do not forget this! When you sleep lay on your side and bend your limbs; this can stabilise the energy. If you are outdoors and it is cold, then sit with both feet facing each other and hands covering the navel, and in this way you won't feel cold. Once you have some accomplishment in meditation then you will forget the cold or heat, so there will be no need at that point to heed this advice.

Building a bridge – the general transmission says to touch the palate with the tongue to build up the liquid, this is 'building the bridge', but I think this is over-emphasising the form and is unnatural. However, my master's transmission is to clench the teeth and purse the lips, so that the tongue slightly touches the palate in a natural way. This will generate saliva in the long term.

Pull down the curtain – lightly close both eyes but not too tightly.

Fix on Dantien – put your intent in Dantien, don't attach your mind to any forms but stubbornly suppress them.

Regulate the breath – let your breathing be natural without controlling it. It should seem like you both breathe and don't breathe, that breath exists and doesn't exist. True breathing is to allow the breath to regulate itself.

Post-Meditation Practice

First, relax the mind. When you want to stop sitting, slowly loosen the mind. Second, take off the bridge. The tongue no longer has to touch the teeth. Third, turn up the curtain. Slowly open the eyes. Fourth, slowly relieve the two hands. Fifth, put the two feet with the centre touching each other, then put both hands on the knees and close the legs. Slowly stretch forwards. After meditation use your right hand to cup the face and lay down on your right side. The right leg is straight and left leg bent. Left hand is on the left knee cavity (Gwai Yen Shr). Right hand slightly presses the ear with the index finger, so that when you rest it won't close the ear cavity.

Dr Serge Augier

The Heritage of Du Xing Wu

Dr Serge Augier of Paris

On a quiet Parisian side street, at the top of a couple of flights of wooden stairs, is an apartment probably unlike any other in the city. It is a place that attracts people from many countries, seekers after knowledge, pilgrims looking for the ancient ways of the Dao, those serious in their personal quest for skill in the martial and healing ways of old China. Step inside and you will feel a subtle yet tangible energy, a force, as if from another realm. Looking around you see ancient-looking Chinese swords, shelves of books on the I-Jing and the eastern arts of healing, hanging scrolls of calligraphy and a somewhat battered wooden dummy. There is the aroma of medicinal Asian herbs in the air...

As if by magic, the teacher appears. He is not, in fact, the white-bearded old Chinese fellow whom you may have expected, but a jovial and rather stocky forty-year-old Frenchman. Depending on the day and the time you may be sharing the room with acupuncture patients, with students of the internal martial arts or with meditation practitioners cultivating the Dao. This man's students have travelled from all over Europe, from as far as Hong Kong, to study with him, and several are already experienced teachers and healers in their own right. Looking at the teacher for the first time you may wonder how someone so young has garnered such respect from so many, but as you spend more time with the man you begin to notice the spirit in his eyes, his special way of moving when he passes through his martial arts exercises, his ability to transmit the most obscure principles of Chinese medicine and philosophy in a way that all of the Western-born students there can grasp, as all the while everything is suffused with a sense of naturalness and easy-going humour which makes the learning a joyous experience.

The teacher is Dr Serge Augier, my main Neijia teacher and a man who has been a huge influence on all aspects of my life. It was due to his great teachings and encouragement that I had the confidence to begin teaching Baguazhang back in 1997, and later to face the inevitable challenges that came with teaching in South East Asia. He gave me the ability to really see how and why an art should be trained to make it effective, the keys which lie behind the forms and techniques, unlocking the ability to develop internal striking power and the ability to enter and finish against a determined attacker. He is a tough teacher for those close to him, and has a very clear sense of his own Way and ethics. As a student I made mistakes which led to some memorable and bitter lessons. Serge gave me plenty of space and time in which to learn from my errors and, although it took years, those teachings led to true insight. It became clear from such learning experiences that the only true understandings of ethics and simple human decency must come from deep inside a person, and refinement must come from genuine change and insight into the nature of natural laws rather than simply being instructed or scolded into compliance.

A real school with an accomplished master will often be the cauldron in which such things can manifest – sometimes from the simple pain of the practice, the demands of the teacher or just the clashing egos of fellow students. And from watching just how much was learned by myself and the other students, our school was clearly one with an expert teacher.

Closed Door Fighting

I recall one time in Paris when Serge announced to my Gongfu brother and myself, 'OK, we will have a little meeting with some fighters from other schools and some guys from Marseilles, just free fighting with no rules to test your skills. These guys from the south are pretty tough…'

I had been training with Serge long enough and had had a few matches with some martial artists in London and Taiwan to be feeling confident in my skills, but I had also heard that Marseilles was a very dangerous place where people fought with blades. There was something in his voice which hinted that it was going to be a genuine test of skill. As a teenager I had been viciously attacked by thugs and gang members dozens of times, being badly beaten on many occasions until the years of training under my Shaolin Gongfu teacher had borne fruit and I was able to start fighting back for real. In the years since then I had made a huge effort to deal with the fear which had lodged in the subconscious from those times. I had trained in traditional systems of Xingyiquan with Sifu Paul Whitrod and Silat with Steve Benitez, powerful martial artists who did fighting drills or free fighting with me every lesson and helped me to find more confidence in my skills. When I met Serge he also taught me many practices to deal with the fear and had battered me so hard in training that I simply no longer worried about street thugs. Once, for example, he told me to put on the head protector and gloves and attack him all out, which of course resulted in him punching me very fast and continuously until I was knocked out. I revived (maybe he revived me, I cannot recall) and then he made me attack again. After the second time I revived and felt too dizzy to stand, so Serge allowed me to sit down for a few minutes until I was fine again. He looked at me afterwards and said simply, 'Good!'

That was the only time he knocked me out twice in a row (and in fact the only other event when I was rendered unconscious was the very first time we free sparred on the rooftop in London a few years before, when I had really gone all out to hit him and he had responded with a blur of hands culminating in a point strike and…lights out) and although it may sound strange, it resulted in another increase in my confidence. The unusual thing with Serge's harsh teaching was that in all the years I never left the class with headaches, broken bones or internal injuries, but only bruises, unlike some Chinese teachers I had met whose lack of control led to many of those things. Serge was masterful at controlling all aspects of his energy and knew exactly what each student needed and when they had had enough.

So when we turned up in the hired room – down some back street, with windows all covered over – the other guys looked as tense and nervous as I felt. There was a sense of uncertainty and excitement in the room. One guy from the south in particular, a rather heavy scowling man who seemed some years older than me, looked mean and intimidating. All the while I was watching my emotions and body state, just as Serge had taught me, wanting this to be a learning experience rather than just a chance to win. I was most curious to see if under pressure the Ziranmen flavour of naturalness would emerge effectively. I have always felt that in fighting we should be able to manifest the flavour and special trademark body motion of whatever style we train, rather than revert to some kind of generic kick boxing. My real concern was that I would be pitted against my Gongfu brother, someone I deeply cared for and had absolutely no desire to hit for real. We often trained together quite intensively and bruises were par for the course, but real free fighting under such pressure was a very different thing and I knew how easy it was for egos to rear up. At that time he already had some skill at fighting and we were probably quite evenly matched. As it happened Serge – who was acting as referee – did not match us up, and that was my first lesson: fears that never manifest can still eat a lot of our energy.

Instead my first fight was against a Taekwondo fighter. The man came in with continuous fast kicks, but I was able to deflect them and kick him in the groin enough times that he became frustrated. The second fight I cannot recall anything about except that I survived and didn't get injured. The third fight I saw Serge grinning as he matched me against the big mean guy from Marseilles. We faced each other and I then noticed that he also looked very wary of me, so we slowly felt each other's range with a few probing shots. I recall at one point going on the offensive with the combinations we trained every day in the school, and actually got my scowling opponent back-pedalling. I have no idea how long it lasted but I do recall the exact moment of my downfall – it was a single thought: 'Ah yes, I am not going to get beaten!'…the man was out of breath and his face had a desperate look on it as I moved in for a take-down and then, Whack! His right hand flailed out in a wild hit and caught me full force in my liver. I can still see the look of total amazement and joy on his face as I doubled over and almost threw up. Somehow I struggled up and did a few deep breaths, keeping him at a distance. But I had no more chance for a take-down and the match finished.

The whole experience had been very interesting to me. I had never enjoyed hitting people for real, treating matches with martial artists as an exchange of skill and a chance to deal with the inevitable emotions and fears which emerged. But having to use our skills in real situations requires the ability to move in with instant definitive action, and when later I had to once again deal with serious street attacks all of these events elicited by Serge's great teaching helped me to survive.

A Lesson

There were many lessons like that along the way, some involving my teacher's ability to help heal serious illness. There was a period when, due to some bad choices I had made, my teacher refused to see me. A martial arts master from Asia whom I knew came to stay with me for a month in England during a time when I had been seriously ill for a long while. It was a painful time as the man would not accept I was unwell and spent the month beating me at every chance. My health worsened, and the day he left I was just relieved to be alone. As so often, my mind went to the years with Serge, and a deep regret rose up again for my mistakes that had led to a distance developing in what was a relationship of deep karmic affinity. And then a strange thing happened. I had told no one about what had occurred between the martial arts teacher and myself, but the next day I received a letter from Serge. 'You look like you are dying, this man's teaching is not helping you. Come to see me and I will teach you to help yourself get better.'

It was the first I had heard from him for some time, but he had heard some things and had been genuinely concerned for me. I immediately booked a ticket and a few days later took a bus to Paris. And there it was again, the school in which so many lessons had been learned and my teacher, grinning and greeting me with, 'Sick man! What is up with you now?!'

I explained what had occurred. He nodded and said, 'Don't worry, we are not going to do fighting stuff. You don't need to be hit! You are forty-two, it's time to go towards other things.'

That was an immense relief. My teacher immediately began teaching me four simple exercises for opening the parts of my body which were blocked. He spent the afternoon with me, gave me much useful advice and handed me a bottle of potent herbal medicine. Back in England the exercises, advice and medicine worked their effect, and within a couple of months the effect of the beatings was reversed.

I have never heard Serge talk about forgiveness and compassion, but he didn't have to. It remains one of the best lessons of my life so far.

The First Meeting

The first time I met Serge many years ago was as a voice on the phone, requesting in a French accent if he could learn some Xingyiquan from me. He had seen some writing of mine in a martial arts magazine and seemed genuinely interested that there was someone in London who even knew that the art existed. I agreed to meet him the following day in a park, although something in the voice made me a little doubtful…

He greeted me the next morning with a big smile and a face full of vitality, casually dressed in blue jeans and a black leather jacket. It was clear from the way he held himself that he trained in something, and in reply to my query as to what that might be he said simply, 'Ziranmen!'

Well…here was an art which I had read about since I was a child, a system whose history was peopled with eccentric and wonderful characters like the wanderer Little Xu and the mystical warrior Du Xing Wu, an ancient method which belonged in the courtyards of Daoist monasteries and the deep mountains of China…and here was a young Frenchman, looking nothing like an ancient Daoist, who claimed to know the art. And then we exchanged a little technique, agreeing to stick to Chin-Na (joint locking) methods. From the first touch I knew I would not be teaching this man anything. His grasping skill was very precise, accurate and extremely powerful, and the range of locking techniques, and his ability to flow from one to another with speed and accuracy, was inspiring. Next up was a little form, and Serge started with a short set from Fujien White Crane Boxing, then an explanation of how each of the Xingyiquan animals had at least five variations, and then a little demonstration of Fajin from an inch away which rattled my body, and then…and then quite simply I knew I had found a teacher. Without any fanfare he agreed to teach me whatever I wanted to learn, including the healing and meditational aspects of his art.

The next morning I turned up early at his rooftop apartment in East London, and thus began a long period of training which was to cover so many methods of Daoist boxing that most days I would return home after hours completely overloaded with information. The first thing he taught me, as I stepped into his front room, was simply to kick the doorframe in a particular way; the kick had to be delivered from a short distance and always from the front leg, and it was to be done in a somewhat relaxed and natural manner with power coming from the hip rather than the leg. Now, you know the thing about doorframes is they are quite hard, and my bare foot was just a little softer than the wood... Serge demonstrated with a force which made the doorframe rattle, and I soon found out that from years of Ziranmen training his toes were able to grip and kick with a steel-like force.

It was these 'little exercises', seemingly simple and basic drills, which were to give me a new ability over the next few years. Serge taught me hundreds of such methods covering the martial and meditative aspects of the arts, and as it turned out the only secret was in actually doing them, day after day, month after month, in a natural manner. In fact Serge emphasised that I should do all of my training in a slightly 'messy' way, since it was closer to the reality and chaos of combat and life. This messy way in fact hid the many details that had to be worked, so that one found not only internal power increasing, but also the ability to apply it spontaneously against surprise attack. I was told to choose a natural weapon and then shown how to develop it – some Ziranmen practitioners specialised in the palm, others in the claw, and some in the thumb. My choice was the Phoenix-Eye Fist, which was central to the Shaolin boxing I had learned as a child, but now instead of hard conditioning I was given a practice that seemed almost too simple, and told to do it during any periods of free time. Thus I found myself doing the practice whilst riding the bus or train, or sitting down after dinner. And something unexpected happened. During exchanges with other martial artists it would take but a light tap of the Phoenix-Eye Fist to produce a big reaction, and whilst I never hit an area which could cause possible long-term damage, even a close range strike to the arm would penetrate through to the bone and stop the other man in his tracks.

The difference, as I was to see with all of Serge's methods, was in the type of penetrative internal force which one slowly acquired over months and years of 'natural' training. The practices somehow enabled one to direct power deep into an attacker's structure, and in more advanced stages added various emotional qualities to the mix to give the enemy an emotional as well as physical shock. Moreover, the footwork and body methods encouraged a loose but precise response to attack that had far more chance of working in reality than a classical or formulaic type of training. Simply put, it slowly started to become clear why the Ziranmen fighters of old had acquired almost legendary reputations as fighters.

Every week brought new teachings, and I was so fortunate to be studying with Serge at a time when he was just beginning to teach. Wan Lai Sheng's emergency acupuncture system, Du Xing Wu's sword skill, Daoist Neigong… I knew I was learning rare skills which were held by only a handful of men even in China.

The Shen-Fa or Body Method of what I was taught was contained in eight short combinations of striking and kicking. Each had to be trained daily in order to find in oneself the specific principle and Fajin, and then later I had to start combining them in a free way using various footwork patterns. The stepping included highly deceptive ways of shifting the feet in a way which was intended to baffle the enemy and disturb his perception of where you were in time and space. Little tricks played upon rhythm, beat and half beat, blind spots, lines of intent, and methods such as 'trapping the eyes' which left an attacker feeling as if he had picked a fight with a ghost who suddenly vanished from his sight. Many of these methods would be impossible to teach in a book or film, requiring hands on instruction and feeling the quality and depth of the impact. I spent a decade teaching the methods learned from Serge, eventually closing my school to focus on practice and 'owning' the art, but the lessons with my teacher continued.

Serge's Studies with His Teacher

Serge Augier is not your normal martial artist. He is recognised by three separate sects of Daoism as a Tien Ran, a Heavenly Teacher, a spiritual adept, holding lineage in one of the oldest extant schools of internal practice. When Serge was still just eight years old his father – an Aikido black belt – employed a cook for the family, a refugee from China who happened to be an adept in the internal arts. The young Frenchman received this rare Daoist system, known as Da Xuan, during two decades studying with this man, who was not only the head of that lineage but also an early disciple of one of the most famous martial artists of the twentieth century, Ziranmen Grandmaster Wan Lai Shang. Serge's teacher had also met and studied with Wan's Master Du Xing Wu, and the equally legendary 'Lightning Hand' Zhang Zao Dong. Moving to France he taught his young apprentice a vast range of skills, with the rare Ziranmen (Natural Boxing) being his most prized martial art system.

Since his teacher's passing Serge Augier has taught a growing number of martial arts and Chinese medicine students in France and Hong Kong under the banner of his school – the White Crane Institute – whilst continuing to refine himself through constant practice and research. When I asked him what led him to practise he told me his story.

'The big motivation in the beginning was that my father gave me to this crazy old Chinese man, and I wanted to be less hurt by him! Second thing was that I actually felt good. From being a weak kid I went to actually not being sick at Christmas for the first time. Then later when I started looking at the older girls I had to contend with the older boys who wanted to stop me, so I had to be able to fight with them. As time passed I knew I wanted to do this as a job, and by the age of sixteen I knew I had no choice. But at that time this stuff was not fashionable like it is now, they all thought I was crazy!

'What stands out about my teacher was his personality. Still today, after all the others I have seen, he still had something else. No one else had this. The first thing was fear. In his presence of course weaker people felt this, not that he was mean just…so much power. Same as an animal, even though he looked mild and smiling. He had a crushing presence, but then in a moment it could vanish and he could be gone even while he was sitting in the same room. This is vital in the training. He could connect from another room and know what I was doing wrong. This kind of intimate knowledge of body and mind is gone today, and in him it was very much from the spiritual work.

'I met other teachers, of course. In California as soon as I met one teacher and shook his hand I knew I would stay and learn from him. Within a week he had asked me to stay and teach something at his school, although he had no idea what I had done before.

There I learned Muay Thai, boxing, weapons and so on. There were several with good skill that I worked with like this, but none of them were free of the things which made them unhappy. The man in California was so bored teaching it was a chore for him. Recently I was with one famous Bagua teacher in Europe and he was defending himself against his wife on the phone just like a child. He had to run everything by her before deciding! When problems came with his students due to their arrogance, he didn't want to deal with them in case it affected his workshops. But my teacher was different from all of them in that he was always happy, even when his life had real problems. This came from his immersion in every step of the spiritual work again and again.

'Today, as soon as someone becomes a teacher they stop training. They don't want to be judged so they don't show their stuff. The way of my teacher, simply his presence, is the most vital memory for me, and even now some of my students dream of him. And of course with the dream work I still see him most days...

'Ziranmen has a much longer history than most people think. It comes from a Daoist clan system of spirituality and the boxing is only one part of the whole system. The name of this system may be changed by certain lineage masters, and before Little Xu [the known founder of Ziranmen] there were many systems which used the sword as the basis for boxing. My teacher was very good at sword, and this will tell you something about the nature of the system. The hand motions then become very efficient at being able to pierce at the end of each strike.

'Also the magical aspect is important for the whole system, and the boxing trains the Neigong. The magic or shamanic power adds intensity for using the medicine skills or fighting, linking you to something more subtle. The reality of internal, call it magic or the esoteric knowledge, is that it is only possible if you are working internally. People say that they can see auras, chakras, earth demons and so on, but this is just refined perception.

'My teacher was the "Killer of Demons" in our Daoist lineage, and in fact our ancestor is the Demon Slayer God. Our system is from the Clan Daoism, totally apart from religious Daoism which wanted power in numbers and copied the Buddhist way of monasteries, rituals and so on. A small number of clans who were totally against visualisation and other Buddhist type methods kept the original ways going over thousands of years.

'The tradition of my teacher is still alive in China, but the teachers are very old and have no disciples. I take care of the expenses of about twenty of them so they have an easier life, allowing them to go into town for supplies and so on. When I was in China some people invited a man who came from near Kunlun, a man I had heard of from my teacher. I arranged to meet him and told him that my teacher knew of him, and asked him if he could show me the special Daxuan Qigong. He then demonstrated some kind of flapping exercise, completely different to our style. So I showed him the real thing at which point he was very surprised and said, "Oh, you are really from our school!"

'The government nowadays treats those monks well who sell the image of Daoism, but they don't care for the old monks. White Cloud Temple in Beijing does a good job of keeping so much knowledge, and I respect this a lot, but it has very little relationship to what we do. There were two very good teachers there, but one has died and the other one is very old.

'With what I do there are three ideas – first is the religious aspect where I am small and God is everything. Second is the animist way where I fuse into the Nature, animal totems and so on. Third is non-duality where we try to go back to the Yuen Shr [Original Spirit]. It is emptiness, complete nothingness.

'I once asked my teacher if there was anything after death. He told me this story. Once his teacher was asked the same question by a man, and his teacher asked the man if he really wanted to know. The man said yes, and his teacher took a sword and chopped his head off. After hearing this I didn't ask my teacher again.'

I asked Serge about the relevance of the Eight Immortals of Daoism, and how he linked with the long chain of masters in the lineage.

'The Eight Immortals give an example of energy and a way to put everything together like a catalogue. Eight big principles are linked to the Eight Immortals. It is like a book of symbols, nice images before each chapter. In Shen Gong [spirit work] you call upon all the lineage. My teacher was linked with many mystics; he permitted me to learn Kaballah, Sufism, Western Mysticism and so on. Now I can teach using Western concepts and jokes, which we need to explain in the West. Then I slowly slide towards Chinese terms and words, and in this way you can experience what it is. This is "in-life" teaching; it is for life, you can still have a job, family and still manage to practise. There is no need at all to be a monk.'

Serge Augier teaching in Holland Park, London 1997

An Overview of the Daoist System

When I asked Serge how important technique and power was his reply was succinct and clear. 'We need three things – power, intent and finally technique. My teacher said the mental aspect is vital, then you can go into the fight with confidence – but this kind of aggression is not using emotion!'

Aggression without using emotion? Most people would consider that almost oxymoronic, but his reply in fact hints at the multi-levelled and somewhat complex nature of the teaching. The first thing to understand is that his Ziranmen is a system comprised of clear stages, each one developing a different facet of the whole human being.

'We want to develop the body, the energy and the mind,' Serge explained to me. 'The work of the body will give us good health through the exercises for relaxation, strength and rooting. Then for energy circulation we also have three stages – to realise the internal feelings, to mobilise the will and to make natural and conscious exchanges. After this we have the work of the mind which enables us to see who we really are, again through three stages – observation of the self, observation of the world, and having global perception. All the practical application of the teaching must go in the direction of relaxing the body, to allow energy to circulate or bring peace to the mind, sometimes all three together. You can only practise with that in mind. Without realising this, there is no practice. In this realisation, you are in the simplicity of the Way.

'All of this follows eight principles – the principle of alignment, of non-resistance, of balance, of breathing, of natural cycles, of intention, of development and of evolution. All of these principles connect with each other, combining and not separate, but to avoid confusion in the beginning we work each one separately.'

There was much more to be discussed, but at this point we should look more closely at the eight stages of practice. What follows is a very clear explanation of these stages from the writings of Serge Augier.

The Principle of Alignment – Awakening of Conscience

'Not to be content with a little.'

This principle is connected mostly with a physical sensation: the sensation of holding ourselves right, but also with our vertical alignment. In the centre of the body and in the centre of the practice we recover the spine. It is composed of vertebrae that we are going to try to stack like in a game of cubes: if not done correctly, one will have the stack lean toward the right or left, toward the front or back. On the energy level, the idea of holding a straight back permits the correct alignment with the celestial energy in relation to the terrestrial energy. This Daoist teaching continues to say that if the mind affects the body, one would also consider that the body influences the mind. That is why while starting to work on the physical alignment and while thinking as well about the energetic alignment, we will help our mind find its centre.

This first stage corresponds to our desire to be better, to change our daily life and no longer be puzzled by our 'deep being'. Therefore, when searching for our centre it is obvious that we must look at ourselves as we really are. The method of 'centring' also helps us concentrate and focus attention. During this process, we realise the work is to be done by us alone and no one can do it for us. We also realise at this moment that to observe any change and to submit to a fully conscious daily practice, it is necessary that we integrate the practice within our way of living.

The awareness that corresponds to this stage is so simple and so difficult: it all must become conscious. We look for the attention to our manner of breathing, position, manner of walking but also watching how we take a shower, at what moment we are stretched, at what moment we are relaxed, what our sensations at every instant are. Once again, it is a stage where we will learn not to believe anything of what is established, to put everything to a test because only our own experience would permit evolution.

The practice of Qigong that corresponds to this stage is called the Stance of the Tree. It is our favourite static position; it is the first and the last of the Qigong exercises. It is also in the practice of the static positions that one recovers the concept of tree stance, but one is going to go farther through bringing dissociation between the right and left, refining the sensations and beginning to see the body as a block under seal, constituted of several controllable sections.

In the next stage, we will begin to use simple pictures to amplify energy generation. These pictures permit us to 'live' in the stances. It is also the beginning work on the intention.

The meditative practice is also one of the most important: it is the conscious breathing. One of the acts we are most unconscious of in life is breathing. It is obvious that most of the time one pays no attention to this. The idea that becoming conscious of our breathing, the important and vital action, allows us to be more in contact with our body. Often, the people who begin this kind of conscious meditation can feel a sensation of suffocation, anguish or light-headedness: this says much about the unhealthy rapport that we can develop with our body if we do not pay attention!

Indeed, this uneasiness is only the refusal of our mental side to feel the body, the fear to see us as we really are. It is a primordial work.

In order to understand the principle of alignment, developing the respect for structure is necessary: understanding that all comes to the centre, the spine, the back. We will see well later that all this comes down to Earth in relation to Heaven. Of course, at this level of practice we will try simply to feel our body; this is already an enormous task! An important stage and the backbone of the body-awareness is the simple exercise of holding our space: we try to occupy the maximum space possible with our back, chest and shoulders, instead of remaining shrunken like a scared or injured animal!

All these practices will be detailed later; the goal here is to explain what we do and where we are going. Physically, we will try (by the immobility of the static stance) to feel and get in touch with our body, also try to fully occupy the space that is ours. Mentally, the work will be in looking at our actions and daily movements, in order to become present and conscious, as much as possible, of the daily events. On the energetic level, we will try merely to open up and experiment with the vital energy sensation, this breath of life that resides in us.

As for this first principle, just like in all the Daoist teachings we find a revelation but also a sensation of inability and helplessness facing our problems. It is not at all a theoretical teaching but a teaching of daily practice: because the only way to understand the theory is to practise without cessation.

The Principle of Non-Resistance – A Passive Activity

'Don't push the river…'

Here we find one of the least understood principles, but one which we are talking about the most. Much has been made of this principle as a way to do nothing and simply wait, like a metro ticket pushed by dirty water into the gutter to go somewhere. The idea of non-resistance is not the idea of doing nothing but the idea of going in the direction of events instead of resisting them. One who can find this in their life finds things become simpler. There is a Chinese saying: there is no need to push the river.

Again, this is a method which requires concrete application and one's own experience. In martial arts basic concepts explain it well: always go straight to the point; if you are stopped in trying to reach your target, stick to the barrier; if the barrier is too high, let the force take you back to the goal.

Awareness which corresponds to this level of training is the realisation that life is fluid and can be part of this flow. This is the time when you have to concentrate to listen to your feelings, accept the signs that life may send and following your instincts. This is the time where we will try to get in touch with the part of ourselves that is already known, this part of us that we never listen to.

Physically, practice is that of coordination, and the only real way to test it is through the relaxation ability of the union of body and mind. This is a fun practice that helps to account for the lack of coordination and for any tension stored in the body, especially in the joints.

It is at this point that we begin the meditative practice of observation. This method of active meditation allows you to view, analyse and understand how your thoughts are activated in the brain, how you operate internally and how the body can affect the mind. This is a practice in which we complain the most because it requires a daily effort and a lot of time before being settled. But we do not have much choice, do we? This observation of our own mind can help us to know it better. It is also a practice that will prove to be the basis of all the others. It must be realised at this time that it is necessary to relax: relax and enjoy life.

One of the first concepts which is easy to understand and almost impossible to apply is to accept what cannot be changed. If an event in your life brings you stress but there is no way to change it, or to soften the influence, then you must understand that you must relax. This can range from the simplest things to the most horrible things that life will concoct. An invoice, a death in your family, or a disabling accident are examples, among many others, where you cannot do anything except accept what you would rather push away. However, if you have the opportunity to change an unpleasant situation, it is important to understand that this is the time when we will also react. This is the stage where we will stop to let it go, to be a victim, and to do everything possible to change what we do not accept.

You also understand that this is the stage where we will understand the need to stop taking ourselves so seriously, to stop being so important, and once again you will have to relax. Energetically, it is the discovery of Qi. This period is when one develops and strengthens the body's defensive energy. By listening to the body in motion, we realise the sensation, the movement of energy in the body.

The Principle of Balance – Stability in Movement

'Find in every thing the happy medium...'

Balance is a concept that we find in all spiritual teachings and most religions, the physical and mental concept that is easy to understand and difficult to apply. In the Daoist system of which we speak today, one first tries to understand and master the physical balance; that will bring us easily to the mental balance. Once again, we start to work on the body before the mental. We do it this way for a reason: we can rarely deceive the body whereas we can always deceive the mind. Incidentally, if you understand what you must reproduce with your body mentally, as you will do it – you will know if it is real or not. If you try solely to acquire the mental balance, without going through the work on the body, then the odds are you will not recover quickly from the illusion: you will not have any reference to know whether you are in the real or fake.

One will become aware here of the three energising centres that shelter the instinctive, emotional and spiritual. These centres are as much physical as they are energetic. By precise exercises, Qigong and meditation, one will learn to wake these centres, become aware of them and utilise them on a daily basis.

We will try to balance the three centres that we discovered in the previous stage to arrive at our being's global sensation. It is an important stage where one is not going only to try to practise occasionally but to practise in a continuous manner, in every instant of one's life, while keeping the developed stability. The awareness here is of our movement in space, falling in every step but controlling our movement and the transfer of our gravity centre. This is done in order to put the body not to a precise place in space any more but in all the space.

The Qigong will be the work on movement. Each of the measurements explored will let us verify the tensions that always exist within us, the lack of stability that we suffer once we leave the static position. The movements start with 'the basin', then 'the wave' and finally encompass the whole body. The movements of the basin produce different circles in different measurements in order to loosen and soften this usually stiff part of the body. The exercises of the basin are recommended to increase the circulation in this region. The wave is a curling produced by the foot on soil and that reverberates in the whole body, along the backbone, finishing in the nape. These motions are done very slowly at first, like a dance, to arrive at brief and exploding movements that go successively in all directions.

In meditation, we will become aware of three circles; the existence of the three energising centres of the body in relation with the internal organs and emotions as well as the meridians of acupuncture. We look at the lower centre, which corresponds to the Yin, to the animal instinct within us and to the Earth; the middle centre, which corresponds to the Man and emotions. The highest centre corresponds to the Sky, to Yang, but also to the strength of the Divine Spark, which is within us. In the meditative practice, we will want to feel and open those centres. The latter will be possible through meditative exercises. Every opening corresponds to a 'small enlightenment' on each of the three levels: physical, emotional and spiritual. These changes may be challenging for someone with strong religious concepts; nevertheless they remain a necessary stage.

We realise during this period that walking is a succession of falls forward, with no awareness on our side. Thanks to the practice, one is going to change it and to learn again to walk appropriately and consciously. Identifying where our weight and centre of gravity are, we will learn to feel them and put them to a test. All transfers of weight will then be made consciously. This very soothing practice first takes place in a straight line, then in a circle. The Daoist idea of the three powers (the Heaven, the Earth and the Man) helps us find that if the Heaven and the Earth are steady enough, the Man on the other hand finds it difficult enough to control his own legs. This practice allows us to change that and, as a pupil said, 'acquire new legs'.

In the fighting arts or Qigong, the ground is the source of all strength. The use of hip strength is a first stage that brings us to return to the origin: the ground. The expression of movement, the fact that we occupy our space and that we 'lean' on the Earth – it is the Man's expression. For the tie between the Heaven and the Earth to be strong, it is necessary that the Man is strong as well. The energy can only circulate in the absence of either physical or emotional tension. For the energy to circulate between the Heaven and the Earth while passing by the Man, it will be necessary therefore that this last will be simultaneously strong and flexible. In every movement, the expression of the three Daoist powers will be present.

It is in motion where we see that, for the perfect balance to be acquired, we do not need to follow rules but that it is sufficient to find 'the happy medium'. It is the concept of re-creating after the effort, the decision to work better. A Daoist concept says it is necessary to take a rest before work, necessary to relax in order to be receptive. For that to be applicable in our complex life, it is not important to follow rules but always to know how to find the balance. We explore the excess and the extreme so that we can find the stability of the centre better.

The Principle of Breathing – The Exchange with the World Around Us

'Practise at the heart of the society.'

Breathing is par excellence an act of exchange. One goes every instant to establish a relation with the world and the environment, by the simple inhalation of the air that surrounds us and the exhaling of personal air. When we inhale we take the O2, the oxygen, and when we exhale we reject the CO2, the carbon dioxide. The difference between the two is that the carbon dioxide possesses one carbon besides the oxygen, the C. The carbon is therefore a particle of matter; to every expiration we add a little part of ourselves. We do recover these carbons in food. Therefore, the saying that we are what we eat is literally true. Before you eat without thinking what you have on your plate – consider every time the fact that this food will constitute your new body, one that is in perpetual evolution. The two main sources permitting the acquirement of energy are the breathing and food. To know how to breathe is fundamental to not wasting all exchanges we make with the world.

The practice of the Qigong is the test of voice. A scream, which often results from this practice, is only the outcome of the internal work. Thanks to precise stances and specific work, we force the breath out and a sound will result from that. One does not shout just to shout, but only to recover the sensation of the hurled down air exiting our body. This can be tough for the students who have difficulty expressing energy. The regular practice permits the expression of our fears and frustrations and the affirmation of ourselves. It is very invigorating and makes for the defensive energy around the body; a very quick practice of lots of Yang.

In meditation, we are going to learn to increase the raw material that is called breath. Therefore, we are going to begin to concentrate energy – what we call 'the compression of the breath'. We are going to learn to press a certain spring, by means of a particular meditative and respiratory state, to condense the vital breath when exercises that ask for more energy are being done. It is a method that requires a teacher to be constantly present; he will make sure the pupil does not become a victim of blockage or stagnation of energy. It is a very interesting meditative stage, because the ensuing increase of energy brings the churchgoer to surprising realisations and visions. As an outcome of this practice, one can feel an increase in strength and resistance and pulmonary capacity.

This awareness of exchange with the world is very important. The breathing is a way to be close with our environment but at the same time a way of being detached from it. Let us take a closer look at this very Daoist paradox. By the action of normal breath, we exchange with our direct environment. In the same way, when we want to separate ourselves from a stressful environment, we can accomplish that while decomposing the respiratory movements. For example, before a marvellous landscape, one will want to inspire a big puff of air as if one wanted to take a piece of this landscape inside oneself. On the other hand, when facing a stressful situation one will make a big inhalation/exhalation to calm down. Breathing is a regulator of emotions. When one laughs, the expiration is superior to inspiration. It is an action Yang, positive. When one shouts or pushes something heavy, it is again an action Yang because the expiration is bigger than inspiration. When one cries, afraid or startled – it is an action Yin, the inspiration is more important than expiration. Understanding this, one can play on the emotions by the means of breath control. The control is never the idea of a practice. It is in the sphere of understanding the emotional mechanisms that one is able to live well.

It is also the concept of not isolating ourselves from the world around us. The breathing recognises the constant daily exchange with the environment; therefore, we become aware, because our practice and work are done in the world and not an isolated place in a cellar. This Daoist school requires certain periods of isolation but the outcome of that is the sharing with people in the world. It is easy to be a big master of meditation isolated from all civilisation but more difficult to keep our calm when we barely miss being run over by a taxi.

The Principle of Natural Cycles – Maturation of Teaching

'We must allow time for time.'

'We must allow time for time' could summarise the principle of natural cycles. Even if you work every day for twelve hours a day on your personal practice, even if you are very talented and you have the best teacher in the world: it takes time. You can understand a concept very well, a practice, but it will be truly your practice with a little time. Acceptance of maturation, the realisation that even when we have understood it will always be better understood in some time. Only over time can we completely integrate practice.

The Qigong of the five elements is directly linked to natural cycles. Each primary element of the Chinese cosmology corresponds to an organ, an emotion, a season and a Qigong exercise. There are five exercises that can merge to balance but also to better understand each of these concepts. The Qigong of five starts like a gym, and then becomes a meditation to finally prove to be a fairly complex Qigong to meet the needs of most practitioners. There are three levels of understanding of its practice, each level being taught when the previous level is fully acquired. The different levels are the physical, energetic and spiritual.

In direct relation to the Qigong of the five elements, the meditation on the fusion of emotions is very important. Upon successful connection of the breath and movement we will occupy ourselves, for these practices, to regulate the emotions. Each negative emotion corresponds to a positive emotion that can be stimulated by physical, energetic and spiritual exercises. Meditation of fusion of the emotions is very important to be able to live without being a victim of the emotions. We learn instead to live with them without having them pose problems. The energy saved by the regulation of negative emotions may be redirected in order to feed the intention. In Daoism we talk about two types of control: the emotional will, which is compared to a young monkey, and intentional will intentionally used to focus the attention. Emotions are compared to a young monkey because you cannot force or control and of course we can never predict what will happen. As an attempt at taming a young monkey, the only way to regulate these emotions is in the art of understanding, not dominating or controlling. By letting go and relaxing you can understand the emotional mind and redirect the energy to feed the intention. The practice is more important than theories, further proof that the Daoist art of teaching is action rather than theory.

Being aware of the need to allow time to put in to commitment of the success in practice; realising that in any case it's time that will integrate the practice, there is no need to rush: here we find the circular Eastern vision of the world: 'The important thing is not where you go but the journey.' It is a time when you learn patience since you have already worked for some time and know that there are not necessarily immediate results. If, on the contrary, there are many results it's time to say that all this is not important. Everything changes quickly; apart from that one cannot predict the next change, so just enjoy the ride without worrying about the final destination. Be aware of natural cycles but also respect the fact that everything that is created can be destroyed, and that whatever is destroyed can be rebuilt. Each renewal is a destruction and to live in these changes we must adapt. Adaptability is an important component of emotion regulation.

Our place in the world is central to this awareness. It is man who must be integrated with the seasons and the rhythm of Nature and not the reverse. He must respect these conditions, the food and air we breathe. A number of problems and seasonal discomforts can be avoided by following the rules of natural energy. Knowing and regulating the principles of Nature is an integral part of the Daoist teaching.

The Principle of Intention – Live in the Present

'It is the intention that counts.'

When we have a good teacher or master and begin our training in the arts of fight, meditation or Yoga, we are usually taught to practise some exercises on daily basis. If you are a pupil or regular disciple (which is rather rare), you then begin to execute what you have been told to do and work a few times each day in your discipline.

Yet it is not because we train every day that we train correctly. I explain to myself that we could say that two ways exist (or more) of training: the deep manner and the superficial manner. The first brings us more toward the being's total practice while the second would rather bring us to a vulgar work of the body and mind without real investment of oneself (but that is still more than only practising once, or from time to time).

To train in 'a deep manner' is to take the being's totality in consideration and therefore to work on several planes: physical, mental and spiritual, one could say. In this view, one practises some exercises with conscience, which allows one to better observe the small adjustments or even the changes that operate within the body. In the exercise of 'the tree' for example, one will be able to listen to the tensions that block the breathing, the rises of heat that turn the whole body into a bubble, the pains that paralyse the arms, the muscles that are weak, the irritation that goes up to the head, the different emotions remaining stuck, and so on... Other exercises will bring us to other sensations and observations and we will be able to work with a clear vision of our limits and desires.

But to train with 'depth' we must also look after what we do just for ourselves and know why we decide to do it. To train this is not to stupidly repeat exercises, imitating the professor or master, or to be able to attain a level that will allow us to build our reputation. To train deeply we need the intention to make it 'here and now' and not the intention 'to win' something. The intention is what makes the whole difference since it is going to bring us to a true presence rather than to any projection.

The practice of the fighting arts with intention is nothing else than to quiet ourselves sufficiently so that we no longer lose ourselves in the 'surface'. We return towards the interior instead. It smells like the progress of the answers of the body facing the practices, it is to be there in what happens, to dare to feel what one knows usually to avoid. And for us to be able to do that only one thing is important: the intention. According to the direction that the intention will take, she will propel us either toward a deep discovery of our interior being or toward a pleasant, rather banal repetition work that won't drag any real change into our life.

To train in a superficial manner is to imitate some exercises without the intention of the moment but with the idea to 'get something', to reach an ultimate stage. Then one gets to it every day, grants a moment of practice and waits for the results with impatience. Most of the time one does that in front of the TV, while listening to music or chatting with those that surround us, and it can be even while cooking! One diverts oneself from the exercise through taking care of other things. Of course, this method can be used, but only when the practice has been integrated in the daily routine, not before. Unfortunately, it is also this shape of practice that rarely stretches toward being integrated in our everyday life.

Indeed, since practice is a means to get somewhere, it becomes an isolated means which slowly becomes a daily habit.

Training of this sort presumes 'a good muscular level' or 'an advanced meditative capacity' which is then compared to people who don't practise anything... Then one seems to be in a pretty good shape and one has good fun. But at the end, no real transformation takes place.

We are always unsettled when we must face an emergency, we are frightened by the idea of having to make a decision and we are always sad when we hear bad news. Generally, the basic problems still exist and in the difficult moments we dive into them just as well as before, but at least we have more of a good form! With this type of practice one can solve a certain number of dysfunctions, without touching a true détente or interior tranquillity. It is a little more than sport and a lot less that a serious spiritual practice.

To practise superficially is to just 'participate' in the world; whereas to practise in depth is to 'invest' in the world. It is not to just 'be there' but it is to be completely present.

Finally, it is the intention that makes all. We can decide to train for and with ourselves and we can decide to train to get recognition and momentary appeasement that will grant us good conscience. The choice between these two ways is very clear; there is no hiding from this fact. But it is not necessary to be mistaken about what we do; training superficially will never bring the transformation of self. The illusion of change without sincere and honest practice is large and good numbers lose themselves in it. But doesn't one want to change indeed when one begins?

The Principle of Development – Increasing Energy

'Knowing to empty the trash.'

You should know that at some point in the training we will be faced with a lack of energy. Indeed, if we train a lot physically and we add to this meditation and Qigong, it is possible to feel exhaustion and quickly get the impression that there was not enough energy to do everything. Even if everything goes well, there comes a time when, older in years, you simply need more energy. In the fighting arts we will certainly need more power. This need for energy is the principle of development. You can practise and stay at the same level for a long time if you do not know how to increase the physical and spiritual vibration levels. For this is simple: we must simply accumulate more energy.

The meditation corresponds at this stage to the large circulation of energy throughout the body. After successfully leading the energy with our will and after learning how to compress the breath and release the voice, we will use all free energy to project power to the outside of the body. The energy stored in the centre will be able to leave the body through the extremities. This is a practice that allows us to gain a lot of energy but also to give. If we can get energy from the body it is clear that we will be able to do the opposite by turning it into energy inspiration. Imitating the principle of the sponge, it will expel its defensive energy creating a vacuum that is filled with inspiring energy from outside. The aspiration of the external energy can be dangerous if it cannot be fully assimilated by the body. This will require a further step by practising the 'breath of the five-doors'. By force of intent and in the stillness, we will push the conscience to the outside of the physical body. This is a spiritual practice that allows us to recover a lot of energy from the outside and send it toward the inside. This practice asks that the physical body and energy are strong enough to be able to share things with energy recovered from the outside. Like all advanced practices there must be a teacher present for the success of this exercise. This is the start of the first real spiritual practice.

The practice of Qigong 'Eight Mother Palms' is an exercise that takes place in a circular motion that combines an understanding of the eight trigrams of the Book of Changes with an alchemy of inner energy in motion. It is a combination of the eight starting positions, with a circular motion, moving towards one another on the circle. The evolution of these changes is a regulation of subtle energies of the three dimensions. This practice becomes precise, free and spontaneous rather quickly. This requires a good understanding of Qigong precedents.

We need to understand an important point: if one seeks to increase his energy it is better not to waste what we have already.

Therefore attention must be paid to the two primary sources of energy: the food we ingest and the air we breathe. Emotionally we also must be careful to let go of our emotional garbage. The image of garbage, when understood, becomes very useful. As we must throw out the garbage of the day or week, we have emotional garbage which must also be addressed. It is very rarely amusing to dig into our garbage. But if we fail to do so for too long we will have neglected those moments when we have the choice of action; then we will be confronted with the obligation to deal with it. Indeed, the garbage overflow eventually begins to go bad or even explode. It will be harder to act out of necessity than choice. An unpleasant action that one is forced to do is always worse. But if one empties the garbage every day it becomes simple and less painful, even when making the gesture at a time chosen consciously. Emotional garbage is very similar to this image. It is obvious that the first time is always difficult but if done more regularly this act becomes easier. Anyway, if we do not do it voluntarily, life will make us face our responsibility to clean up. It is a simple practice which amounts to not accumulating stress, or at least only the minimum. Emotional stress is a major consumer of energy. Moreover, most of our energetic actions become a vector of universal energy rather than a donor of personal energy.

This need to accumulate energy demands, of course, economy. The senses often consume a lot of energy for nothing: we talk too much, we look too much, we listen too much, we taste too much… Avoid too much. We need to learn how not to spend too much energy in the use of the five senses. This is also the time when we learn to control sexual practices in order to generate force instead of spending its energetic capital.

The Principle of Evolution – Towards a Different Ethic

'Respecting the world beginning with oneself.'

This stage of development is possible only under certain conditions: it must be that the practice is the most important thing in one's life, that it is fully integrated into one's life and that one has practised long enough. If these conditions are met, the move to a different life is practically a requirement. This leads, in general, to changes that can sometimes be difficult and painful but necessary. After some length of practice one cannot remain under the same conditions as before.

All practices of Qigong are just exercises to sensitise the body and mind to all possible variations of energy. It is an education of intent and to develop the muscles and tendons of the body. But the essence of Qigong lies in simplicity. All the Qigong we did before was a preparation. The merger of the 'dragon and the tiger', the Yin and Yang Qigong, is the ultimate of our school. This is the only true Qigong, the others are only a repetition of techniques, not spontaneous. This Qigong, which is very simple from the outside, condenses everything you did before. If Qigong has not been trained previously, it is a waste of time to engage in this exercise. Internal Qigong is complex because it aims to make all the years of exchange of natural energy spontaneous. This is an advanced practice.

The meditation of the 'golden path', the last practice we learn in the school, is simple, without form, with nothing particular to do, which means it is the most complex. This meditation is one of the most advanced and will be addressed in the company of a teacher who himself practises this exercise. (In some practices it is not necessary that the teacher has done what he teaches. For example, some great boxing coaches were poor boxers.) In these advanced spiritual practices it is dangerous to follow a teacher who has not himself experienced all the pitfalls and benefits of each practice.

We are here at the point of synthesis of all that one has learned in the system. We must have integrated all the other practices to benefit fully from the spontaneous practice. Traditionally we regularly omit to mention this step, so that the student is not too eager to achieve, or simply to avoid having to teach a student who is not really committed on the Way. Now the time has come no longer for Chinese secrecy but for sharing. Anyway, it is impossible to practise freely without having beforehand attended a teaching.

The freedom to practise the level we are talking about is the whole point of the Daoist school. It allows a daily diverse and varied practice throughout life. There is no more formality, no more rules or error. One practice is all. It is often said that before one is in the Way of practising, a mountain was a mountain and a stream was a stream. While learning about the Way all of a sudden the mountain is a mountain and the stream is really a stream. But having mastered the Way, a mountain is a new mountain, a stream a new stream. While learning about the Way it is clear that each practice is something complex. But this is not the essence, because the essence of the practice is always simple.

It is interesting to see that after a minimum time involved in a practice it is not possible to live the life one lived before. Training causes changes which lead to evolution that cannot be denied. We must abandon the old to the new and switch to a new ethic of life. After practising enough and noting the changes brought in and out of oneself, it is often difficult to be satisfied with the life one had. Becoming a human being in one's own right one cannot be content with life as a frightened animal. Recognising the change of state one must move in that direction. One may be faced with a misunderstanding on the part of one's circle, an inconsistency in one's employment or other such inconveniences. A long and painful rebirth process may be the result of a serious practice. This is neither bad nor good, it's changing. This change can happen very early on the track but one may not be aware of it for years. In any case what will happen will happen.

The path of the 'natural school' is not a moral way and still less a moralising. It is a Daoist Way based on simple rules that are not fixed or static but simply crutches to help before one can walk alone. It is obvious that we can succeed without crutches but it is less easy and we tend to fall more often. This is a course that teaches respect for the world and the acceptance of one's own role in it.

While some changes are necessary in life you must know the risk of taking them rather than giving up your 'personal legend'. This is when we can no longer be content with a little but decide to bite life with the teeth, do what we must do to be what it should be.

~ ✳ ~

So…was that not a very clear and logical approach to practice? Let's see how Serge approaches the four main Chinese internal fighting arts.

'Taijiquan and Xingyiquan are both percussive boxing methods, Xingyi starting from a distance and Taiji from touch. Bagua is mostly focused on the palm and wrapping energy, so its motions are all round – there are very few straight line motions and even these will go up or down. Ziranmen has all of the different forces.

'The skill of timing comes from playing with non-cooperative force. There is no way to develop timing without this. You really need to play, first in a comfortable way, then in a way that offers resistance, and soon you will discover that on certain lines everyone will react in two or three ways. Actually this skill is not a problem of style but a problem of teaching. Many teachers of these arts cannot use it in reality. For example, Xingyi has very formal exercises but in reality it's not easy to parry and hit someone like that. Baguazhang has very nice two-man forms but much too planned. Taijiquan is simply too focused on root and not moving the feet, putting themselves in very weird positions from where they think they won't fall. In Chen style Taiji, for example, they are very good at using the grappling in push hands but when it comes to striking, and I mean real striking, it is not so useful. I think this is partly due to Chen Fa Ke having a bad stutter, and when he taught he rarely spoke of the principles, so his students ended up only with the form and techniques. So, first develop timing, then fighting skill can come. Play is the vital factor: with this you will develop timing and see how the other guy reacts in different settings, then you will simply know by instinct. I know some internal martial arts teachers who never touch anyone in six years; they say "It will come later…" Sorry! It will not come. Maybe they get healthy but they will not have fighting skill. Timing will not come from form, but form will make you move better and have more mobility.

'Ziranmen uses half and quarter beat as you move and hit, and cultivates calmness in a fighting situation – if the enemy doesn't move then you don't move, if he moves then an avalanche falls on him! This is why I realised that my Bagua, Xingyi and Taiji are not great, because I use my concepts of my family style to understand them. Nowadays many martial artists can fight, but few can fight with the real flavour of their art because there is so little need to really fight in our times. Then you will find the good fighter who cannot teach too well; often they are not so healthy as they just want to fight and so have many problems and pains. In our life how often do we really need to fight? But we always need to breathe right, be happy and so on. However, knowing this should not be an excuse to be lazy about fighting skill!

'The big change in me is that I no longer believe in different styles; that's the big difference between now and ten years ago. There are excellent Karate and Aikido teachers, for example. But it has taken me a long time to realise this! If you don't go deep, then the art is empty and cannot be useful. The teacher must train more than the students, if not, he will not progress. Now I practise and teach what I was taught by my teacher, and I no longer do all the Bagua and Xingyi. I have succeeded in forgetting all the Lui He (Six Combination Boxing) and the Jiang style of Bagua which my teacher showed me. The Zhang Zao Dong Bagua I still do because it is so simple! And for Xingyi I do a little of the Neigong, but we already have most of it in our style. Every day I do a minimum of four hours training and more if no one is around. Before I had to keep static postures to feel the energy for Qigong and meditation, but now I can find the same with motion. It is a big change. I am working the last part of the Ziranmen training which is called Wuji Taolu or the formless form. Everything you do goes in there.'

On Baguazhang and Zhang Zao Dong

'There are really two big schools of Bagua; the first we can call "body exercise Bagua" and the second "fighting Bagua". In the first one people cannot fight, but if you are honest about it then it is fine. But if you train body exercise Bagua and then one day find yourself in danger then you will get hurt. Some schools train Xingyi first and these people tend to be capable fighters, so when they go on to Bagua they can hit really well. The Gao Yi Sheng and Zhang Zao

Dong styles are like this. You can take a mixed martial arts guy and show him Bagua and he can use it to fight, because he can already fight! But I have met hardly anyone who was using only Bagua to fight well. Real Bagua fighting ability is in the Neigong, the Ligong [strength exercise], all of the little exercises…not in the form. Each of the old systems has these exercises for fighting. But nowadays many people do lots of form and think that if they do it enough then fighting skill will emerge over time. No it will not! Where are the three years of circle walking, the inner qualities? In Beijing I saw one famous master, and his student – a French man – looked so miserable. He was half way through three years of just circle walking and could not stand it.

'In Zhejiang Province I saw these Bagua men who were hitting trees; it was not internal but very simple, and after this they were hitting people. It worked well but these guys had no need to do Bagua! With the Yin Fu style it was just not circular enough to be enjoyable for my body, plus the forms are very long and boring! As soon as the form is more important than the training of the quality then it is dead.

'I studied with two men who were Gongfu brothers under the same Taiwanese master many years ago. One was incredibly fast, but through these very fast slapping type combination attacks he lost power. If you stood still for him, yes, he might kill you, but as soon as you were right in, his lack of grappling skill gave him problems. The other man was the best throwing guy I have ever met, also very fast but with a Beng Quan (crushing fist) which would kill you from a few inches. I learned from him all the sixty-four changes, straight line forms and so on, but in the end it was all just information, too much stuff to be useful. He keeps it since he has many Western students, but the funny thing is that none of them can fight even though they think they can. I think the reason is this focus on forms and the fact that he does not hit them for real.

Dr Serge Augier with Single Change Palm of Baguazhang

'My teacher met Zhang Zao Dong in 1925 in Tienjin and was very impressed. He always told me stories about Zhang's tremendous power, the fights he had against gangs armed with his chain-whip… and knowing that my teacher was already so strong made me think. Also as a kid I kept seeing this photo of Zhang with his beard and it always stayed with me as the archetypal Chinese master image! He was doing very nice Bagua but with Xingyi power, which I really like. Zhang style Bagua has three stages, and each of the basic palms is so clear. Each one relates to a striking exercise on the post and a

Neigong, and there are five striking directions and three lines. For the eight changes you first have the technical one where the form is clearly defined. The second stage is where you link the postures in motion, and the third is the fluid swimming dragon stage where there is no stopping. With Zhang's Bagua, if you do the Xingyi first you get a very clear idea of the power being used. So many people do Bagua and after five years they have very little power or skill. Just form… Very few can really fight using just this style, it is all show.'

Applications of Single Change Palm

On Xingyiquan

'For Xingyi power is important but it is not the only thing. I recall once in China we met this killer Iron Palm expert, and my teacher just smiled and said, "Come here!" Of course the man would not. It is one thing to have that skill, but how do you get in and do it with someone like my teacher waiting to hit you? It is the same with the Shanxi and Dai Xinyi which I saw, very impressive power but you still have to be able to move and change well to apply it. With both, yes, you can be excellent. My teacher's Xingyi was very powerful, and he would use Xingyi to explain all of his Ziranmen and martial arts.

Serge Augier practises Xingyiquan's Piquan Splitting Fist Form

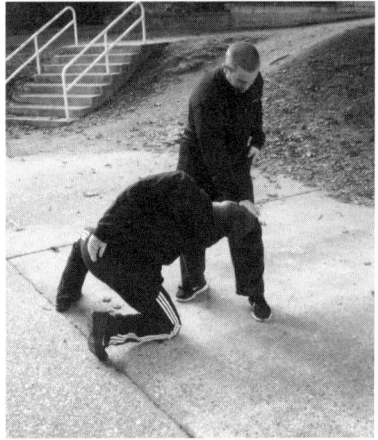

Application of Piquan

'Our Xingyi comes from Li Cun Yi, a friend of Zhang Zao Dong and one of the most skilled disciples of Lu Qi Lan. This style is very clear and powerful, loose and fluid, and has no empty movements at all. We begin with static stances and Neigong in order to develop good structure and rooting. After the basics come the study of the five fists – Pi Quan, to separate, Zuan Quan, to drill, Beng Quan, to smash or saw, Pao Quan, the explosion, and Heng Quan, the crossing or horizontal force. Each fist has many different types of Neigong to develop the forces combined within each movement. Next we have many little combination forms of a few motions each, and then there are several linking forms which combine the fists in a natural and loose way and also eight basic ways of Fajin. Following this the student learns the Twelve Animal Forms, each of which has several variations and includes various Neigong exercises. Finally there are several advanced forms for one who has accomplished the Twelve Animal skills. From the very basic stage one will practise all the skills with a partner to express the forces one develops, and to make all the training practical for combat.'

On Taijiquan

'Taijiquan is my favourite! I can explain all of my Ziranmen using Taijiquan, it is a very rich style. General Li and Du Xing Wu were friends and exchanged knowledge, so the General Li Taijiquan my teacher got was very clear; he learned directly from them.

'For teaching it is really painful to watch students learn this style! Everything has to move together and until it does it is no good at all. I need to correct one thing, then another, then another... very difficult. But once they get it, this is the style where I see their body change the quickest, the structure and strength changing so much. For sure it is the most difficult of the three main arts and the most complete – every technique from any martial art I can find in the Long Form. There are three stages to my teaching – the first is technical where I teach the Yang style form. Next comes the stage of slow and fast mixed, where you train Fajin. Then finally we go to the Li form, a boxing type form with plenty of grabbing, clawing... It is more free as a form and there are plenty of parts where you can repeat something and do it as a loop. For example, you can do Peng as a loop and really play with it in terms of size, force and so on. Chang San Feng Taijiquan has loops going from small to big, and from big to small again, but I don't like it so much and don't do it often.

'The founder of Yang family Taijiquan was Yang Luchan, and he was forced to teach his art at an Imperial Court of the detested Manchus. For this reason he taught them a changed version, transmitting the true art only within his family. His youngest son, Yang Jianhou, learned this old method of Taiji boxing and in turn taught Li Fang Chen the hidden style. Jianhou's third son,

Yang Cheng Fu, popularised a health exercise method based on the movements of the family style, a kind of martial-inspired choreography lacking in real inner training.

'The traditional style, on the other hand, develops Ligong (strength exercise), Neigong (internal power exercise) and combative exercises before any learning of the form. The three basic levels of this Li family style are first, training the movements of the thirteen postures, second, practice of the partner exercises and the fast forms, and, third, the Long Boxing. There are four principles of combat – Peng, which is to occupy space; Lu, to draw; Jie, to crush; and An, to push. There are then four supporting forces – the elbow, bump, catching or seizing, and splitting. These eight concepts of combat go in the five directions, thus we have thirteen postures.

'Each principle, such as Peng, has some dozen or so Neigong, Ligong and partner exercises. Amongst the sixteen partner exercises are methods such as to bore, to carry, to seal and to smash, all developing the force of impact in various angles. Then come the twelve fast forms, little forms with three to five movements which test the force and penetration with speed and motion. Only now, with all of this preceding knowledge, will the student move on to the Long Form, which is a kind of summary of everything learned before. The three forms of the Li family style are the Long Boxing, the Spiral Boxing and the Cannon Fist. Long Boxing is learned very slowly but later done with many changes of speed and rhythm to develop the real usage for fighting. Spiral Boxing produces a powerful body and martial qualities, and develops the Fajin. Cannon Fist is the combative form of the style where you combine stepping with internal force and apply the Fajin for real application.

'There are three stages of evolution within the training and the practice of the Long Form – developing the structure, learning the forms and acquiring freedom. In the basic stage one should keep in mind five points: first, loosen the body and calm the spirit; second, keep the correct posture; third, pay attention to each technical detail; fourth, keep a light, nimble and balanced body; and fifth, be loose, natural and flexible.

'Then in the second stage of training there are three key points: first is to co-ordinate the movements through the whole body; second is to move with grace, softly and naturally, and third is to move each part of the body during each movement. In the final stage of practice there are four further points: first is to direct the body with conscious feeling; second is clear awareness of empty and full; third is nourishing the Qi and combining inner and outer forces; and fourth is to let the Shen [spirit] link the body movement.'

Taijiquan Grasp Sparrow's Tail shown by Serge Augier

Application of Grasp Sparrow's Tail

On Ziranmen

'With regard to Ziranmen, the first big thing to understand is that it is a spiritual system, not a boxing art. From Du Xing Wu we had a spiritual system. You may ask, how can we learn to be natural? Surely by its nature it cannot be taught, right? Actually what we do is to feed more knowledge to our natural being, and as soon as it is digested our natural being can express itself. In the boxing we train the lines, tricks, Fajin, and then we let the natural motion come out. Like when I grab you…' Serge reached out and grabbed me, causing a shock to go into my bones… 'this is a natural motion but fed by all of the training I did for that thing. Ziranmen feels different in application because of its capacity for letting energy go through the system. It comes from sword skill, putting energy on the tip of the sword so the energy goes far.

'Technically we have little forms to teach the good lines of motion, then one form as a reminder. The stepping skills are vital, and the secret training is all the kicking. We have a very specific way of using our legs, the difference being the very clear way of slowly getting to know the leg. Most people just kick. We use Qigong and medical knowledge to know the leg. I can kick with my big toe, lock you with my toe, so even if I kick slowly it will still hurt.'

Serge has me hold a heavy pad on my leg against which he gives a slow round kick. It feels like a horse has kicked me.

'As with punching we learn how to multiply the power with the hand or foot by turning certain parts, by collapsing the weight. There are lots of exercises to Fajin with the legs which people do not have in most styles. It is a secret method and only given to students once they are close to the teacher.'

I then asked Serge about the founder of Iquan (mind boxing), the famed Wang Xiang Zhai, as I had heard that he had learned from Du Xing Wu and been influenced by the Ziranmen system in creating his own style.

'Yes, Wang saw Du's training and was influenced by the ideas, but he was already too much into his Way, and Du's work was very complex and difficult. Du Xing Wu had a lot of very slow repetition of motions. It goes from motion to set two-man drills, then to reaction training, then half free/half sparring. There are reactions with three hits, two hits and one hit. Then there is stepping through and stepping across. We spend a lot of time in nourishing the technique, since the reality is never in the technique.

'My teacher learned from Du but officially he was a disciple of Wan Lai Sheng. Wan studied some Buddhism and Daoism but he did not get the clan Daoist teaching, he did not have a Daoist name. As a martial artist he was great, and when I met him what really impressed me was the internal power of his strikes.

'Ziranmen strategy is very simple – how do I position myself, take his attention, and set up my heavy strikes with kicking. I learn

to trust in my hands. If I can touch someone I am home! In reality
I know I will get hit, so we go from very far to very near but never
in between, never in the sparring range. You extend and then you
vanish. Our low kicks can separate the bones of the leg, and if one
part of the kick is stopped I simply change to another joint and it
changes the line of the kick. All the kicking is just like stepping
through someone.'

At that point Serge showed me his leg, how he has trained the
muscle such that it covers the cavity behind the knee and over the
shin, most unusual! He then launches a front kick which I stop, and
within a fraction of a second the same leg changes to a stamping
kick which hits my knee. His leg changed faster than most people
can move their hand.

'You see, we train the muscle so it blocks the cavities, and at the
same time train sensitivity so that the legs become as quick as the
hands. When I was small and skinny I wanted to prove to myself
that it was working, but I was not so sure. In my dreams I would hit
someone but they would just laugh. Then I started to see that it was
working but it was down to luck. Sometimes they would scream,
sometimes nothing. Slowly I started to see how to make the power
slide, to penetrate, hit and go through. In real fighting you always
look for the dangerous stuff to finish the guy, but at the times I used
it I had no choice in the method, it came out by itself.

'Qing Gong is the lightness training, it is vital to be light
because it goes with the happiness! To kick good you must be light.
I am ninety-five kilograms so how can I be light? I must be to have
quickness in motion. We train for openness of the joints, softness
of the muscles and strength of the tendons. The low stance training
is good when you are young but when you are older there are more
important things. The lightness training makes you understand
heaviness.'

I then asked Serge about the special types of Jin or trained force
in the system.

Serge Augier shows a Ziranmen combination

'We can say that there are three basic types of power in Ziranmen – shocking, penetrating and breaking. Each has different training and ways of applying it. With the first we throw the intent or give a big slap to the chest such that he cannot even think about the hand hitting his nose! You shock him first and then hit. It is very powerful and takes away his desire to fight. The second way we choose where to send the force, it is very precise. The third way is for when my life is in danger; I physically break or rupture the enemy's body, artery, bone and so on. Even if he continues to have fighting spirit at this point he cannot physically continue.'

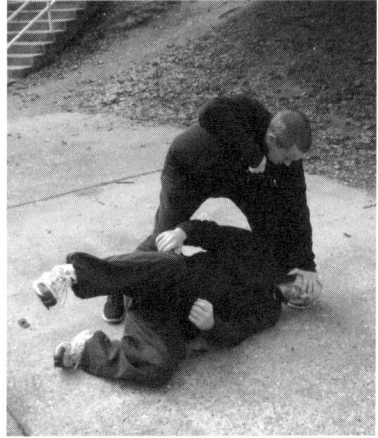

One application of Ziranmen combination

And how about the mental and emotional aspects of training?

'Sure, first we have to be able to separate the spiritual, emotional and mental energies. In our way emotion appears like a cold wind blowing through; we are really feeling it but not concerned, and in this way our body reactions are good and we go much faster. We let it rise up but without analysing it. This is very important to understand because in Chinese medicine the emotions are considered to be the first disease.

'The mental mind is very useful but only for doing things like planning a trip, doing sums and so on. Emotions are between the spirit and the body and are nothing to do with the mental mind. But we cannot help ourselves, and we end up putting mental energy into the emotions. Slowly people get hooked on the emotion and feel alive through it. Twice a year I lead a retreat to help people understand and separate out the various energies. I explain it in pieces, from breathing to posture to emotion, using Qigong. People can hear this stuff without their brains exploding, it is clear.

'There is not one right way to see things. Is the Chinese, Tibetan or Western way the best? No! We are not a body with meridians or cells, we are a complete mind and body. The systems are not complete, just tools to see things. The real thing is the experience of life, and the exercises we do give us experiences. Some people say that only what you feel is real, but maybe this feeling was due to tension or sickness. Then what? If a man is a real alcoholic he may listen to his body and figure he needs more drink... I need it now! He really feels this, but should he follow it? No, he is sick! Do not believe a sick body. First we must bring the body to balance. By balancing the mind and body then we can listen to what we feel. Yin and Yang nourish each other. If you train only the mind the body will get weak. If you train only the body you will weaken the mind.

'I must emphasise what I consider the most important thing, the point that we should not be confused. What do I mean? Well, almost everyone confuses the exercises of Qigong with the real Qigong. Real Qigong is an exchange of energy. They confuse the exercises of meditation with real meditation, and they confuse martial arts with fighting. Also, people today do more and more, learn more and more, but they do not practise! They always want something new as a distraction. Learning is learning, but at some point when you forget the motions you really begin to practise! We want new forms, methods, spiritual ideas... It is exactly the spiritual materialism which Trungpa [a famous Buddhist master from Tibet who taught for years in the West] wrote about all those years ago. It is just another kind of television. This year I will make a week-long retreat on boredom, giving the students nothing so that they will simply have to be with themselves, making them confront themselves. Because if you are really present, really in the feeling, there is no boredom!'

I asked Serge about his own evolution through practice, and what stood out in his mind.

'The most vital thing is that when I started I noticed changes with my body and energy almost every week. Then after some time I stopped noticing the changes and thought, "Ah, now I am done!" Then of course the changes came only each month or each year, and with every change came the insight that there was so much more to be accomplished. For me now the most important thing is the pleasure of simplicity. I enjoy the training and it is nothing special. I enjoy sitting! No need for entertainment, television, sex, books and so on. This comes with a quiet mind. I see so many students creating things with their minds and having so many questions... For me when I speak it just comes out. This is the purpose of training, to find happiness in simple things. We are basically happy you know!

'In Asia the accomplishment of a human being was traditionally wisdom, not money, it was being happy. Today of course it is the size of one's wallet. Practice brings happiness for us right now, no matter that later on we will go to the Daoist heaven or be eaten by worms – right now we are happy. This simplicity makes life simple. For example, this month I have little money, down to minus, but today someone turned up and gave me a big sum he owed me for a year. This result from the training is very interesting, because it shows that in fact you have no choice in life. You think you can choose, but really you cannot. Martial arts develops intent, and with intent comes pride, the pride that we decide or choose what happens. But no, you cannot choose, life happens. This idea starts to work in each art. Medicine starts to be simple, because when you meet people you already know what is wrong. Disease is then just an expression of this wrong thing. My teacher said that martial arts is about intent and power and then with time comes technique. No fear or planning will help you fight well. Meditation is the same, it is silence and simplicity, just like the famous one hundred character scroll which says that without a goal your life will be good. You are just melted into things. Between hitting people as a martial artist and curing people as a doctor, I still have to walk, sit and breathe – this is life!'

Serge demonstrates a second Ziranmen combination

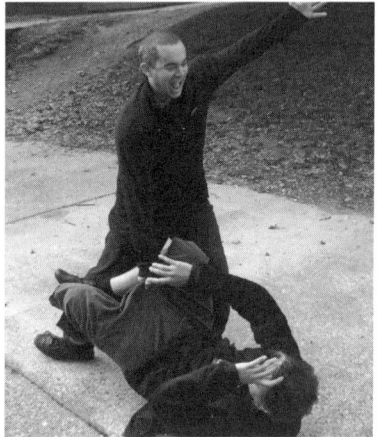

This sequence shows application of the second Ziranmen combination

So, I wondered, what made a system complete and authentic?

'With the old systems, especially the Daoist clan systems, there is a coherence centred around principles such as Yin and Yang and so on. These are principles applied in every facet of life. For example I have a very complete set of teachings for the knife, sword, medicine and so on, but I also teach how to sit, how to shit, how to place your stuff in a room using Feng Shui, how to work. This teaches you how to live and brings you close to the energy of the world, how to go with it and not against it. We have ways to use the energy of the changing seasons, how to breathe. Today people seem to only want the shining stuff, they can do a jumping kick but they cannot walk! Breathing and walking are closer to reality, so a complete teaching is one which will show you how to go into the things of life. In these arts we learn techniques and then forget them, this is the natural way. The practice must fuse you with life, it is not a ritual. Look at how so many martial artists do their stuff so nicely and then fold their clothes like a shmuck! When I was in the temples in China I was shocked, people rushed in and out, they didn't take time to breathe the incense, to appreciate the sky.

'Our practice is complete because we train qualities, how to breathe and walk, to make the body strong. Then comes the fighting and so on, which are just tools. Practice must melt us into life. You know how people from boxing or mixed martial arts make fun of martial artists? They are right! Technique does not work. If you train the rigid way it will never come out in real life, which is a mess, a chaos. So train qualities, not techniques. This can only come from a complete system.

'If you practise well you will see and perceive things differently to others. If you train with too much tension you will feel differently. If you train well you will recognise that they are different but not be bothered. Everyone wants money but you are happy simply breathing! You will start to see the people in the office as part of you.

'The Shen or spirit has two parts. The Hu is the liver energy, the most Yang and light part coming from the Original Spirit. In there you have a little part of everyone. You start liking people, start to recognise them because you can feel them. For example, from the start of my training until my time in Japan, about fifteen years, I felt really separated from people. Then I started to see the unity. Now once a month I need to have time alone, because if not it takes me twice as long to pass to the next level.

'You also start to see that there is nothing you can really do to help people except to simply be there for them. If people are very sad no need to do anything. Is it cruel? It is just reality, only they can help themselves, and we can just be there. Even a surgeon, for example, is not doing anything to help, he simply gives the body a chance to balance and rearrange itself. That is why some people die after surgery and some people live. The same with our teaching, it just gives the tools – for some people it works and for others it doesn't.'

I then asked Serge how the medical, spiritual and martial aspects of the system were linked.

'You have energy, in you and everywhere else. Medicine, fighting, astrology...these help us understand how it works and how you can create balance to make it work better for you. Against aggressive energy in a fight you will be able to cut down the violence by counter-violence, but without emotional involvement, without fear or anger. It is the same principle for all things. By understanding the mind, spirit and energy you see how to make balance. In Qigong you make space for the energy to enter. Without having a teacher who really practises it is very difficult to get this, he must have been doing the work to be able to teach it.'

I wondered if certain systems could produce deeper or higher skill than others. And indeed, what defined skill and its various levels?

'Some systems are very old and passed through many generations of evolution, so they see the easier way to do things. But any Way that you do diligently and daily will succeed. The older systems tend to be very precise within a tiny space, and have a knowledge of sky and Nature, all the energies. You still have to work but you are very clear about what you are doing, you have complete understanding of what you are doing.

'Take this soft punch, for example...' Serge demonstrates a totally relaxed striking action which seems to come out of nowhere. 'This uses a complete understanding of body structure and that is why it works so well. Every student has different questions about himself, and so the teacher with deeper understanding can answer with more precision. He can give details for that one student's technical needs. Skill is the ability to use what you want to use. Mixed martial arts fighters have skill within set rules, they have complete control within those limits. Traditional Chinese martial arts skill is different because you react as you train, and those that train to always miss by one centimetre will probably in a real situation also miss by one centimetre! So we can say that skill has two factors: first, being able to use the method, and second, not being confused. This second point is vital, because skill will be blocked by fantasy.'

So, did that mean my teacher considered mixed martial arts skill to be more practical than traditional Chinese martial arts? Was it not the case that many of these modern fighters relied on their size and weight to win fights rather than the deeper skill we see in the internal arts?

'Well, skill is the deciding factor only up to a certain point. If two guys are equally skilled then the bigger guy will win! Take a normal human being who gets stung by a wasp. OK, this guy will get hurt a bit but will survive. He gets stung by ten wasps, he still survives. A hundred wasps…mmm, probably OK. But a thousand wasps…he will probably die! This is the limit of the human body.'

Then why, I asked, do we spend so much time learning all of the obscure skills of the internal martial arts? What, if any, are the advantages?

'The arts such as Bagua see the enemy as a big water bag which can be upset. How to do this? We use a drill, a spiral, because a screw can penetrate this bag. Even my palm can have a spiral. This kind of power is very different from modern fighters' power, as it can be applied very close in. The ways of developing these types of power are also very different to modern training methods, and will not ruin your body by middle age.

'From my own training I can also see that with skill comes the ability to do it precisely without depending on luck. I know how to put myself in a good position, not relying on luck. I can trap his eyes, catch his intent…these are from the traditional training. In our system we have plenty of things like this, where we trap the eyes and then they cannot see the hit coming. Or we throw the intent so that we transfer an emotion, such as fear, into them…with this not many people want to continue fighting so they stop. Real fighting requires commitment, and without this the fight is over.'

Common Problems Along the Way

I asked Serge what were the common problems he had observed with students of inner cultivation and the internal martial arts, knowing that he had taught those from complete novice level to fighters with decades of combative experience.

'It's a strange thing but because the way we train brings internal power very quickly the problem is how to make the body strong enough to keep up with the power. For example, last week one of the students did a push on another student and his wrist fractured... he couldn't believe it and neither could the doctors, but I checked it and sure enough the bone had sheared clean through as a result of the big power coming out. Normally you would need to have a bad fall to break it like this. This shows the need for preparing the structure to take the power you develop. The action is Yang, the physical structure is Yin, they need to feed each other.

'Another big problem faced by internal martial artists and people involved with alchemy is how to keep the energy, how to stop it dispersing. We train, feel a lot, then stop...and it is gone! We have a neuro-muscular trick with the mind to keep the energy in when we are not training; without this you can train for years and never really get much. Internal martial arts is nourished with Neigong from the centre to the outside, and with external styles first you make the arms and legs strong and then go to make the centre strong. It is internal only if you are nourishing the centre.'

At this point Serge stood up and demonstrated the difference between external and internal striking, using a right hand horizontal palm slap against my extended right palm. The first sends a heavy power which makes my hand and arm full of pain. The second merely stings my hand ...followed half a second later by my body reacting painfully to a heavy force in my spine and centre.

'To have this second kind of force you need to have at least gone through the emotional training. Emotion is a big wave and we learn how to surf. Most people live in the emotional-mental energy, but with this training we can at least feel what is emotional energy. It is separate from mental energy. I will talk more about this in a minute but first I will mention some recent incidents which let me see how my own emotional and mental training have affected me when under pressure.

'I had a problem this year on the subway with three guys. Immediately I punched the first guy in the face and he was knocked out. I then slapped the second in the balls but my hand slipped a bit and I only managed to get one, the sound of it crushing against the bone was horrible. I saw the third was scared after that…it all happened very fast without thought.

'Last year I was on the bus and saw this guy bothering a woman; as they got off the bus I followed them to make sure she was OK. The man was really abusing her, and as I tried to calm him the woman turned on me. I was a little impolite to her…but as I was speaking the man on the left of me reached towards her. Without any thought, as if acting by itself, my hand did this rear slap to my back' – Serge demonstrated a motion which I was happy not to be on the receiving end of – 'which knocked him out and to the ground. I wanted to stamp on him but realised at that moment that the bus driver had stopped and fifty people were staring at me with open mouths. I crept back onto the bus and tried to hide myself in my bag…

'Fear is the only emotion, all other emotions come from that. Fear and the survival impulse are not the same. In the same way, love is a natural state of being, or should be, it is not an emotion. When we feel "in love" it is mostly a sickness coming from fear of dying or loneliness or pain. Emotion is always more visceral, physical, our hearts beat faster, we get warmer, more energy. But mostly we add to that the mental process. The first problem is determining a good vocabulary to discuss this matter. Emotion moves us away from the centre. People who only do fighting tend to block the emotions. Those doing only spiritual work are doomed, like the Buddhists who block the emotions with their mental mind and don't deal with it…they will destroy the body. I had a friend who just came back from Siberia and was full of claims that he had become deeply enlightened. I got a bit annoyed as he would not stop so I hit him and he screamed! I then asked him why he was suffering!

'It is like having sex to be a virgin, or fighting for peace. Unless the body and mind are trained together we cannot find the reality. So to start with we have these very simple exercises to feel the difference between thought and emotion, because to start this work we really need to know what is what. In the same way we do dream work – all day long we work, keep our presence, then suddenly for eight hours we are plunged into darkness and the water stops boiling! I take my students into the forest to train this type of thing. They will swear that the earth is shaking, or I will make a force field inside the dream and they will not be able to escape a certain area. Once a year I will take a few students into the desert for a retreat where we can do this type of work.

'We do fighting practice to protect the temple we are building; it is not the first thing but it is important. In medicine you start to see that in fact you can do acupuncture on a room, on a house, it is all related.

'My medical speciality is all the mental and emotional problems. In the fifth year of training my students learn the Daoist and traditional medicine for treating psychiatric and psychological problems. Unless someone's mind is peaceful I will not teach them the magic. When you do things like the desert retreat you will have to confront a lot of fear. But there is only one energy, no good, no bad. It is only different in your feeling of it. In reality there is no such thing – a church and a torture chamber have the same energy, only you feel different.'

I asked Serge about the relationship between teacher and student in the modern age.

'I ask a lot from them…they must be punctual, respectful, but they do not have to wear special clothes! Respect must be there, that is essential. For Qigong I don't care, it is up to them how they learn, it is exercise. But for fighting I only teach a couple of people who are really interested. I teach openly just like my teacher, but it is not a relationship of friendship. One of the big secrets of martial arts is to be able to feel the impact, since then you can reproduce it. So I only hit the people who I want to teach. If a student does not ask me questions and talk to me, then I cannot help him. If he is honest, I can help him.'

What, I wondered, was the relevance of training with traditional weapons for the student of the present day?

'With Bagua and Taiji weapons we have only drills, not forms. I don't believe weapons should be done with forms, with empty hands OK, if you mess up you may not die but with weapons any mistake will cost you your life. Even with my little plastic knife I can seriously damage your arm. The knife is very serious. My teacher told me that I was not gifted at martial arts but that I trained hard. But he said I was really gifted with weapons!' Serge stood up and walked over to a wall on which hung many different swords and other weapons. He pulls out a Chinese straight sword which has only the very last part of the tip sharpened and begins to demonstrate expertly the small circular piercing actions using just the very tip. The energy in the room changes dramatically as he continues to manipulate it. 'There are two types of straight sword: this one which uses the very tip for piercing, and the other which has the first third of the blade sharpened and uses both cutting and piercing attacks. The usage of this first one can be extended to some of the special Ziranmen weapons like this one...' He replaces the straight sword and then picks up a small, silver needle-shaped weapon, the end of which looks razor sharp. It is clear as he demonstrates with it that you would be in extreme danger getting anywhere near him. I back away quickly and he nods. 'I don't like seeing students play with weapons, they are extremely dangerous, even practice ones. Against a knife attack it is best to run or kick him to even have a chance. If you have the skill there are other possibilities.'

Giving me a knife, he invites me to attack, and as I do so he already has control of my slashing hand as he steps to the side. His grip is very strong and seems to pierce into the bone.

'We treat each method, such as gripping, striking and so on, as a tool which we have to train to have maximum efficiency...since we know at some point we will grab, this is natural in a fight, it always happens...then we want to grab in a way which will make him scream.' He grabs me a bit tighter and the pain becomes excruciating. 'Or the same with the feet...look...' Serge lifts his right foot and shows how he can manipulate each toe individually, even the small one. 'We train the toes like the finger, look, I will show you why...' As I attack he makes contact with both my arms, and in the very next moment I feel the tip of his right big toe in the pit of my throat, striking with enough force that I almost choke. 'See, everything is a weapon!'

It had been a long and very enlightening conversation with a remarkable teacher, and before we concluded I asked Serge for his opinion of the level of Chinese internal fighting arts in the West.

'The level is really bad, especially in the USA, where they are so focused on pretty moves and totally forget the real thing. It is not Yoga. Real internal martial arts is very clean, you bleed on the inside.'

Students' Stories

Over the years I took many friends to meet and train with Serge. Some felt disturbed by the crushing impact that was his trademark way of teaching and never returned, others 'chewed the bitter' and came back enough to slowly gain his trust and learn the deeper methods. Everyone who met him, though, had his or her stories…

One friend who was raised in a North American ghetto, and severely bullied by gangs for years until he was almost scared of his own shadow, had avoided any kind of martial or violent activity until he met me. We were sharing a house at the time, and as Serge frequently came to stay with me it was inevitable that my friend would meet him and see our training. After their first introduction, which was a simple handshake and smile, he decided suddenly that he wanted to take the next day's seminar that Serge was to hold in our little courtyard. The seminar was to be on Xingyi fighting techniques, hardly the gentle first experience which my friend perhaps needed, but when I explained that it might be a somewhat brutal experience he simply nodded thoughtfully and explained that even though he was scared there was something about Serge that he trusted. The next day, during the first few minutes of the training, Serge picked my friend out of the group and asked him to attack with any kind of punch. He had a look of abject fear on his face, but he did indeed try his best and swung a rather ungainly cross toward the teacher. Even I was a little shocked at what Serge did next – he struck my friend with what looked like a very hard palm strike in the chest, sending him reeling back onto the paved stones of the courtyard, and then simply turned back and continued teaching the rest of us. I made a motion towards helping my friend, but was then surprised to see him burst out with laughter. He sat there for some time just laughing to himself, then stood up and threw himself into the training for the rest of the day as if he had been doing it all his life.

Some time later, after Serge had returned to Paris, my friend told me that the palm strike had shocked him to the core for a moment, and then as he regained his senses it felt as if all fear of violence had left him. It was not that he was no longer afraid of being hurt, but simply that he was more than willing to confront and defy the fear which had haunted him since childhood. Something had changed in him that day, and it was elicited by a big slap.

Another friend was invited to a throwing seminar given by Serge behind closed doors in a matted area, but hesitated to go since he had suffered from a chronic spine injury. Mentioning the matter to Serge at the start of the training he was called up minutes later as the teacher's demonstration partner, and was in the next moment sent flying through the air and onto his back – in fact the impact hit him on exactly the part of his back which was injured. The rest of the day was spent in much the same manner, and Serge seemed to have forgotten completely about the spine injury. The next day my friend called in to see me, and was full of amazement that his spine was now completely free of the pain that had bothered him for the past few months. The impact of the throws – especially the very first one – had released something in the upper back and shoulder areas that had corrected the spine problem.

One of my Gongfu brothers, a Chinese man, told me how once he had been with Serge when they had returned to the latter's apartment in the heart of Paris, only to find that a key had been left inside the door which effectively barred them from using a key on the outside. The problem was that the door was not only made of thick solid hardwood, but had been reinforced with steel to make it bullet-proof. My Gongfu brother recalled his amazement when Serge hit the lock with a short-range palm strike and sent the key flying out the other side, saying that it would have taken a huge force to do that.

One more story, told to me by Serge's girlfriend. She had left their apartment, which is several stories up, and just outside the block was confronted by a strange man who seemed about to assault her. Serge, who had been standing on his balcony waving goodbye, let out a tremendous shout from on high which sent the man reeling. The stranger than ran off, a terrified look on his face. That was a superb application of the Voice Gong, one of the special arts within the Ziranmen system, and one that requires great inner force to accomplish.

'Being light goes with being happy...'

Cheong Cheng Leong

Guardian of Shaolin Phoenix-Eye Fist

Grandmaster Cheong Cheng Leong of Chuka Shaolin

Penang, Malaysia 1972. The annual Penang Pesta Committee martial arts display is in full swing, the large audience glad to be seated in the town hall and out of the scorching Malaysian heat. One of the observers is famed martial arts researcher and teacher Donn F. Draeger, there to discover the traditional roots of Chinese Gongfu. The various performers take to the stage and go through their forms, all duly noted by Draeger and the rest of the audience.

A lone figure steps up and began to move through an empty-hand form. Absolute silence fills the hall as Sifu Cheong Cheng Leong of the Chuka Shaolin Phoenix-Eye Fist style performs his art with incredible speed and power. The big American Sensei sits up and begins to take notice. As Sifu Cheong ends his performance the room erupts with applause. The form is called 'Phoenix-Eye Fist Guarding the Mountain' and the display leads to a friendship with Draeger which lasted until the American's death nine years later.

Cheong Cheng Leong, the present Grandmaster of Chuka Shaolin, began his study of the art at the age of ten in Penang. For ten years he trained daily under the watchful eye of his master, Lee Siong Pheow, eventually reaching the level of master in his own right. Upon Lee's death in 1961 Cheong became the fifth generation head authority of Chuka Shaolin, inheriting not only the fighting skills of the old teacher but also his methods of herbs and healing.

Another disciple of Master Lee is Sifu Tan Hun Poey. He also learned Chuka's unique finger slapping method used in the treatment of old injuries and other ailments, especially useful for chronic problems of the muscular-skeletal system. Well respected in his quarter of Penang, Master Tan dedicates his life to healing others, often for very little money. He and Grandmaster Cheong stand as unique figures in the world of healing, having consistently healed patients who have not responded to other types of medical treatment. Draeger travelled to Penang each year after 1972, bringing with him several martial arts friends with seemingly incurable conditions. These included an American Judoka and a Japanese swordsman both of whom had severe shoulder problems; after treatment by Sifu Tan they too were cured.

One young girl who could see only nine feet ahead of her was brought by her parents to Sifu Tan and after a session of massage and some herbal application she was able to clearly see forty or fifty feet ahead of her. I met an octogenarian – informed by doctors after a bad motorcycle crash that he would not walk again – who told me that Cheong worked on him daily for a month until he could finally walk around just as before the accident. The locals swear by their skills, and both men are respected as much for their kindness and generosity as for their healing hands.

I always love my trips to Penang, the 'Pearl of the Orient' sitting just off Malaysia's west coast, feeling as if I am stepping back in time to a previous century. Many of the buildings and even whole streets date back at least that far, and everywhere you look are the written Chinese characters for old Chinese clan houses and Kungfu schools, traditional bone-setters and herbalists, craftsmen and artisans who still ply their trade beneath hand-painted signs. As a thirteen-year-old child I read the book *Phoenix-Eye Fist*, co-authored by Grandmaster Cheong and Draeger (Cheong and Draeger 1977) and a year later began serious study with his student in London. It was a very traditional system, one that I dreamed of studying under the guidance of the Grandmaster. Finally, in my late twenties, I was able to accomplish that dream and make the first of several visits to train with him in Penang. Being in my mind since such a young age, it felt exciting each time I stepped foot in his school, for it is still in exactly the same place as the photos in *Phoenix-Eye Fist* show. The sign at the front gate is old and peeling and opens onto a training area where for decades people have trained in the centuries old skills of Shaolin Gongfu.

The sign at the front gate of Grandmaster Cheong's school

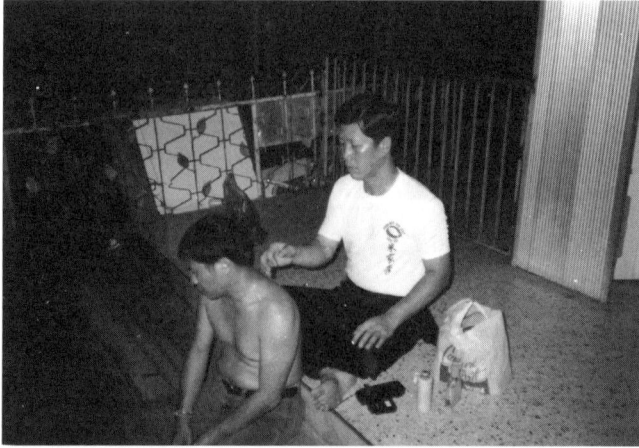

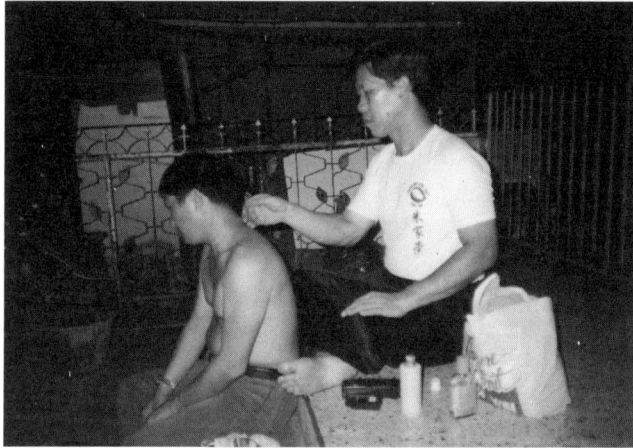

Grandmaster Cheong applies slapping massage at his school

High on a mountainside overlooking the rest of the island is the
district of Ayer Itam, crowned by the famous Kok Lek Si Buddhist
monastery with its towering statue of Kwan Yin gazing out
compassionately across a vast distance. Leading up to the monastery
is a winding stairway flanked by gift shops, one of which belongs
to seventy-year-old Grandmaster Cheong, who is known locally as
Brother Leong. Next to the gift shop is the area which for decades
has been the school of the Chuka Shaolin system, and to this day a
small but serious group of students train here under their teacher's

expert guidance. Several nights a week they gather to practise the empty-hand and weapons methods of this very traditional style.

Watching the Grandmaster it quickly becomes clear just why a man such as Donn Draeger, already a highly respected authority in the traditional Japanese weapons arts, would see fit to visit him each year and bring with him other martial experts from Japan both for training and to receive medical treatment. His movements display that certain 'something' which hints at the attainment of real depth of skill and power; when he wields a thick hardwood staff he sends force out in such a way that only the very tip of the weapon vibrates as the rest of it stays relatively still, something which very few can emulate.

Cheong Cheng Leong demonstrates Long Pole, Penang, 1997

There was another big reason I was so happy each time I met him – despite his skill, which seems to come from the old times, he is a genuinely humble and easy-going man who deeply loves both his Chuka Shaolin and the family and friends who are his constant companions. Sitting around a table with Grandmaster Cheong and four of his old friends who have known him for more than sixty years, the light-hearted banter is like a group of school-mates who have not a care in the world. It is the special way of the Chinese, or even the Asian race as a whole, that they can make eating become a time where humour, news, information and wisdom – and more than a little Gongfu knowledge – all flow freely back and forth between friends and teacher and students. Times like those I always wondered what it must be like to have spent one's whole life in a single neighbourhood, surrounded by the same people and smells and sounds. Ayer Itam was where, as a youth, Grandmaster Cheong had spent ten years training under the strict guidance of the late Grandmaster Lee Siong Pheow. It was where he had married and raised four children and twelve grandchildren, and where he had for decades taught the Shaolin art to young and old alike. Walking around the crowded streets with him, it seems that everyone is his friend, and I attributed his tangible aura of happiness in no small part to the sense of stability that such a background must have engendered.

Here in Ayer Itam I could see how the Grandmaster's art had truly merged with the environment in a living example of the harmony so prized by Asian culture. The new generation of Chuka practitioners, some as young as eight or nine, were now devoting themselves to the art. Martial skill, healing ability and ethical behaviour, the fruit of much sustained effort, were respected by – and benefited – almost everyone in the neighbourhood.

A Conversation with Cheong Cheng Leong

On a recent visit with the Grandmaster I had the chance to discuss various aspects of Chuka Shaolin with him and I began by asking him how an aspirant should approach practice.

'Chuka Shaolin should be practised in a relaxed way. I always tell the students, but often they don't listen and practise too hard! My teacher would often teach the first form – Kai Shan – in a slow, smooth way, so that even older people can practise it. The meaning of this form is to "open the mountain", and this tells the student that a long challenging journey is ahead of them. Kai Shan has many fighting techniques which are very useful for self-defence. Most important are the nine basic Shou Fa, hand techniques, the stances and stepping and all these basics; it takes many years of training these to make a good foundation.'

I then asked about his own training all those decades before with the late Grandmaster Lee Siong Pheow.

Grandmaster Cheong and students, Penang, 2006

'I would train with my teacher two or three times a day, almost every day, his place was nearby so I could walk there. When I was older he would take me and Tan Hun Poay up the mountain to collect herbs, then we would observe him treating people for different kinds of problems, and that is how we slowly learned the healing methods. But now we can only find about fifty per cent of the herbs on the mountain due to all the building and pollution, the rest we have to get from the herb shop.

'My teacher was famous locally for his Phoenix-Eye Fist, he specialised in very close range fighting and his hands moved too fast to see. Once he was in close then you couldn't stop him! He could strike with the Phoenix-Eye Fist and leave a dent in steel. But later on a customs official became his student and gave him lots of money and too much rich food and drink, and he had a stroke and died. So slowly I began teaching and have carried on ever since.'

He showed me one of his notebooks from the time with Lee Siong Pheow, full of diagrams showing the vital point locations and the times to strike them.

'This art is very dangerous. I always tell the students that if possible they should run away from an attack to avoid hurting people. But if they have to fight then they must go in very fast! Chuka Shaolin is a very close range fighting art, the hands are always changing where they will hit and you are always moving so that your enemy cannot see your strike.'

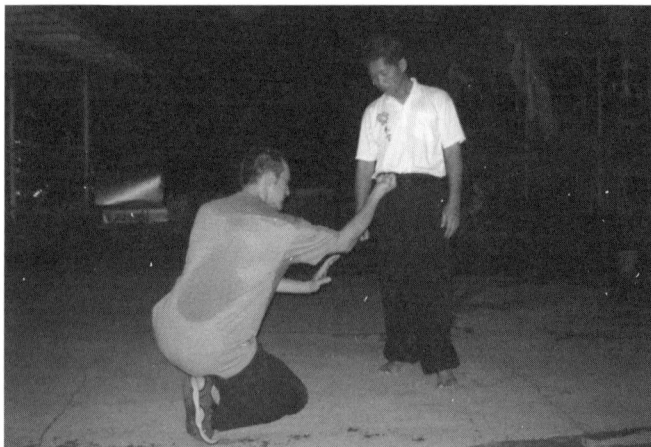

Grandmaster Cheong teaches the author, Penang, 2006

I also asked Sifu Cheong about his relationship with Donn Draeger.

'Yes, Draeger was very big and strong, his chest and arms so strong and he was very skilled at the Jodo, Japanese pole fighting. Actually back then I also tried Karate, and had a black belt. I remember one of them challenged me so I had to use Chuka, after that he was injured and complained to me that I didn't use Karate! So those days if someone wanted to fight with me, sometimes I would demonstrate the long staff and after they watched that they would not want to fight! Draeger was very interested in our pole fighting, and we spent time comparing the Japanese and Chinese arts, how similar or different the techniques are. When I heard he had cancer I prepared some very special Chinese herbs for fighting cancer to send to him, but by then sadly he had died.'

And what about the internal side of the art: how did Chuka Shaolin approach the topic of Qigong? At some of the classes a sprightly octogenarian Gongfu brother of Sifu Cheong would come and practise his breathing exercises.

'Yes, yes, this is important but first students must make the basics strong. Then we have the training for bringing energy in and out of the Dantien, how to make your stepping more rooted, and your strikes have more force. There are different Qigong exercises and these are good especially for older people to keep healthy. Then we have forms like the Shih Ta Hsing Hsian, Ten Animals Fighting techniques, which is for keeping you in good health and has methods for making the rib cage much stronger. Qigong is very important and now I focus mostly on this. Also, when we do the slapping massage we need to be able to pass our internal energy into the injured area. One of our treatments can have more effect than ten normal massages, but the problem is it can feel quite painful so for older people is not always so easy.'

Sifu Cheong with his senior student Ong Tatt Lin

Grandmaster Cheong teaching in his Penang school, 1997

Today Grandmaster Cheong continues to teach Chuka Shaolin to a select group of dedicated students. Widely respected for his superb skills as a fighter and healer, he is understandably concerned that his Phoenix-Eye Fist art stands intact for the next generation, and watching his senior students practising the forms and fighting skills with tremendous speed and Fajin it is clear that he has managed to transmit the Chuka without any dilution. But what of the future for the art in Malaysia? When I asked him Grandmaster Cheong shook his head and sighed.

'My senior students here all have careers and family, so busy life, they practise for themselves because they enjoy it but they do not want to teach. Now we have a committee to try and keep the standard strong. So for the future... I hope the seniors can keep it alive!'

The Training System of Chuka Shaolin

Basic Stances: Horse Stance, Hanging Horse Stance

Basic Stepping Patterns

Shou Fa (Hand Training):

1. Drawing the Bow – an important exercise for developing whole body power, strengthening the tendons and ligaments and learning the correct use of relaxation and tension in striking.

2. Golden Duck Striking Drill – teaches the correct technique for short power striking and deflecting using the Phoenix-Eye Fist.

3. Stealing Hands – a punching skill which steals the initiative from an enemy by launching a Phoenix-Eye Fist punch.

4. Aggressive Hands – teaches seizing and grasping of an enemy whilst closing in on him and striking.

5. Dodging Horse – develops a fast and fluid side dodging step followed by an immediate counter-attack along a different line.

6. Side Body Horse – builds the skill of fighting multiple attackers using swift evasive stepping and multiple punching techniques.

7. Plucking the Moon from the Sea – the core of this skill involves suddenly dropping the body to a crouching position from where one plucks at the enemy's groin with a Tiger Claw strike.

8. Thrust Penetrate Catch Tear Hand – a very vicious attack using grasping and tearing type actions.

9. Deflect Strike – teaches how to make use of openings created from a deflection to launch counter-attacking strikes.

Tui Fa (Leg Training):

1. Lightning Kick

2. Heart Penetrating Kick

3. Leg Stopping Kick

4. Deflecting Kick

Conditioning and Strengthening Exercises

Two-Person Pre-arranged Sparring Drills

Empty-Hand Forms:

1. Kai Shan (Opening the Mountain)

2. Er Shih Sze Tien 1 (24 Points)

3. Er Shih Sze Tien 2 (24 Points)

4. Hu Chao Chien – Shang Shan Hu (ascending Tiger Claw)

5. Hu Chao Chien – Sha Shan Hu (descending Tiger Claw)

6. Loong Hu Chien (dragon and tiger)

7. Ta Choong Koong (stamping inside, the palace being surrounded)

8. Mei Hua Chien (Plum Blossom)

9. Lien Huang Tui (continuous kicks)

10. Tong Tze Pai Kwan Yin (boy pays respects to the Goddess of Mercy)

11. Yin Yang Er Sien Ku (two positive and negative heavenly ladies)

12. Ta Ooh Li (strength performance)

13. Shih Ba Lorhan Chien (18 Hands of the Lorhan)

14. Foong Yen Tin Sun Chien (Phoenix-Eye Fist guards the mountain)

15. Shih Ta Hsing Hsian (Ten Animals fighting movement)

Two-Man Fighting Form no. 1: The basic partner form which develops courage, timing, distance, defence and counter-attack skills and puts into use the basic techniques.

Two-Man Fighting Form no. 2: Using the Yin–Yang pattern, this is a very complex set which trains evasive skills and footwork and advanced striking techniques.

Weapons Forms:

1. Liu Tien Ban Koon (six and half point pole)

2. Mei Hua Koon (Plum Blossom pole)

3. Sho Ho Chien (neck locking spear)

4. Shih Sun Chien (thirteen points long spear)

5. Chu Toe (farmer's hoe)

6. Tze Mu Tao (twin knives)

7. Tieh Cher (iron rulers, same as Japanese sai)

Weapons Fighting Form:

1. Koon Twee Chai (pole vs pole)

Qigong Breathing Exercises

Healing Skills

Although it is a very extensive system, Grandmaster Cheong stressed to me several times that the stance work and nine basic Shou Fa drills had to be trained continuously over many years to provide a good foundation for everything else. We can only hope that this rare fighting art can flourish and be passed down for future generations.

He Jinghan

Guardian of Baguaquan

Master He Jinghan of Baguaquan

Meeting the Master

Summer 1999. It was a typically warm and bright afternoon in Taipei, the capital city of Taiwan, and I stood under the massive pillars of the Chiang Kai Shek Memorial Hall watching a middle aged man teaching martial arts to a small group of women. Laughter and smiles punctuated the lessons from both teacher and students, and I observed that the man had a tremendous openness in his posture – most noticeably his hips and spine – which was reflected in his demeanour. After a couple of hours of coiling and twisting their way through a series of demanding exercises the women left, and I took the chance to introduce myself.

'Master He Jinghan? I heard that you taught here at this time and wondered if you are willing to discuss your Baguaquan with me. My name is Alex, and I have been looking for you ever since I saw your photos in the *Bagua Journal* some years ago...'

'Sure! Let's go and find a cafe...' Master He grinned and shook my hand. A short time later I was having my perception of martial arts turned upside down over coffee and cheesecake. The smiling Bagua master held his arm level over the table, asking me to hold it firmly, and then proceeded to explain how he moved the tendons, flesh and bones individually, and why that was important in how his system expressed power. It felt as if there were multiple cogs turning one within the other inside his arm. He then explained how each joint generated a force which led to the next joint, how potential power was always stored in the posture ready to be used at any moment, and how the walking in Bagua developed a 'vertical force' which depended on exact alignment of feet, hips, spine, chest and head.

'Most people take up the Neijia arts thinking that they can develop subtle power, but it is impossible unless they have first Ming Jin, obvious power. This obvious power can take ten years or more to become real, and then slowly that will be refined into more subtle force.'

I then enquired about the use of spirals and circles in his Baguaquan, and if Xingyi and Taijiquan used them in the same way.

'No! You have to understand twisting and spiral force. If you twist, which means that there are at least two directions of movement in your arm or body, then a spiral force will be developed. Xingyi uses a very direct power in straight lines, containing spiral force in a narrow range of motion. If the Xingyi man twists too much then his body will start to spiral and spin, and then he needs the stepping of Bagua – Baibu and Koubu – to allow this spiral force to manifest. This explains why many Xingyi fighters wanted to explore Bagua, to go deeper. You can see that the footwork of each art allows its special trained force to be expressed. Taijiquan, for example, is constant expansion and contraction of the sphere, whereas Bagua takes the sphere and turns it in three hundred sixty degrees of stepping, always using at least three dimensions of power. Actually what most people call spiral is not really spiralling, it is merely turning of limbs or body. To really spiral you must have a deep twist, and this is the speciality of Baguaquan.

'However, it is important not to try to mix the energies of the different arts; they all have their own basics, stepping and way of developing force. Many people have tried to mix the different martial art energies, but all have failed.'

Learning from Everything

It was a lot to think about. Since I was planning to be in Taiwan for a few more years I asked Master He if I could study with him, and he told me the times of his classes. Over the next several years he not only taught me in class but used all aspects of life as a means of explaining what was good or poor skill, and to convey a whole range of teachings. Once, emerging from the Taipei subway with myself and two fellow students, he suddenly stopped in front of a huge advert for a Chinese ballet troupe who were performing in the city. There were four male dancers, all of whom had exceptionally strong looking physiques, and all doing different dynamic postures or leaps. He asked us which posture we liked the most, and then gave an extended teaching about the alignment of their limbs and heads, which of them had the most force and their direction and way of movement. He then related these things to our martial arts forms and basic training, revealing points which I had never heard before. From a simple advertising picture I came away with an increased understanding of posture and motion which could directly be applied to my Bagua practice, and with Master He this was an ongoing experience – music, dance, fighting, the play of animals, human relationship and the movement of the elements, anything and everything became part of the learning, part of the Bagua.

But that was all to come later. My first few lessons with this most unusual of teachers – raised by a master of the old generation, immersed in the ancient philosophy of China, yet enjoying playing saxophone and appreciating the spirit of jazz – were full of a new kind of pain as I worked through a series of twisting exercises for loosening the shoulders, back, hips and spine. The basic requirement for these, as for all the training methods in Baguaquan, was a fine awareness which put the attention deep into the body. These early classes, running four or five hours in length in the sweltering Taipei heat, also emphasised other Jibengong (foundation exercises) and training of the fundamental stances – Mabu (horse stance), Pubu (squatting stance), Gongbu (bow stance) and Hanjibu (containing chances stance), which was a very challenging posture which involved keeping all of the weight on one hip whilst wrapping the soft tissue of the limbs into the centre and still keeping all the correct alignments. These stances were first held as static postures, then sometimes later trained with a single step, and finally with a sudden and dynamic leaping type motion which was very close to how one might apply the method in real combat. That sudden, almost explosive release of force came from all of the storing, wrapping inwards type movements. The process could not be rushed or hurried; it took a long period of time to find the special power which Master He could so obviously and effortlessly express in both simple and complex forms and techniques.

The process was clear enough in theory – first open up the body parts, especially the major joints and spine, then integrate all the body parts. Only true opening could lead to true integration, and trying to push out the power, as in some people's way of constantly expressing Fajin (emitting force), would only damage the practitioner, according to Master He.

GRANDMASTER GONG BAO ZHAI

MASTER HE JING-HAN

TRANSMISSION OF THE BAGUAQUAN EIGHT MOTHER PALMS

Gong Bao Zhai and He Jinghan with Eight Mother Palms

'Fajin comes naturally, we do not train for it. Some Taiji people trained for Fajin after watching their teachers express power and damaged their body and nerves. They didn't realise that the teacher was just naturally releasing what was built up. Others did Fajin continuously and became exhausted. Actually what we need to do is to open a clear pathway in the body, and then allow or lead force to naturally travel down the pathway to the extremity and beyond. If we talk about using Fajin in combat, it is only used after you have destabilised the enemy's balance or centre of gravity.'

That process of 'opening a clear pathway' became my major challenge, learning to be soft and open enough whilst simultaneously keeping a certain integration of the Jing (connective tissue such as tendon and ligaments). From the first lesson onwards I was aching in places I had never felt before, such as the connective tissue joining the two legs and running through the crotch and hip region. Training this area developed what He Jinghan called 'Deng Jin' or the propping up force of the crotch, a crucial part of being able to express the vertical rising force which was so critical in every part of this particular Bagua system. The value of this could be clearly experienced during another fun and somewhat risky type of practice, walking from stance to stance on top of house bricks turned longways up. I began, in fact, with the bricks flat on the ground, which presented less chance of breaking the ankle joint but still allowed me to feel if the vertical force in the legs was lacking. If there was any forward movement when stepping then the brick could easily slide on the earth. Put the brick on its side, but not yet standing up, and already the difficulty factor was doubled – a slip now could really hurt the foot. Stand the brick up vertically and I moved very slowly, emphasising the lifting up and placing down step with great caution, well aware that any movement off the vertical could make the brick fall and lead to twisting or even breaking of the ankle. Keeping relaxed amidst all this focused stepping was an even bigger challenge! The difficulty was compounded exponentially when the bricks were placed in a circle and I began 'walking the circle' with Baibu (toe out step) and Koubu (hook in step). This was really difficult, and to watch He Jinghan doing it with such nimble and accurate foot placement made one realise the countless hours he had put into the foundation exercises over decades of practice.

'Baguaquan is in the step.' So goes an old training dictum of this martial art, and since my teenage years I had loved the practise of circle walking learned from the Spectacles Cheng branch of the system. Now, immersing myself into the branch passed down from Grandmaster Dong Hai Chuan to his closest student Yin Fu, there were new leg skills to learn. Spectacles Cheng had been an expert in Shaio Jiao (Chinese wrestling) and so his Bagua is full of forward and backwards reaping sweeps, legs hooks and low kicking. The Baguaquan from Yin Fu's line had used the Shaolin Lohan system as a base on which to express the Bagua theories, and this was reflected in the stepping skills which often utilised the Ding Bu (half horse stance) in very swift dodges to the eight directions or side to side, the stamping step and also various types of jumping and leaping footwork. Even though they were very different from those of Cheng Bagua, my body felt surprisingly comfortable with the new postures due to the fact that my early training, from the age of fourteen to twenty-one, had been in Shaolin Lohan Quan. It was exactly how my teacher explained it – the old generation had taken Lohan as a base and added to it the deep twist and spiral motions of Bagua. It was fascinating, like a more refined version of my childhood Shaolin, and at the base of all of it was the embodiment of certain principles. The first of these which I learned was 'change and unchanging'.

'Freedom means you are able to change,' Master He told me during those early weeks of training. 'The ability to really change, be it fighting or in life, requires a free mind which rests in the changeless state. The reason we get pain, stuck, need to control or to argue, is because we follow a certain concept, an identity or ego. I see myself like this or like that, I can only do this or that. Toxins and illness get stuck in the body where we cannot release them, they are hiding in the corner due to our stuck thinking. Even the concept of fighting, of being a fighter, limits us in real fighting and certainly limits our life. You need to understand that Bagua is not for fighting!'

I pondered on those words and then asked He Jinghan if he had ever taught the fighting skills of the art, or was rather only interested in the exercise and mental aspects of Bagua.

'We have many training drills and exercises for developing fighting skill, but this is in the post-birth stage of practice. First we work on the pre-birth stage, which develops the body method and mind. We open up each body part, creating a good environment for practice, and by this ability to feel every part then you can produce real Neijin or inner power. If you can really release your physical and emotional blockages, and can go deep enough, your body becomes a gateway to the spiritual world.

'The fighting skill of Baguaquan uses eight different directions of force, and to discover these we practise the Ba Mu Zhang (Eight Mother Palms). Once your body can produce these forces, then you begin to combine them, moving from large circle motions to small circles, until eventually you can change from one force to another in a tiny space. This ability to change freely requires a very open, relaxed and integrated body and mind, so you simply cannot rush to the fighting methods without first training at the Pre-Heaven stage.'

It made a lot of sense. My previous training had been very combat orientated, with the Eight Mother Palms, the forms and the basics having direct application to fighting situations. With the exercises I was learning in Taiwan it was often difficult to see how they could be applied practically, but as the months and years went by it became clear that even the most simple methods – such as the stepping or arm swings – did indeed contain the potential to be very effective fighting skills. But more than that, above and beyond fighting, was that the exercises were beginning to produce new feelings in my body, of openness and internal connection, and revelations about how the principles of the art were as relevant to every other aspect of daily life as to the combat situations which I had previously been fixated on.

Walking the Circle

I was introduced to the Ba Mu Zhang as eight postures held whilst walking around the circle, and a short while later was also taught the Single Change Palm with circle walking. Using what is called the 'crane step' developed a very unique feeling of circling; at each step one leg crossed over the other, always moving directly up and down, allowing the limbs and body to be moved forward through giving in to gravity rather than the actual motion of the leg. The feeling whilst doing this is somewhat like pedalling a bicycle down a slight incline – although an initial effort is involved in pushing the pedals, after a short time one feels that the bike itself is doing the work, helped of course by gravity and momentum. The first time I really felt this whilst circling was an absolute revelation. I kept my body posture fixed according to the principles of structural integrity, stepped onto the circle and made an effort to walk using the hips in a pumping up and down action, inclining my body slightly forward whilst also twisting into the centre of the circle, all the while using my eyes and intent to lead the whole work around and around. Within a few revolutions of the circle 'something' took over my structure, and I was being carried around by that force until I felt my legs were barely able to keep up with the speed.

'Exactly!' was He Jinghan's response when I told him what I had felt. 'The challenge when you can circle well is whether or not your legs can keep up with the speed. We call this Shr, a potential force which is inherent in everything in the Universe, and in every unbalanced posture this Shr is what can make you move. When Gong Bao Tien walked the circle, his queue stood out horizontally, such was his speed, because his legs were fast enough to keep up with the force being generated by his body. The principle is, first the steps move the body, then the body moves with the steps, then the body leads the steps. In a similar way you must integrate the three factors of Xing, Shr and Shen, or posture, force and spirit. All must be connected along with many other factors to produce the correct movement. The eyes, for example, also have their way of being used – you intend to do something, your eyes move, your head follows the eyes and then you have motion in your body which twists and completes what you intended to do.

'The two steps used in circling – Baibu and Koubu – draw strength from the pelvis, hips and crotch area, and although we lift them high in practice for real use in fighting they are applied low. The key point is that when circling you have total control over where your feet are at any moment, you can change no matter where your feet happen to be, even if they are in mid-step or mid-air. When my teacher Gong Bao Zhai stepped on a hole in a pitch black street one night, his body instantly jumped without thought straight out again, although his feet had not touched the ground! This was also how he and his teacher were able to walk on water.'

It sounded fantastic. 'But then without Qing Gong (Light Body skill), we cannot expect to do that kind of stepping?'

Master He shook his head. 'Actually Qing Gong needs to be started as a child to really fulfil its potential, or else you can damage your energy and body. But we can train certain aspects of it that can help us develop special types of stepping. Think of how a dog leaps to catch a frisbee, and then grasping it in its mouth it twists its body around before landing. This shows us that we don't need the ground to have structural integrity. In fact what we need is to connect all the Jing (connective tissue such as tendons) as one big web all over the body to make it move like that. For example...' He leaped into the air and kicked forward, and then ran forward before landing...my eyes stared with disbelief! From a vertical jump he had somehow managed to run forward in mid-air. That should be impossible.

'Try...you can find it!' Master He laughed and left me to practise.

Single Change Palm

A few weeks later in the Sunday morning class – which now numbered about ten, mainly Taiwanese, students – Master He began teaching some of the combative theory of the system as it related to Single Change Palm and circling.

'Old time fighters did Single Change Palm for five to ten years since their priority was fighting, and this exercise is for fighting. The body and centre are always kept still with the energy remaining in the Dantien. The Li [force] can go out of the limbs but the Qi must stay in the centre. In between the push palm postures we can put various combinations of fighting changes, every day will bring new changes. Also you must keep your awareness like a sphere, as in the old times your enemies would attack in a group and have weapons, and fighting was a matter of life and death. You must never allow your knees to straighten as they would be open to a leg break attack which could mean disaster. Don't look at your feet, feel your feet... no matter if the terrain is level or uneven you should stay the same height and be balanced on whichever side or part of the foot is on the ground.'

We were told to practise around some trees which had big roots sticking out in all directions, and the experience certainly taught me a lot about how the step had to be able to adapt to any terrain. A while later I visited Beijing's Imperial Palace in mainland China, and was able to practise in the vast stone courtyards which were similar to those where Dong Hai Chuan, Yin Fu and Gong Bao Tien would have honed their skills. The stone floor was very uneven, with big gaps here and there and sudden erratic changes of height. This must have been how people lived their lives before the advent of cement and concrete laid flat by surveying gadgets, and their everyday experience would have been of having to find stability and balance in their own way of walking and moving about. Practising in this environment – or on a beach, in water, around a tree with roots – gives one a much more acute sensitivity to changes of pressure on various parts of the feet, to the need to change swiftly and surely in both a vertical and horizontal sense and with the whole body moving as one unit. I was to find from such practice a rather practical benefit – if I tripped over something in the dark or in a crowd, I still stumbled but didn't fall down, and my body instantly righted itself without conscious thought.

Fighting Skill in Bagua

'The problem of fighting is basically the space between two or more people.' It was a few months into my training when Master He first began speaking to the Sunday morning group about the specifics of fighting. 'Speed is not ten strikes in one second, but using time and timing and space correctly. Just to punch someone does no real damage because he will move back with the impact. The skill in Baguaquan is to strike someone as they move towards you, to find the tiny opening in his defence that you get through to reach him, how to jam his space and put him in an inferior position. If you simply step back and block it is no good as essentially nothing has changed in the dynamic.

'If possible you must run away from a fight, apologise or do something else to diffuse the situation. But if you really have to fight then it is life or death, and you must empty yourself and give your life up to the situation. You may be surrounded with many attackers, they may have hidden weapons. If you have the concept of fighting then you will be separate from outside and from the enemy. If you harmonise with everything then you will have the whole world with you!'

*Against a low sweeping attack He Jinghan steps
forward and strikes with his knee to the body*

He Jinghan then gave me my first real taste of Bagua technique as applied to fighting, using a Koubu step to simultaneously evade and enter into my space as I attacked. It felt as if a mule had kicked my leg, with a force spiralling up through my spine and causing me to fall off balance, though he made very light contact. It was certainly a shock, as I had more or less begun to think that my teacher had no real interest in sharing the fighting skills and had never felt him deliver power before. That day I had a glimpse of why he didn't like to show too much of it in the park, for it was brutal and dangerous work and quite clearly developed by serious warriors in a time when a fight meant probable death for one or other of the combatants. All of the principles and techniques worked in such a way that had the attacker or attackers been holding blades, no modification was needed. Vital areas were always protected or kept out of harm's way, constant motion and evasion off the line of attack were emphasised so as not to present a sitting target and to prevent 'stuck on the spot' syndrome, and the mental aspect – so crucial a part of any encounter – was dealt with in a way that made it very clear how the Pre-Heaven training was developing the totality of the human being to prepare for all eventualities. But what I was seeing that day was still but a taste of what was to come – there were far deeper skills which I was soon to experience…

The Old Bagua Masters

'We modern people have the wrong idea about the old masters,' said He Jinghan on the following Sunday morning, 'somehow thinking that they were always fighting. No! People such as Yin Fu, who was a bodyguard for the empress, would maybe have had three fights in their entire life, and only then when there was a very good reason and when they were sure they would win. If Yin Fu had to fight, he had already failed. His job was to keep the Imperial family safe, not to get them caught up in violence. He would have been expert at all kinds of terrain, geography, weather patterns, local customs and much more, all kinds of strategy and ways of travelling, to ensure that he never had to fight.

'Real fighting is completely unlimited, which means we cannot guess how the fight will go. There are certain factors which we can know, and others which are beyond our ability to know. For example, if I punch you I know that there are certain ways you can block this, up or down, left or right, but you may also do something totally wild such as throw something at me. We need to understand the known factors, and then develop the intuition or extra sense to deal with the random forces. In the same way, we need to learn all the forms and techniques, and then forget everything. The goal is freedom – but we nurture that freedom within the discipline of Bagua's boundaries. The freedom of Bagua is within the limits of Bagua.'

A lot of the skill in Baguaquan is refined through dozens of semi-free exercises or, as He Jinghan called them, 'games', practised or played in a somewhat natural and loose manner. The first one I learned developed the ability to 'turn one arm into three', in other words to be able to skilfully and smoothly use wrist, elbow and shoulder to strike and deflect: a student stood with eyes closed in the centre of a ring of four people who grabbed or struck at random targets, slowly at first and only picking up speed over time, with the student deflecting from the nearest joint to the attack. Another one had two students working only the stepping, one attacking with Baibu and Koubu to the other's legs, and the defender using the same steps to evade, dodge and encircle. As well as teaching us a wealth of knowledge about technique, variations, sensitivity, softness and how to blend with an attacker's force, they were highly enjoyable!

'Baguaquan nurtures a hidden potential,' He Jinghan explained during one class. 'In fact we don't know what we can do until need brings out our skills. It is like a bell, the harder you strike it the louder the response. This kind of loose and fun training is similar to the way that animals will learn fighting as they grow up, bringing out all of one's potential in a natural way.

'A fight between two experts in the old times would have been like a chess match, positioning, evasion, different ranges, strategy, timing, angulations, connecting then separating; it was all about skill. In Baguaquan the three piercing palms contain the essence of the fighting strategy – make contact, change line and rhythm and then hit! If, for example, I am attacked by a southern stylist such as Hong Gar, I cannot go directly against his very powerful direct punch. I must change myself, hit his vital points and make him change, in that way his greatest strength is overcome. Sometimes I must sacrifice one part, such as my stomach, in order to finish him by hitting a really vital area such as his eyes. Baguaquan is very sneaky, you will never know how you have been hit. In a fight you keep the mind like a sphere, seeing everything, when you need to focus you focus.

'The bodyguards such as Yin Fu were very different from those of the present age. Nowadays bodyguards have all kinds of technology to rely on, there is much less danger, the same as modern hunters with all their powerful weapons and tools. The old hunters would have been in the same danger as their prey, the old bodyguards would have had to have extraordinary senses to keep people alive. I remember once I was visiting a tea-farmer near Taipei; as I went in and he began serving me tea and talking it was raining. After some time I asked him if he was concerned about his crop, since tea is such a delicate plant. He shook his head and replied that the water was only eighty per cent full. I asked him how he knew that, and he said that he could tell from the sound… That is the kind of special ability that the old ones had!'

The Sword

One night He Jinghan took me to begin training with another group in a different part of the city. He told me that this class was an experiment – they were members of a Daoist association who, amongst other practices, travelled to towns or countries where disasters had happened to perform rituals for the eradication of suffering. They had asked if they could learn the straight sword and, although it is normally a weapon which requires much previous preparation of the body, He Jinghan had agreed. The training was on a rooftop overlooking the neon lights of the city, with six or seven people mainly in their twenties or thirties. It was a friendly and fun class. We were taught the sword from as much an energetic as a physical perspective, the first exercise being to feel and understand the way that energy travels along the weapon. Then with a partner we began to 'tune in' to the energy of the other person's sword using our own as an 'antenna'. This was a truly fascinating work, with the others seemingly as engrossed as I was, and fairly quickly everyone was able to sense a tangible, magnetic-type force emitting from their partner's sword. This appreciation of spiral force then led into the unique basic techniques of the weapon, using stepping on the circle along with simple cutting and pointing motions. It was easy to see how Baguaquan empty-hand methods had grown out of the sword.

'The sword moves like a dragon,' He Jinghan told us. 'Every joint and the Kua [hip] spiral to produce this movement. Since it is a short weapon it is very quick to return and cover, so don't worry if you thrust it a long way. But with a long weapon like a spear you must keep it close to the body as it cannot quickly return and cover.'

The next exercise was very revealing about the potential of that spiral force. He Jinghan pulled a very long, thick and extremely heavy water hose from the side of the roof, the kind that takes two hands to pull. I held one end and my partner, a bright-eyed young chap with a Daoist-styled wispy beard and top-knot (quite unusual for a Taiwanese), took the other end. We then had to use a spiral motion of the right arm to send a wave along the hose all the way to the other end. Well, our first few attempts had all of us laughing, as the waves travelled less than fifteen feet (4.5 m) before fading out. He Jinghan took my end and gave a motion of his right arm, and a powerful wave went some thirty foot (9 m) to the end of the hose and had the young Daoist back-pedalling from the force. That was really something! Actually it is of the few ways you can tangibly see internal force manifested externally as a spiral wave. After some experimentation, using more motion from the body and legs, we were able to increase the wave, but He Jinghan decided the time had come to work the tendons – and so it was back to foundation exercises.

On Gong Bao Zhai

It was Chinese New Year, and He Jinghan had invited me to his house. For Chinese people all over the world this is a time for the coming together of loved ones and the sharing of food and gifts against a backdrop of firecrackers and lanterns and lion dances. His place was full of wonderful old swords and calligraphy and carvings, and as we munched on the myriad little snacks which are found everywhere during that festival he shared some memories about his recently deceased master, Gong Bao Zhai.

'My teacher observed everything about my life – my friends, my girlfriend, what books I read. A master and student is like a farmer and his crops, even when he is home he will be concerned, is it sunny, is it raining? He was from the old generation and found it very hard to trust anyone, you know he passed through war, very difficult times where he had to fight for his life… When he fled to Taiwan he had lost everything. He used his ability gained from Bagua practice to learn to be a locksmith, to make a life for himself. The art helped him survive in the same way that it helped Yin Fu and Gong Bao Tien survive the pressure and politics of life in the Imperial Palace. He never spoke about martial arts, but one day an old friend came who knew he was Gong Bao Tien's disciple. Slowly he began to teach a little. Every weekend he would have a group in his hardware shop, people would just sit there and if they didn't ask him anything he would just make small talk! He said it was like a bell, if you hit a little there would be a little sound, but if you hit a lot there will be a loud ringing sound! He said that what we develop from practice is unknown even to ourselves until we are tested, until we really need it. Even my teaching is like that, often until a student asks me I won't know that I know something.

'My teacher was from Jing Shan Village in Shangdong Province. Gong Bao Tien had gone back to Jing Shan after retiring from serving the emperor as a bodyguard, and in his old age he just had fun there, playing tricks on the women and playing with the children. This was his way, he just did what was right at the time, simply what he needed to do – he had killed men in his earlier life but now he just relaxed and enjoyed himself. My teacher was very sickly as a child so he learned Baguaquan to try and get stronger, he studied with Gong Bao Tien for twenty years. He was a spiritual man but in a very practical way. For example, he told me how one night he was walking back towards the village on the mountain and a big monster came towards him from within the trees. Picking up a branch he shouted at the monster to go back to his own world, that he didn't belong here!

'Another time he was on the mountain and he saw, some way below, a well-known martial arts practitioner from the district sword fighting with a woman dressed all in white. The woman had incredible skill and completely defeated the man before she simply vanished! There were many strange things like that which he related to me. He told me that he was very good at shooting with this old German gun which they had in the village. One day the villagers spotted a gigantic bird, a very strange creature with an enormous wingspan, taking a small animal up into the sky. My teacher shot it and it must have injured the creature because it began to lose height; everyone took the dogs and chased it into a forest. By the time they had got to it the bird had crashed but had already killed one dog. They killed it, chopped up its parts and sold it for food or for medicine. That was the type of people they were, very practical!

'In Taiwan life was difficult, food was scarce. Because he ate so much salted meat back then, later in life he had heart disease. His three arteries were blocked, but he refused to let them operate. Instead he began training his Baguaquan again and used his inner force to unblock the arteries. Whenever he felt lack of oxygen or dizzy he would go into a back room for ten minutes and do a certain exercise, and then feel better. This is the spirit of the martial artist, to take their health and life into their own hands and not rely on others.'

This was one of the most extraordinary stories I had ever heard, and one of the things that inspired me to use Neigong and meditation to fight against a serious illness which developed some years later. I asked He Jinghan about his own training with his teacher.

'My work in the army was with communications, you know, listening to signals through headphones, codes and those things… so I had plenty of time to practise. Martial art was for me the most important thing. My teacher's house was like my own home, I would go there and sweep the floor, he would teach me through many things like Chinese chess, telling me stories about the old times, Chinese classical books, always teaching the principles of life. Sometimes he would wake up in the middle of the night having dreamed about some movements which he had long forgotten, so he would teach me from that experience.

'Even as he got older he was still very strong, once he carried a very heavy wooden beam for his shop on his shoulder, all the way from Lio Jang Li to Hsin I Lu [across several city districts]! I remember one of his students came to see him from America when my teacher was very old, and asked him for a push hands match… Well, the student tried to Fajin and my teacher's body instantly reacted and sent the young man flying! This was his hidden power. When he was dying it took four doctors to hold him down, even though he was unconscious on his deathbed. I felt two very strong pulses up the sides of his body; these are developed from the Qing Gong training. They tried to put a breathing tube in his mouth but accidently knocked out a tooth which he swallowed. The next day he unconsciously reacted, his body sending the tooth shooting out again. This is why he insisted that you cannot train fighting skill, it is something that will simply come out from correct practice when you need it.'

I was very touched at He Jinghan's recollections, and thought in silence for a minute or two as he poured green tea for us. Over the years as I got to know him more and more, it became very clear that he didn't view death in the same way as most people; to him it was a completely natural event and simply another change. He told me that his teacher had been happy to depart, since his wife had passed away not long before and all of his old friends had long since gone. I wondered about his view on lineage and discipleship and its relevance in the present day, and if he would take disciples. His face took on an unusually serious expression.

'Actually, a few years ago I took two disciples. But after some time they no longer came training with me, and one day I saw them training with a man I knew. He was a martial artist who focused on the fighting skills, and he told them that he could teach them those things much better than I could. So…'

I felt sad at the look on his face and asked him what that experience had made him feel.

'Sad. Just sad that both of them and myself had lost the chance to go deeper together.' He poured more tea for us and handed me a plate of small round bean-cakes. 'People don't understand what lineage is. After my teacher died one of my Gongfu brothers came to see me. He had started training a little before me, and came every year or so to visit our teacher. He said to me, "Now that teacher has passed away I am the senior student, so I should be the head of the lineage." I replied that, "Lineage is a burden we bear, not a crown we wear." I said that he was welcome to be the head.

'The ceremony or form is not the vital thing, what is important is the spirit of responsibility for taking the knowledge forward to the next generation. Lineage is like being married, rather than having several girlfriends. Actually, to take a disciple is not to take him for myself, but to bring him into the Baguaquan lineage. He becomes a family member, one line of family being blood relatives and the other line the martial art family. It is a big responsibility to take a disciple!

'Each generation of Bagua practitioners has a unique mission. Dong Hai Chuan brought Bagua out of the mountains and into Beijing. Yin Fu protected the Imperial family. Gong Bao Tien took the art out of the Palace and into the villages, to the common folk. Gong Bao Zhai brought the art to Taiwan and gave his treasures to disciples who teach in other countries. For myself I want to use Baguaquan to uplift humanity.'

Sipping my tea, I reflected on the stories and their morals. He Jinghan writes in his book *Bagua Quan Foundation Training* (2009) about the need to deeply hide one's true skills to avoid the pitfall of arrogance, and how the energy developed through practice can destroy the practitioner if it is used to satisfy lust and material greed. Having made so many mistakes in my own life I knew how very hard it was to be a truly virtuous person.

But I had seen also much kindness and goodness, in situations where there was nothing to gain by being kind or good, and received incredibly generous gifts of love, knowledge and material support from teachers, friends and complete strangers. Martial arts training and spiritual cultivation will present us with many choices as we walk along the path, and every single choice we make will plant good or bad seeds which will grow in time. Just being a lineage holder or even a monk is no guarantee of having good inner qualities. Monks and great warriors are men, struggling along the path like the rest of us until the final fetters are broken and liberation dawns. For years I blindly followed those who appeared to be spiritually advanced, simply because they had superb fighting skill and could recite the teachings of ancient wise men. In my middle years I have stopped having any awe or respect for people with power, be that martial or energetic or 'spiritual', unless it is tempered with genuine kindness, humility and simple human love. I needed to study spiritual work from men with absolute honesty and sincerity. It was why I deeply respected Serge Augier, Paul Whitrod and He Jinghan – there was not a trace of difference between how they acted and how they were internally, no pretence just to impress upon others how spiritual they were. Also, and very importantly for martial arts masters, none of them ever used their great powers to dominate students, either psychologically or physically.

This brings to mind a story told to me by my good friend Gary Roba, who had studied classical Indian music in India for seven years with some of the greatest living teachers. One of his teachers was the disciple of a deceased Guru who had three famous students – Gary's teacher, who was famous in India, another man who was an international superstar, although nowhere nearly as skilled as the first, and then the Guru's daughter who was a hermitic woman of almost legendary reputation living in an apartment in Bombay and said to have almost supernatural ability in music. But then there was a fourth student, rumoured to be even greater than the other three, but about whom little was known. After some years Gary found the man, quite by chance. He was living in utter simplicity and materially very poor – but when he played the flute, Oh! It was truly incredible. The man had a way of playing where the fingers were spread out far more than was usual, allowing him to play with much greater sophistication than normally possible. This was a very difficult method, and although Gary wanted so much to learn from him he knew that it would mean starting all over again. But for someone who could – the results would be unlimited! Gary was most struck at how much deeper this man's practice was than his famous counterparts, and particularly at how very humble the man was compared to the others.

It was a story I have pondered on many times over the years.

The Courtyard

It was four years since I had met He Jinghan and I was renting a room on the street where he lived. This meant that I was able to train with him most nights on a large courtyard area beside his apartment. Actually, this was his personal training time, late at night, but he generously agreed to let me practise there as well. I had many memorable experiences in that place but the one which stands out above all happened about a week after I moved to the area. He Jinghan and I began to walk the circle together on the same circle, standing opposite each other with the classical push-palm guard stance facing into the centre. As was usual when training with him I was able to 'borrow' some of his force which meant that I began to walk very fast and with a deep twist in the torso. Everything outside the circle blurred and all I could see was his two bright eyes looking directly at me…my steps were going faster than I had ever felt before…the eye to eye contact was a deep telepathic connection between the spirits of two people, beyond thinking…and I just knew a second before he wanted to change direction although not a word was spoken…a swift and fluid change of palm, walk the other way around and once again the speed increased to very fast, my eyes connecting with his and feeling a strong transmission of energy. It really was like being in a vortex of power which was somehow being summoned by a Bagua master, and I was aware of generations of adepts of our beloved internal art being behind us all the while. When at last we stopped

I realised that I had never walked the circle so well in twenty years of practice. He Jinghan grinned at me and said simply, 'That is circle walking!'

A couple of days later I was alone in my new apartment when He Jinghan made a visit. Ever since meeting him I had often asked about the fighting methods of Baguaquan, and he had indeed taught various such skills in the group classes, and showed me various things when we were alone. But this day I was to see something quite different.

'OK, since you always ask me, today I will try and show you how we really use Bagua for fighting.' He shut the door behind him. 'It is very difficult to do without hurting you, but I will try. But you must attack properly and not hold back.'

I didn't need a second bidding! I launched a right fist strike to his face and…there was something like a massive spring exploding out of the stillness where He Jinghan had been, a flash in my eyes and slight pressure on my throat and I was thrown backwards. Clearing my vision I saw him releasing the Lion posture, which is basically two piercing palms launched simultaneously towards the eyes and throat. I attacked again and again and each time I fell into an empty space or was thrown backwards. The first big difference from what he had demonstrated before was his use of releasing force like a huge steel spring. It was extremely fast, disorienting and fear-inducing, and I was certainly happy that he had superb control. He Jinghan then showed me how he would change if I had somehow managed to stop his first attack. This was to be the second revelation. His way of shifting from strike to strike occurred within a very small area as he changed 'on the web', fluid and yet each time releasing this spring-like short power. Everything was so clearly based on the Mother Palm energies, and kept very much within clear Bagua flavour technique. No matter what I did he never resorted to generic punch-kick type actions. His Baibu and Koubu footwork, combined with the very close-in short movements, were deployed in continuous changing steps often only an inch long. Every movement had the whole body connected as a cohesive unit, and yet capable of rapid and fluid change when presented with a barrier.

After that day's lesson I had a much clearer idea of how the Yin Fu branches of the Bagua system used their motions in a real fighting situation. One of the most interesting points for me was that very little needed to change if the attack came with a blade; the same postures and changes would be utilised. Yet again it was made clear that no matter how beautiful the forms of Bagua, and how deep the philosophy underlying it, it was still a very dangerous method of fighting.

A few nights later on the courtyard I received another lesson, also memorable but for a different reason. That night He Jinghan taught me the importance of releasing the muscles which we normally hold ourselves up with, and relying instead on the network of connective tissue (Jing). Of course it was something I had heard many times over the years, but that night something really clicked. This came about because earlier in the day we had been watching some videos of various martial artists, one of them being an American man who had made a documentary of himself and his teacher in China. The American was a typically large man whilst his teacher was a small frail-looking oldster. He Jinghan pointed out the difference between them when they moved through various Taiji and Bagua postures. In the movement where they shifted weight backwards in the heel step or Seven Star step, in the Taiji posture called 'Play the Lute', the old man's force went directly downwards into the earth, whereas the Westerner's force went horizontally, thus disconnecting him from the earth. In the Bagua postures the oldster used clear twisting force whereas the American merely turned one dimensionally.

'These small details tell everything about the depth of the practice,' He Jinghan commented. 'This man has better fighting skill than many Westerners, partly because of his size, but he doesn't understand and cannot do the things he is talking about. However he explains it very well!'

When the old man on the film did push hands his structure was totally supported by connective tissue, but when the Westerner did 'Fajin' strikes on his students he tensed his neck and shoulders and had a deep furrow between his eyebrows. 'This kind of tension is very bad,' He Jinghan commented. 'So many martial artists died young from high blood pressure caused by this tension, or by too much Fajin. Very few can release the muscles and use the Jing to support the structure, but if they can they will melt into the earth and have great power even in old age. This kind of tendon power is what we use in Baguaquan; it is very sharp and bound inwards to the centre and can release like a huge steel spring. Muscle power will make you tense. When your face and neck tense your Qi will rise up, which we must avoid. Anger also brings the Qi up, but in fact we want the Qi to stay down and the Li to go up and out. My teacher took many years to help me to bring my Qi down.'

So that night in the courtyard he continued the theme, teaching me a series of exercises which helped me feel where I was stuck, and how to release the bound tension and instead use the Jing as a support. One of them was to outstretch the arms and lean the palms against a wall while inclining the whole body at a forty-five degree or more angle with only the balls of the feet touching the ground. The spine and head had to line up and be totally straight. This was very difficult! Within a minute or two the entire musculature of the body began shaking, sweat pouring from my skin. The only way to keep going was to relax the muscles and feel the tendons under the armpits coming into play to support the thirteen stone (82.5 kg) of body weight. When the correct tension of the Jing suddenly manifested it was a totally new feeling, as if an entire web of thin steel springs were criss-crossing my body, most prominently in the armpits and arms, crotch area and the feet. It was a revelation!

However, feeling this web of Jing was just the beginning. Now I had to learn how to keep it in play in all the postures and, most challengingly, whilst in motion.

There were many great training sessions in the courtyard, but that was one of the most memorable.

Therapeutic Aspects of Baguaquan

One day I asked He Jinghan about a chronic hip pain which I had had since pulling the connective tissue many years ago during low stance training. What he told me and the method which he taught to heal the injury is what I have used and taught with much success ever since and is worth relating.

'Look on this as a way to learn more about your body. Go into the painful area, do not struggle against the Jing. Go into the pain just enough and then exhale as you release the tension. There is fire in the nerve, too much heat, so you need to let it cool down for a few months. If you avoid doing low stances you will not find the original place of injury, but you must work through this very slowly and with deep feeling. Actually, some people never go very low in their martial arts training – they will get power and skill but not the deep skill! But the correct alignment is the vital factor, better to go only as far as you can without losing the alignment.'

He spent a lot of time writing articles for martial arts magazines about this very topic, and his understanding of human structure and motion was profound.

'From the Baguaquan training I am half a doctor! The other half is the study of herbs, which I did not learn. But through Bagua you can learn how to heal the body of external and internal problems. Qigong will create space and pressure inside of the body, the space will allow the Qi to flow and the organs to work naturally, and the pressure will massage the organs. If you practise the Eight Mother Palms well then you can feel when certain organs are out of harmony or when the Qimai [meridian] is blocked, and through practice you can adjust them.'

Qualities of a Martial Artist

One day we were taking the evening bus from downtown Taipei to the Yong Her district where we lived, holding on to the hanging handrails as the packed and somewhat battered bus bounced and lurched over the pot-hole filled roads. The traffic was at a snail's pace much of the way back, but to me every day in the city was a magical adventure and even the horrible pollution – so bad much of the time that it left a metallic taste in one's mouth – did nothing to detract from the experience. I was there to understand Chinese culture and the roots of Baguaquan, and a bus was as good a place to do it as any. As we swayed along with the seventy or so other passengers we began talking about a film we had recently seen called *Crouching Tiger, Hidden Dragon*. I mentioned how much I enjoyed the character of Li Mu Bai, the main hero played by Chow Yun Fat. He Jinghan shook his head.

'His character was not a real martial artist. Several times he had to stop and think about what to decide. He had wavering thoughts. A martial artist cannot do this, he would die if he did! A real martial artist must act and react instantly.'

'So what are the most vital qualities of a martial artist?' I asked, trying not to be distracted by the smile of a beautiful girl on my left hand side. There were some good points about crowded buses…

'First is perseverance,' answered He Jinghan. 'Second, he must be able to put himself beyond his own life, without fearing death. And third, he must be aware of everything around him…'

Happy that I had at least the third quality I continued on a related topic. 'And what makes a good teacher of martial arts? Is it his fighting skill?'

He Jinghan raised his free hand and gestured with an open palm in the small space between us. 'A good teacher will consider how he can shape his student. His reason for training, his motives, his approach to practice and his life philosophy – all of these things will shape the way that he does a form or his basic training. For example, when you see the Single Whip posture of an old Taiji master, what is inside of that movement? All of his life is inside! So the deeper a master's life experience, the deeper he can teach. But…then it is up to the student to be willing to learn and accept the treasures! You know that when most people see a great master do something skilful, they will be amazed but not be inspired to do it themselves. When Gong Bao Tien lived in his home village he would ride a donkey to the top of a nearby mountain, and then carry the donkey back down again. He said it was only fair to return the donkey's effort! But still, people saw this but didn't become his student.'

I laughed at the image of old Grandmaster Gong carrying a donkey, but the moral was very clear. It made me think again about how stories of the masters had led me around the world to train with some great teachers, such was the power of the written and spoken word. I thought about the Single Change Palm of Bagua, which had been my main daily martial arts practice since my mid-teens, and of the hundreds of thousands of times I had circled around, striving for an elusive and obscure goal which would have seemed pointless to all but a handful of people. My motivation was still pretty much what it had been back in my childhood, just a simple fascination and unstoppable love for this beautiful and challenging spiralling martial art, a feeling that it was a connection to the sacred as well as a method which had stopped me getting my butt kicked by bad guys.

Keeping aware of everything around me, I smiled back at the beautiful girl and wondered what was inside of my Single Change Palm.

Visiting Britain

In 2003 I returned to Britain, and rented a house in Wales where a small group of students could practise full time. It was a period when I was training very intensively in the forest near my place, feeling full of vitality and doing practices such as bounding at full speed in between the trees, using the evasion and tumbling skills to avoid being hit, even trying it at dusk and night time when the lack of light made trusting in intuition a necessity. I had been inspired by the tales of Gong Bao Tien's son and Liu Bai Chuen who had done similar practices, although with Gong's ability in Qing Gong he could also leap up and swing on the branches before continuing the run.

Three months later He Jinghan flew over and stayed with me for the first time, teaching every day for four weeks. The first evening he asked what I had been practising so I showed him.

'Why is your face so serious!?' He Jinghan laughed. 'You have been training continuously for a long time, now you need to relax a little, forget martial arts and rest a few days. This will give your body a chance to transform, to move to the next level. It is like baking bread – first you mix the flour and yeast, then knead it very well, and then you need to leave it for a while before it can be cooked. But if you just leave it, it will rot!'

One of the students who was there asked how to change one's thinking and concepts, as it seemed so difficult to really do that.

'Don't try!' He Jinghan stated. 'Just listen to the master's words and stories over time, change will come, the way you see the world will change. Change equals freedom, the ability to change requires a free mind and body. If you think you are anything, or have any idea of yourself, you will not be able to change.'

It was going to be a month before I would be doing any resting, as we had full time training planned for every day of He Jinghan's visit. During the first week in London he gave a series of seminars to twenty or so students from various systems, sharing a lot of detail about bodywork, Qigong and the principles of Bagua, but showing very little in the way of fighting. Some time earlier I had disbanded a close group of friends and students who had studied with me over a several-year period whenever I was back in London, and these men, all serious about their practice, had continued training with other masters. Attending the seminars, they seemed impressed with He Jinghan's control of his body but disappointed that he did not appear to have great fighting skill.

'He is a very nice guy but he is not a fighter!' one of my friends complained bluntly.

'When we did sword there were openings I could have hit him through,' stated another.

I understood their feeling, as He Jinghan gave very little in the way of real martial teaching that week and came across as more of a bodywork or Yoga teacher. Of course, the bodywork teachers who attended thought he was amazing, and the fighters thought he had little genuine martial skill. I mentioned this to him one evening as we rested back at the house, and he shrugged.

'None of them can even walk properly. Why do they want to learn fighting?'

The next week we travelled to Wales. There was a three-day retreat focusing purely on the Eight Mother Palms Qigong and Neigong methods. Afterwards four of my students and I gathered at my house for a two-day teaching on Sixiang, one of the forms of Bagua which had a lot of combative applications. After lunch on the first day He Jinghan turned to a student named Andy and said simply, 'Attack me any way you want, try and hit me.'

The student looked surprised but followed the instruction. He Jinghan proceeded to show some of the cleverest and swiftest fighting techniques I had ever seen him do, and the students were in awe of his skill. Andy, who had travelled to Taiwan with me before and knew what the master was capable of, said that it was like fighting a ghost. That evening I asked He Jinghan why he had decided to show only these five students what he could really do, and yet chose to leave a large number of my friends in London doubting that he had martial skill.

'I trust these people here.' He smiled. 'I do not want to attract people who are looking to be great fighters. If people want that, then fine, but I am not a trainer of fighters. Whatever martial art is to you then that concept will make you stuck at that level. Do you want to be a king, a general or a soldier? The Jiang Hu members in China were mostly soldiers. When a teacher meets you he will decide which level you will learn, but don't be stuck on the level of a soldier.'

Another student asked him why he hadn't hit the London students to show the special force of Bagua. He Jinghan stared at him as if he had lost his mind. 'Why would I want to hit them? I have only just met them!'

The next day we revised what we had learned so far of the Sixiang form, and were then shown how – once one was adapt at the form in its fixed step version – it then transformed into a continuous and very fast sequence where strikes whipped out like wet towels and linked one to another fluidly and without any break in the force from start to finish. This way was close to the power one would actually use in real fighting, and had some very useful applications where the palm cut through the attacking limb and immediately bounced up to hit a vital area as the body moved nimbly aside from the attack.

'Some masters forget the forms,' commented He Jinghan. 'That is fine, because the form is only a tool. Don't be obsessed with any tool or system, always look for the essence. The same with this Sixiang form or any of our forms, you must understand what it wants to teach you.'

One of the motions of the form is a leap and spin through the air, and it brought up the topic of Qing Gong. Several of the students there had never seen He Jinghan demonstrate this, so he agreed to show a little of its uses. First he ran three steps up the side of the house before landing lightly, and then, leaping up, ran three steps forward *through the air*. He then asked me to make a low bow stance, and as I stood there he ran up my back with such lightness that it felt like a squirrel's feet. The strangest thing was when we piled up three huge cushions and he leaped on and off them – the top cushion was dented barely an inch. When anyone else tried it they simply fell off or the cushions collapsed beneath their weight. Later I was one side of the large kitchen cooking at the stove and someone had asked him about footwork as it related to Qing Gong – the next thing I knew the whole wooden floor was shaking as he began stamping on the spot with extreme speed and force. That kind of vibration force is something quite extraordinary.

He Jinghan teaches in Wales, 2003

The students had received some excellent training in the seminar and had many questions about how they could use the principles of Bagua to make their lives better. That evening we had dinner together as He Jinghan said to all of us, 'Don't struggle against your own life. Everything that comes *is* your life! Don't expect that things will happen in the way you hope, because they rarely do. This body is very precious because it is the reflection of your soul in this world, so no need to separate soul and matter, all life is a gift from God for us to use and grow by. We must have a big trust, a great confidence in life, that God will give us what we need. Bad pushes good, dark pushes light, Yin pushes Yang. If things come, OK, if they go, it's fine too! This is the same as Bagua for fighting, we don't try to attack someone but just see what he gives to us. In this way you can be relaxed and happy!'

One student asked about anger, and mentioned someone whom he was very upset with. He Jinghan gave him very clear advice.

'If we see a person at a certain time and get angry, we only see that moment and not the long cycle. It will change. The wise man sees it all as a transition and knows that everything has several causative factors.'

Someone else asked He Jinghan if he was a Daoist.

'Baguaquan comes from Dao, but all religions are man made systems of thought,' he replied. 'Truth is Truth!' And having said that, he then proceeded to give several hours' teaching on the meaning of the Trigrams, which are one of the major symbols of Daoism. I finally went to bed in the small hours of the morning, with his voice and laughter still resonating in my ears.

Several of the students left the next day, leaving two young men who had been living and training with me the past couple of months. These two were almost polar opposites – one was a very serious, driven and macho kind of guy, very closed as a person, whereas the other was very laid back, gregarious and very soft in speech and mannerisms. When they asked He Jinghan what they could do to improve their practice he observed them for a while as they went about their day to day tasks in the house. The woman I was sharing life with at the time, a Taiwanese teacher of sacred and folk dance, was teaching in the house, and He Jinghan advised the serious macho guy to join her class. That evening I saw him with the group of girls, twirling his hands and fingers and trying to copy their graceful poses, and it was to his credit that he did it. It is never easy on the ego to do something like that when your friends are watching. Looking back I can see how it gave impetus in what was to be a long, slow journey towards finding himself.

'By going towards his opposite extreme, towards Yin, slowly he will come back to the centre and find himself,' He Jinghan commented as we watched him dancing in the front room.

Mr Soft, on the other hand, was given a very Yang practice – he had to go up and down the length of the garden doing a very direct and powerful punching action called 'chain punching'. Once again He Jinghan was helping someone find their centre by going to an extreme, but in this case it brought up so much emotional energy for the young man that he vanished at midday and we didn't see him until the following afternoon.

One of the first things He Jinghan had noticed when he walked into my house was a picture of a Buddhist monk, a well-known religious figure. 'It is easier to be a monk,' he said quite seriously. 'Let him try and be married, that is much more difficult!'

I had to agree, being in a far from harmonious relationship which was about to dissolve. It was an intense month for everyone involved, as it always is around a true master, with many learnings, and the seeds being planted which would later bear fruit in He Jinghan's annual visits to his students in Britain. When eventually I waved the smiling Baguaquan master off at London airport I had no idea that it was to be almost two years before I would see him again. I would soon be flying off to Thailand where I would end up living for three very happy years, and where a whole new series of adventures awaited me.

The Land of Smiles

Summer 2005. I had been married for a year and was running a retreat centre in Chiangmai in the north of Thailand, teaching Bagua and Xingyi to students from all over the world in a neighbourhood surrounded by palm trees and populated by friendly people. My wife was from a traditional Thai Buddhist family and completely appreciated that practice was the centre of my life, and she was happy cooking for the students and taking me to meet meditation monks in various temples. I frequently visited a Chinese man who was highly skilled in an old Shaolin system, and my retreat centre had many interesting and talented students who I could practise with. It was a truly contented time of my life.

Although known as the Land of Smiles, Thailand has many serious social problems which most tourists simply never encounter. Corruption amongst the police and government is so rife that when you are stopped on your motorbike you simply give some bank notes and get waved on again. Terrible violence happens seemingly out of the blue and often en masse, and there is a huge problem with drugs, alcoholism and, in the south of the country, daily killings of ordinary folk and Buddhist clergy by an unknown group. But despite all these factors life in Thailand can be simply wonderful – a widespread appreciation of Buddhist values, many highly accomplished meditation teachers, year-round sunshine and some of the friendliest people in the world.

He Jinghan and his lovely wife visited us for a week's holiday during the summer, and although it was a laid back and fun time I once again learned a huge amount. I was at the peak of my fitness and vitality, and He Jinghan seemed happy to share many fighting drills and concepts along with various other teachings. After the first day I told him that it seemed I was learning a completely new style of Bagua.

'With my teacher, every few years I also felt as if it was a whole different style of Bagua!' he laughed. He then began explaining the fighting theory from yet another angle. 'The highest level of Baguaquan is "Entwining Palm", which is like two snakes coiling around each other in embrace or around a bamboo – if you can contact the enemy like this then you have the potential to change his heart, because you can kill him at any moment but choose not to do so. It is like throwing them a fish line which they catch, or sucking them into your vortex of energy. You dance with the attacker, completely wrapping him and controlling him, and maybe in that way his anger will transform.

'You must begin to make feeling the change of force your habit. Look, see that tree blowing in the wind? We cannot see the wind but we can see the result of its force in the motion of the branches and leaves. You can see this in everything! In fighting there are basically three types of force which you need to feel – the point [which is like a punch], the line [which is like a chopping action] and the circle [which is like a body throw]. These three kinds of moving force must be understood. If you can keep to the changeless state then you can really understand the changes of force. But only change when you need to change!'

In the evenings He Jinghan taught our wives and myself a very old Qigong set from the Yang Shr Taijquan system. It was to be done as if swimming gently in water, and for myself produced a feeling of soft energy circulating smoothly through the body, very satisfying on the joints and spine. He said that traditionally in the style it had been an important teaching until modern times had moved the focus more towards just the Long Form, and that the real secret of Yang style was in the Jibengong or foundation exercises. The first of these was very demanding, involving squatting very low and then back up on one leg with certain motions of the hands. When he taught me the Yang style Long Form in its basic version there was a tremendous amount of detail regarding the directions of force in each posture and the purpose or principles inherent in the motion. He said that this form trained postures and breathing which were short-short-short and then long, making it a 'good form'. Whereas Bagua was a very sharp twist with direction, Taijiquan was a constantly expanding ball. And where Bagua forms each had a clear and specific purpose, the Taijiquan Long Form could be done in many ways and with many goals in mind.

My wife, a very calm but spirited person, had practised Bagua with me for a while, and was happy when He Jinghan gave her some teachings. He told her that in the old days women would have special skills, such as the use of the hairpin to attack vital points and the wearing of steel-tipped shoes hidden beneath long dresses. He also taught her a punching drill and said that she was to attack me at random moments in the house to see if I was alert, which later was to give her endless satisfaction and amusement! She particularly enjoyed the Qigong set and later, when other Thai women joined my classes, I noticed that they too had a great affinity for soft, circular motions and could do them much better than the average man. He Jinghan was pleased that at last I had found a happy relationship, and gave me some good advice based upon his three decades of marriage.

'Marriage is a real test of reality and peace. Our first ten years we were often arguing, very difficult. The next ten years we started to understand each other's way, and the last ten years have been very smooth and peaceful. I discovered through Baguaquan that marriage has the same principle as fighting – we must lead our wives, not teach them, in the same way we join the attacker to change his direction. Women don't want to be told what to do, but they will respect the husband's way and slowly change to follow it. The problem is always this – if your essence changes can your partner accept?'

Certainly He Jinghan and his wife were one of the very few couples I knew with genuine harmony between them, and their humorous exchanges made them a joy to be around.

One day we took a long drive into the mountains and the conversation somehow got onto the topic of death and dying. 'For skilled martial artists dying can be very difficult,' He Jinghan commented. 'They feel very strong but at death they cannot abandon the body, they will struggle. They have put so much energy into their Jing Lo, their tendons are so strong but they cannot move to the next level. At some point you must abandon your strength and power and empty out, and in this way you can transform. I now work on this, letting energy go from the Jing Lo to the Qimai. I train myself to be ready to die at any moment, with no regrets.'

To die at any moment with no regrets…it is certainly one of the greatest abilities a person could have, and one that must surely come only after a tremendous amount of inner work over a long period of time.

On the last day of his holiday He Jinghan showed me the special skill known in some Yin Fu styles as 'Buddha's Warrior Attendant Rolls the Ball'. His hands moved as if playing with a large ball in front of his body, rolling it in every possible dimension and with his body undulating. What was remarkable was the way sharp power suddenly 'popped' from palms, wrists and elbows as he did the motion, really one of the most refined demonstrations of short power with continuous flowing movement I have seen. I could clearly see force from the lower Dantien being led up and out of the arms in a very unique way. I shook my head and told him that I simply could not work out how he was able to do it.

'It is a long story!' He Jinghan laughed. 'My teacher said that Gong Bao Tien was very skilled at this.'

He then told me many details for my practice and taught me a breathing exercise which he said would help me to understand the 'real Dantien'. 'The way most people understand Dantien is wrong, and that kind of fake Dantien can actually harm them. The real one comes as a result of the practice, not something forced. Feel my body…' I put my hands on his lower abdomen. Although the outside seemed to move very little it was as if there was a baby or some creature inside twisting and spiralling around, a feeling of great inner force. He then led the force so I felt how it could travel up the spine and torso and into the arms, changing the volume of power as he moved through various postures. This was the coiling dragon body, and it really was as if a living dragon was moving him! Suddenly the rolling the ball exercise made more sense and there was a glimmer of insight into how it had been accomplished.

We then went into the garden to the tree which we had been using as a training partner that week. He Jinghan had taught me how to work with it to train Bagua's unique fighting techniques. Trees are a potent symbol in Bagua – Dong Hai Chuan's training had begun with him walking around a seedling which became a big tree, and the system is often compared to a tree whose roots are the foundation exercises and whose branches and fruits are the forms and techniques. This week's training with the tree had taught me a lot about how to use an enemy's stronger force to move my body into a good position for efficient counter-attack. On this last day He Jinghan added a few more ideas and then told me the following.

'Remember that these are all tools for you to understand yourself better. After we learn forms and techniques we have to forget everything, just be natural and free. However, the freedom of Baguaquan is nurtured within the limits of Baguaquan. Do you understand?'

I replied that I would work towards understanding what he had given me. It was so much to digest, almost as if a year's worth of teaching had been transmitted in a week, and that is how it is with a real master. Whatever level of insight you have reached, however skilled your body has become, with a few words or gestures the master will take you to a whole new perspective, and make you feel as if you are once again a beginning student on his first day of practice.

It was time to sleep. He Jinghan and his wife would fly out in the morning. I entered the living room to say goodnight and saw him sitting there staring at an old photo of his teacher Gong Bao Tien doing one of the Mother Palm postures. I waited for a couple more minutes and then bade him goodnight before retiring.

The next morning I said to him, 'You must have seen that photo hundreds of times before, and yet you were staring at it for ages. I felt very touched, but also very curious at what you see when you look like that?'

'What do I see?' He Jinghan looked at me and smiled in his typical frank and open manner. 'I see how very far my skill is from the old ones.'

On Gong Bao Tien

Gong Bao Tien (1870–1943) was one of the top students of Yin Fu, and by many accounts had the highest level of Qing Gong skill of all of his generation of Baguaquan experts. His trademark skill was an extremely sudden and sharp power used when quickly turning away from an enemy, combined with swift footwork which enabled him to fight multiple attackers with ease. Once in Shangdong Province he was challenged to a combat by some local martial arts teachers. The location was to be a temple, and when Gong turned up there were twenty expert fighters waiting for him. There is no account of what happened but all of the teachers were found dead with no external wound marks on them. One of Gong's special skills was his finger strikes which could attack with lethal effect, and another was his Red Sand Palm – several times when he hit people it left the print of his palm on their body. Once, to dissuade some bandits from attacking his village, he struck a coin so hard with his palm that it lodged into a wooden post.

Gong Bao Tien had superlative ability with the staff. He could place it vertically and stand atop it, and then invert himself and slide to the ground!

One story clearly illustrates Gong's use of Fajin. Addicted to opium since his time in the Imperial Palace, in his later years he accepted teaching positions from wealthy patrons who were able to fund his habit. One such man was Wang Zhuang Fei, the famous 'Wushu King of Shanghai', already very skilled in several fighting systems. Gong taught Wang mainly fighting techniques, but not the Jibengong, as that was what he wanted to learn. After a year or so of this tuition, however, Wang decided to test his teacher and launched a sudden attack with a punching technique. Instantly Gong hit Wang's arm with his cutting palm, breaking the bone. Another year of tuition passed by and once again Wang tested the Bagua master, this time by attacking with a fast kick. But the result was the same, only now Wang had his leg broken by a single strike from the thin-looking old Bagua expert.

Master He Jinghan and Pendekar Steve Benitez sharing the arts

Master He Jinghan of Taiwan relates a story about Gong's famous fight with a renowned Tang Lang Quan (Praying Mantis Boxing) expert in Shangdong Province. The Mantis boxer had challenged the Bagua man to a fight at midday and waited in the main street of a town. A large crowd had gathered and the Mantis man called out for his opponent to step forward. Suddenly Gong leaped from the crowd and – calling 'Here comes Gong!' – flew at the man with a punch, which the Mantis boxer hooked and pulled using Tang Lang Quan's trademark hooking claw. Following the force Gong span around and sent an elbow strike which was blocked by the Mantis master. Continuing in an unbroken flowing motion – and calling out 'Here goes Gong!' – Gong Bao Tien leaped back into the crowd and was gone. It all happened in a flash and no one was sure who had won the bout. But the next day the Mantis master left Shangdong, the traditional way of conceding defeat. He showed his students the holes left in his jacket over vital areas. Gong had shown compassion by merely tearing the fabric rather than using lethal force.

Li Shi Fu and Lindsey Wei

The Daoist Arts of
Wudang Mountain

Li Shi Fu teaches his disciple Lindsey Wei on Wudangshan

In China the two most famous birthplaces of martial arts are the Daoist site of Wudangshan (Wudang Mountain) and the Buddhist Monastery of Shaolin-Ssu. Both have a long history as places of inner cultivation stretching back hundreds or even thousands of years. Towards the beginning of the Japanese invasion in the early twentieth century Wudangshan was closed down, and all the temples were used as staging posts for the military or were destroyed by the Japanese. All the monks and books disappeared. In the early 1980s the government slowly allowed them back. During these dark periods there were individuals living secretly in some of the sites by themselves, at a time when it was illegal to be a monk, some of them wandering to other sacred mountains and gathering what knowledge they could. Lay people would sweep the altar, no matter the risk which such actions involved. Many of the deities were destroyed but others survived, including the giant turtles in Yushugong, which were saved somewhat miraculously by being underwater due to a flood.

The Daoist priest Guo Gao Yi was appointed head of martial arts when the monks came back, his students studying with him for five years before being sent to teachers in other parts of China whose systems were directly connected to Wudangshan. When he died in his nineties the people said that he had been there since the early part of the century, so obviously, despite all the suppression, cultivation had continued on the mountain. Long Hu Shan, Dragon Tiger Mountain, home of Zhang I Pai,[1] is not far from Wudang. Five Dragon Temple (Wu Long Gong) is perhaps the oldest temple there, several hours' walk from the central peak; from there it is clear to see how the central peak is surrounded by the other peaks which lean towards it. Legend has it that an ancient Chinese emperor visited Five Dragon Temple, and there were five wells said to contain five dragons which, according to local people, could bring the rain. As it was a time of drought the emperor requested them to call the dragons, which they did, and rain indeed fell. From then on much money and support was sent to the temple, and Wudang began to flourish and grow. Whereas Dishaogong is the centre of administration and tourism in Wudang, temples such as Wu Long Gong are the places where real inner work is done.

In the late 1990s I visited Wudangshan and met some of the monks, both young and old, who were enjoying the new-found atmosphere of religious tolerance in China to once again be able to practise openly.

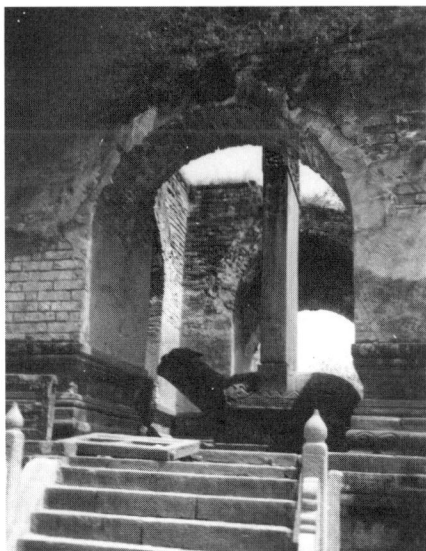

Ancient statue of sacred turtle at Wudangshan

This was a few years before the building of a huge commercial martial arts school and the commercialisation of the mountain, which began drawing in large numbers of foreign students who would come to learn dozens of different 'traditional' forms from a new wave of priestly robed 'Daoist masters'. When I was there it was still a calm, unspoiled place where one could meet real cultivators and learn interesting things. With the coming of foreign money many of these folk simply left the area, moving deeper into the mountains or going to other sacred sites.

Some years later I was back in England when I received a letter from a young man who said that my written accounts of training in Wudangshan had inspired him to travel there and find a teacher. It seemed he had had quite an adventure over the past few years. A very sincere and softly spoken man his mid-twenties, Jon came to visit me a short time later, and as soon as I met him I knew he had been with a real teacher. I felt a strong link both with him and with the lineage he was involved in. He began telling me about his training with a certain Li Shi Fu, a Daoist monk who lived in an obscure temple on Wudangshan, and what he said had the ring of authenticity. The stories about Li Shi Fu were marvellous. He was apparently a very traditional teacher who naturally drew respect from everyone who met him due to his presence, and his martial arts and healing skills were superlative.

Through Jon's introduction I became friends with a Chinese-American woman named Lindsey Wei, another disciple of Li Shi Fu who has spent several years in China cultivating the Dao. She had begun her training on Wudangshan at the commercial martial arts school and later, feeling there was more depth to be found in the practice than was available there, she was fortuitously introduced to her teacher by Jon. What follows in this chapter is a recent conversation with Lindsey in which she describes some of her experiences with her special Daoist teacher.

Interview with Lindsey Wei

'Lindsey, how did you come to study Daoist practices at Wudangshan?'

'When I was fifteen I went on a school trip to China with my language class. I had never practised martial arts before. Daoism and Buddhism were just names of religions I'd heard of. My Chinese heritage had not yet been awoken and I was quite an American girl at the time, rebellious and disrespectful, in ignorance of the humility and servitude that I would be taught in the years to come. However, my whole life I had felt deep chasms and divides in my personality and relations in America. I would later understand that this paradox inside me was rooted in my mixed blood and a torrential affinity with the Dao.

'After high school I spent my first year in China at a Sports University in Beijing studying Chinese Language and Modern Wushu. I recognised that I could learn the language with great ease, which I attribute to my genes. A new voice came out of me, a new person really, another side that had not yet had place or culture to come forth. I found that I felt a kinship with the Chinese around me and they showed me the same affection and acceptance that they show to those they consider Chinese. I recognised that aspects of my nature that had always conflicted with American culture made perfect sense in the culture of China.

'My second year was spent in Wudang, which I had heard about through the circle of foreigners studying martial arts. As soon as the taxi began its ascent up the mountain, I felt like I had come home. Though I had never set foot here in this lifetime, I felt the entity held in the mountain had been my home before, and I was returning.

'After three years in China I finally found my true teacher, whose birth name is Du Song Feng. His Daoist name is Li Feng and his generation name Xin De. Li Shi Fu quickly became like a father to me, as well as the single most important person in my life and a mentor who has dramatically shaped who I am. Though I recognise that he is still only human, my trust and belief in him is profound. This trust and unconditional faith must be present between master and disciple of spiritual teachings, for the master is leading you down an invisible path which you have never walked before. He will tell you where the cliff hangs over an abyss, what you must ignore, and what you must grasp.'

Li Shi Fu holds Horse Tail Whip in front of Five Immortal Hall

'Can you explain about Li Shi Fu's background?'

'Li Shi Fu's family lived in an ancient ruined temple. Three days before he was born, there many crows came to live in the trees around their home. They stayed until he came of age. Many people thought it was surely a bad omen. However, in Wudang, the crow is the spirit of the mountain. One day in the market, when Li was seven, he met a wandering Daoist on the street. The Daoist looked at him, felt his bones, and told him that he had destiny with the Dao. The young boy thought nothing of it at the time… Li Shi Fu grew up in a generation that can hardly be compared to my own. Since he was thirteen he has been training day in and day out in a variety of fighting skills, boxing, as well as meditation, all in the traditional manner of extreme discipline, dull repetition and bitter lengths. The most interesting, or perhaps rare, of these practices and according to him the bitterest of them all, was what is commonly known as "Qing Gong" or light Gongfu. He says that even by the time he encountered it, the style was already falling into extinction. No parent was willing to subject their son or daughter to such hardship. Traditionally the practice of Qing Gong must begin before the age of nine, while one is still in the pure Yang or pre-pubescent phase of life, or at the very least before the bones have fully grown.

Li Shi Fu poses with Seven Star sword

'Li Shi Fu was already seventeen by the time he met a master who knew the method. His master said that it was too late for him and to learn it would be of no use. However, Li Shi Fu was determined to try. They would wake at midnight to practise so that no one would see them. What exactly they did has never been disclosed to me, but at that time, if one practised the authentic method he could jump ten metres (33 feet) straight upwards, run onto the back of a moving car at forty mph (64 km/h), and jump as far as eight leaps in mid-air. These statistics far surpass anything that Olympic athletes can do today.

'I, myself, though I have spent three years on a mountain training mostly alone every day, am completely laughable in the face of everything I imagine he has endured. An example comes to mind. The Pure Yang Sect of Wudang has a type of hard Qigong known as "Da Gong". Through the use of a breathing method, the skin, muscles, fascia and organs can be strengthened to withstand hard blows to the abdomen and other vital target points. Every day we would do many repetitions of the movements, which include being punched, slapped, ramming yourself into trees and hurling your body onto the ground. As a woman I had a lot of trouble with this practice in particular. I would cry when my master whipped me on the bare skin with the bundle of bamboo sticks. It was like a knee jerk reaction, not necessarily due to the pain. For me it was emotional, as illogical as that seems. To be hit as a woman I think must be worlds apart from what it is to be hit as a man.

'One day, my master proceeded to punch me in the gut for two hours until I was black and blue. All kinds of thoughts passed through my head, anger towards him, fear that I would be internally damaged, doubt, mistrust, frustration, sadness. Then I reached a point where none of those emotional reactions were streaming through me any longer and there was a kind of bliss and surrender…a trust in him knowing how far to push me. And finally, oddly enough, after being beaten for two hours, I was left with only a profound admiration for the experience I'd just been put through, the lesson he had given me on physical and emotional pain. He said, "Do not be afraid to eat bitter."'

Lindsey Wei

'Having heard many stories about Li Shi Fu's healing abilities, I am curious as to what powerful healings you may have seen him do…?'

'Coincidentally, the most miraculous healing I have witnessed Li Shi Fu perform was on the first night I ever met him. A woman he had known from his hometown, named Xue Mei, had fallen ill with cancer. Daoists read a lifeline from all aspects of a person's image, including their palms, face and name. A woman with the name of Xue Mei, or "Plum Blossom", a flower which blooms in winter, is destined to develop in conditions of hardship, though there is beauty expressed in her endurance.

'By this time Li Shi Fu had already been a renunciate at the Five Immortal Temple in Wudang's White Horse Mountain for ten years. He rarely heals people, even those who seek him out, due to the strict precepts he has sworn to. At most he tells them he is just a poor old Daoist who knows some herbs, picking one at random and telling them to go home and drink it as tea. He says it is as simple as that when one empowers from the spirit.

'He ran into Xue Mei by chance on a trip to the south to settle an issue with his passport and for one reason or another was moved to help her. The hospitals all said that there was nothing more they could do for her, that she had forty-five days left to live and she'd be better off spending it at home with her family. Tumours had spread throughout her entire body. She had two in the liver the size of a grape and one in the pelvis the size of a small yam, nearly ten centimetres (4 inches). She could not sleep at night for more than a few hours due to her pain, and could not walk more than twenty metres (22 yards) without rest.

'Li Shi Fu says, "It cannot be said that all illnesses can be healed. Though likewise there is no disease so severe that it may not be healed. As long as the patient is alive, there is a way."

'It is not the body which is hard to heal; it is a person's thoughts and the things they have done. The precepts which Li Shi Fu has sworn to follow are his promise to the power of his lineage, both his physical teachers and the eternal ones, for without their allowance, the gates of miraculous healing cannot be opened. First the patient or, if they are unconscious, a representative, be it friend or family, must be in a state of begging. Only in this state of plea are they receptive enough to the healer's magnetic field and willing to change who they have been.

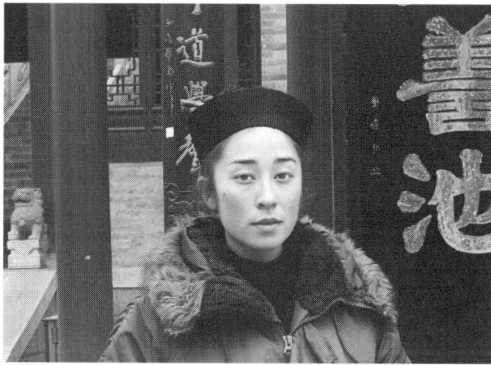

Lindsey Wei, practitioner on Wudangshan

'Second, therefore, the patient must be resigned to use their new-found health or even new chance at life to pursue good deeds rather than crime. And, last, the healer must feel a divine affinity with the patient, or be driven to heal them by a higher beckoning. These precepts are what the Daoist healers call "the promise".

'He told Xue Mei that if she was willing she could come back to the temple with him. She and her husband boarded the train with him that same day and began their journey and last hope for her life. Li Shi Fu performed a small healing on the train and she fell asleep for thirteen hours. She awoke renewed, unlike anything she had felt for months. Previously not being able to walk even twenty metres [22 yards] without rest, she proceeded to walk up the mountain in under two hours [the average person walking it in one hour].

'For the first week, Li Shi Fu arranged all of her daily activities. Despite her bald head and the shadow under her eyes, she appeared to me to be a woman in average health. She swept the temple floor and lit incense twice a day. He had taken her out of her previous environment, changed her diet and changed her way of thinking. On the seventh day he performed her healing.

'We were all sitting in the small dimly lit TV room when he suddenly rose and told her to lie down on the couch. He put an old CD into a portable disc-player that was connected to the TV speakers and a very strange and ethereal music began to play. It is known as healing music and it was being played by one of Li Shi Fu's Masters. I was sort of dumbstruck, having just arrived myself at this temple. He stood above her, with his back to me, and raised his hand in a symbol. I could hear him murmuring words under his breath. Then, as if something had just entered his hand, he moved it with a quickness over her body, writing symbols in the space above her. Then, with a sweeping motion of his palm from her head to toe, it was over. He told her to stay in the room, rest and listen to the music. We were all dismissed and went to bed.

'A few days later he told her to go down into town and get a CAT scan to see how her health was progressing. She came back with the X-rays proving the tumours in her liver to be gone and the one in her pelvis to have decreased by half in size.'

'That is an incredible healing. What about Daoist Alchemy, can you explain what this involves? How does Li Shi Fu teach this?'

'I asked Li Shi Fu what happened to him when he retreated to the cave and almost died. He said he could not tell me because he could only speak to me of the things I am ready to hear.

'Daoist Alchemy is much different than "Dao Yin", or what is often called Daoist Yoga. That is to say there is a vast divide between alchemy and common energy work or even most meditation, and most people never cross it. It is a life work and it is virtually impossible, impossible not just to the many practitioners and adepts but also to the great sages who have come before us, whom we fall infinitely short of. Li Shi Fu says, "Alchemy is to capture life." It is to create another body. He tells me not to pursue it, that I am still in the realm of desire, that I still have a life to live, children to birth. To open too deep a knowledge now, would only make it hard for me to live a normal life, that a lot of trouble would begin to find me out. "If you truly want to know where do we come from and where do we go…then sit and be silent. But if there are still things you want…children, husband, family, love, happiness, even life itself – then don't do it. Because everything you want, they will give it to you, and you will follow them away from your goal."

Li Shi Fu balances above the Wudang Mountains on the Turtle Rock next to the Snake Tree, depicting the sacred symbol of Xuan Wu (The Mystery)

Li Shi Fu in High Ceremony Robes (Gao Gong Fa Shi)

Li Shi Fu and his horse White Dragon in front of Five Immortal Temple on White Horse Mountain

'"Who?" I asked him.

'"The Gate Keepers," he replied.

'My experiences in meditation can only be called preliminary sensations at best, in light of what is possible. If we are seeking the deeper aspects of the spirit we should really stop and ask ourselves how much time we have devoted to it. Because unless it is at least three hours a day for one year without skipping a single day, then it is relative to say that we have not experienced even a percentage of what lies beyond our daily awareness. Throughout all of my practice it was when I sat for one hour every night for one hundred days straight that I truly built something. There were many sensations, and the realisations that come along with them, which seemed profound to me at the time. Sensations such as an inner glow, or light radiating out of my fingertips, the purple universe between the eyebrows... However, when I reported them to my master, he simply told me to ignore them, lest I gain another desire in this world, to use this power that I'd found. "Pay no attention to those feelings. Don't be so curious, just continue, undistracted, else you will become stuck there, intrigued by those flashing lights."

Lindsey Wei practises the stillness in motion of Taijiquan

'So as you can see, the way of the alchemist is very strict. They say that the physical method of transformation is very straightforward, however, it is our thoughts and our nature that take a lifetime of toil to prepare.'

'Is there a difference between Daoist cultivation methods for women and for men?'

'From a very high perspective there is really no difference between them. From the perspective of the average person, however, who defines themselves by their identity and sexuality in all aspects of their being, the two paths could seem to be very different indeed. That is why it is sometimes said that a woman must first become a man before she can enter the gates of Heaven. She must reverse the wheel of reproduction and return to her childlike state, no breasts, no menstruation. It is the same for men, their testicles shrink back into their body and they cease to emit semen. However, we certainly do not say that a man must become a woman before he can become a luminous body. It is better rather to say that both a woman must first forget that she is a woman, and a man forget that he is a man, before one may become a luminous body, which is no longer in the realm of division between male and female.

Lindsey Wei practises Taijiquan on Wudangshan

'The Daoists say that men are Yang on the outside and Yin inside. Women are Yin without and Yang within. What does this mean? Women are more readily peaceful due to this inner Yang or "light" principle. In fact it is said by Daoists that alchemical cultivation takes one third the amount of time for a woman as it does for a man due to this. Men are easily angered and quick to act, like fire; whereas the woman is contemplative and soft. Men are firm in body, whereas women are yielding, like water. And, like water, she is easily lured this way and that. This is perhaps where the feminine Yin principle can be associated with a negative aspect of darkness. She is seduced. So both men and woman equally have their challenges along the path of alchemical cultivation. Albeit that the end goal is to become a pure Yang body, it is a modern misnomer – or perhaps ancient cryptic saying – to say that a woman must therefore "become a man".

'What would it feel like to disassociate with our sexuality? What kind of thought-level, let alone physical transformation, would it take to truly be neither man nor woman? These questions are very simple, when looked at in purity and at the same time extremely complex when we take into context culture, history and human nature. So until we find ourselves on that higher vantage point, we must continue to take into consideration the natural differences between male and female cultivation.'

Lindsey Wei performing at Daoist summit with talisman flags hanging in background

Note

1. Long Men Pai (dragon gate sect) has always been the majority sect in China.

Lu Yaoqin
and Rudy Ibarra

The Legacy of Grandmaster Wan Lai Sheng

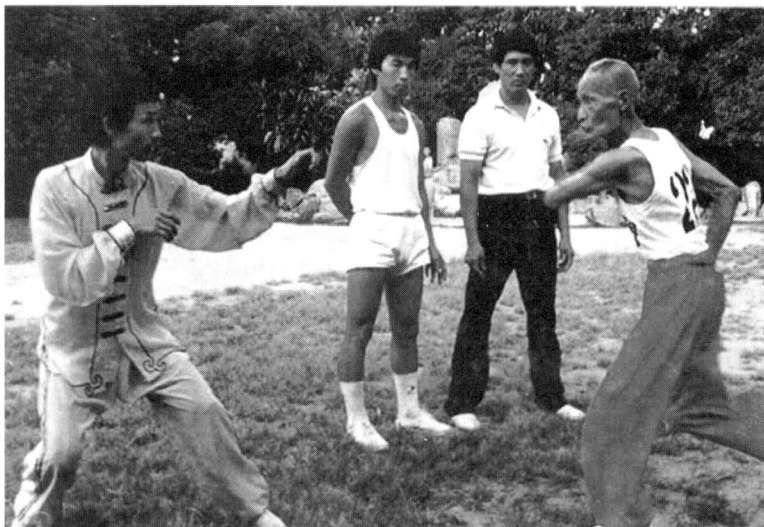

A young Lu Yaoqin learning from Grandmaster Wan Lai Sheng

The great Ziranmen Master Wan Lai Sheng left a legacy of expert students when he passed away, many of whom have begun teaching outside China or to visiting foreign students. The once extremely rare system has opened up somewhat, although there are still only a handful of non-Chinese who have trained seriously over any period of time. One such practitioner is the American-born Rudy Ibarra who eventually found his teacher in the Ziranmen Master Lu Yaoqin. In this revealing discussion Rudy talks about his training and development under one of Wan Lai Sheng's close disciples and gives his own perspective on the technical aspects of the Daoist martial arts.

'Rudy, can you give a resume of why you first started martial arts, what motivated you?'

'Since about age eight, I had been fascinated with the Hong Kong movies playing on the "Sunday Kung Fu Matinee", but what really did it was the television series *Kung Fu*. Not only was the protagonist able to defend himself at incredible odds, but he and his master said profound things that really struck a chord in me; of course, later I learned it was all from Buddhist, Daoist and Asian philosophy. Another chord that was literally struck happened when my parents made the decision to move from a tranquil rural community to the inner city at the beginning of my junior high years to find work. Within my own country this was a culture shock. I saw older kids being held back three years, I saw bullies, I saw gangs and I saw fights. This made a deep and a few times even painful impression on me. Having only two older sisters, a pacifist father who had never allowed me to play with even toy guns and the fact that this would be the fifth place I would live in, I had never learned to fight. So now the practical reason for learning martial arts was driven home and I decided at that time that I definitely had to learn martial arts not only for its artistry and philosophy, but more importantly to learn how to fight and defend myself. I had begged my parents yearly but because of the cost and the violence concern, they had constantly refused. Eventually, at age sixteen, I was able both to get a higher paying summer job and find a school that was actually walking distance from my home.'

'So has the reason changed after these years of training?'

'Something interesting happened when I began training: after having spent most of my young life as a "visual artist" who hated sports, I discovered my body. I found it immensely cathartic and freeing at the same time so I trained every day! Another benefit was that I started meeting people with whom I had common interests and through them I heard of remarkable people, which led me to travel to incredible places. I then became interested in martial art roots and history, which led to an interest in general Asian history, which led to Asian philosophy and religion, which led to Chinese literature study, which then led to language study so I could talk to masters without translators, which in turn led to more martial arts! Eventually what made me continue was not only the practical idea of improving my fighting skills or the romantic idea of following traditions and going through training and motions that someone did five hundred years ago, but what I got from it in terms of mind, body and spirit. Of course the deeper one goes the more one finds, so personally this makes my entire Chinese martial art experience much more culturally enriching for me.'

'What was special about your first meeting with Master Lu that made you want to become his student?'

'Master Lu Yaoqin lives in the Fuzhou City Hutongs [an ancient type of housing]. I was led to his office where he sat surrounded by weapons and photos of his school and his teacher, the famous Wan Lai Sheng. He was slim, five feet seven inches [1.7 m] tall, wore dress shoes, slacks and the typical Chinese Lacoste short-sleeve collar shirt. He looked almost fifty. No bulging muscles, calloused knuckles, swollen hands, furrowed brow or any other sign he was a martial artist. He did not stand and he remained very serious during our interview. I asked general questions about his school and his teacher and he asked about my training. Then came the moment I knew would come, when he asked me to demonstrate. I tried to politely decline but he insisted. So I got up and began the first Ziranmen form of Ying Yong Quan. After my demonstration there was a moment of silence, then he spoke and said it resembled his Ziranmen...a tiny bit. He said mine looked more like a version of a hard Long Fist style. He then stood up and said he would execute the same form slowly, so I could see the differences more clearly. My companion and I stood shocked. The biggest difference was that he shrank so small and then expanded so large. It wasn't just using the "Yao" [lower back connected with waist] but using all from the ground to knees to waist to lower back to upper back to shoulders! There were truly no arms in his movements; it all came from his hips and spine! He brought to life every single thing I had ever read or heard about Ziranmen and Wan Lai Sheng! He explained a few of the other differences in his art as we continued listening in shock.

'As I had planned from the beginning of this trip to the south, I asked about the possibility of coming from Beijing to train with him, even while knowing that new students usually required a formal introduction as opposed to the quick phone introduction from the Fujian Martial Art Federation. After he thought a bit, he explained that because I had been studying a version of his art for so many years, had come from the other side of the world and was learning his nation's language, he would agree to teach me, if I returned. In case I decided not to return, he invited me to write or call with any questions concerning Ziranmen. In this he was very different from the other teachers I had met and demonstrated for around China. He did not try to convince me of how great he was or talk of lineage holding and he didn't go on about how incorrect I was or how very necessary it was for me to study with him! As we were preparing to thank him and leave (while I was still in shock), my companion asked politely if he would mind giving me an introductory class. He agreed and we set the time for that night at 8pm.

'The first thing he asked was if I presently trained Nei Quan Shou. To his surprise I didn't know what that was. He explained it was the first and most important Neigong practice in Ziranmen, to cultivate Qi, work on Yi, improve blood circulation, create the feeling of whole body unity, make one's eyes clear and sharp and basically what made our initial "external" looking forms, internal. It was basically our Zhan Zhuang or pile stance Qigong. The difference is our pile stance is not a stance, it is slow motion stepping where every joint is rotating, turning or bending slightly, with the arms moving in circles, while you also simultaneously step in a circle. At first glance people confuse it with Baguazhang for its circular stepping or Taiji for its slow speed. Like those two arts, Ziranmen is also linked in Daoist traditions. Many people have heard about the circular stepping meditations of the Daoist monks that Bagua incorporated within its practice. Ziranmen also has its version.

'The second thing Shifu Lu taught was an external to internal "Shen Fa" [body method, biomechanics] exercise that worked the inter-co-ordination of the entire body, rooting and structure, awareness of the centre, expansion–contraction of body, substantiality and insubstantiality and Yi [intention].

'The third thing he taught was how to punch with the entire body for explosiveness and snap. This was one of the direct applications of the previous exercise. The entire body moves in circles that start big and get smaller. This was the first time I had seen a traditional Chinese art use this type of punch. From a distance it almost resembles a boxer's punch, but far from it. It uses the entire torso in both horizontal and vertical movement. Another difference was that when Ziranmen boxers punch they also always cover with the other arm and this cover easily becomes another punch, deflection or other appropriate move. So, as far as the rumours that Ziranmen has only Neigong and Ji Ji Fa [combat methods] go, this is somewhat true at the beginning and advanced levels of training. In other words elder Gongfu brothers worked forms as much as combat and Neigong at the intermediate level, whereas my teacher at his advanced level and I at a beginner level concentrated more on Neigong and basic combat-related drills. After class I was soaked in sweat and had an extremely comfortable and energised feeling all over my body. Before he left he told me that if I was still in Fuzhou the next night, I was welcome to come by again. Of course the next night I was still in Fuzhou.

'The second night he checked and corrected the previous night's lesson. His correction method was impeccable. He was very patient and if I didn't understand something he was able to break it down until I was able to understand. When that was over, he asked what form I liked and wanted to work. Thinking myself too advanced for the first form, I asked for the second form. So then he had me re-start what I had previously learned and in every move he added much more bodywork (expansion and contraction of the torso) and waist work (horizontal rotation) to maximise power. Every movement became full, meaning intention in everything, especially transitions, what happened in between moves, which were very important in Ziranmen. After the first six moves I was mentally and physically exhausted, meaning my mind could not absorb everything and my body could not endure the pain of the postures. I stopped the class, apologised for my ignorance and overeagerness and asked him to start at the very beginning with the first form. He smiled for the first time and re-taught me the entire first form, which only has twelve techniques. Once again I was in total awe! I had heard "More Body!" and other martial poems on how one should move while practising Chinese martial arts many times before, but Shifu Lu not only spoke of it and demonstrated it, he also taught exactly *how* to move in this way. He explained teaching this was especially important in the beginning stage so one would understand not only how but also why and the method to instil and allow it to become natural. This led to him explaining the concept of "Bu Ziran Dao Ziranmen", from the unnatural and un-spontaneous to the natural and spontaneous. After my second class, as a parting gift, he gave me a copy of the very rare 1928 reprint of Wan Lai Sheng's book, *Wu Shu Hui Zhong* (*The Common Basis of Martial Arts*) which was a treasure I had been seeking for years, out of print since the 1980s. He then wished me well and once again reminded me whether I returned or not, not to hesitate to call or write with any questions.'

'Can you describe your teacher's special skills, and tell some story of your time with him?'

Master Lu Yaoqin with Sword Posture

Master Lu Yaoqin teaches Rudy Ibarra (left) and his senior

'Training with Master Lu Yaoqin is always intense. He lectures, he explains, he corrects, he leaves no stone unturned. If something is difficult to grasp he breaks it down. If still not understood he will break it down even further. Nothing is just "Higher! Faster! or More Body!" He teaches exactly how and why you are doing something. As he says, Gongfu has to train your entire body and mind, otherwise you're not doing anything except moving your limbs around. Once, as he was demonstrating a movement from a two-man form, one of my Gongfu brothers asked if it was similar to a certain fighting drill we had been practising the night before and Master Lu paused. Other students who were working on different things came over as he began to give a lecture about form and combat being complementary and how the forms, two-man forms, weapon and combat training are and must be connected and similar. Even our Neigong has similarities to everything else we do. Master Lu explained that because Ziranmen was not an empty art for beauty's sake, what we were working on was an internal to external connection and natural feeling that eventually becomes completely spontaneous. So the answer to the student was... Yes, the two-man form is and had better be similar to the hand drill, not only in theory but in practice, otherwise we were wasting our time. Everything in the art is connected. He had heard of certain new styles in the West that had discarded forms in their training and he explained that the way certain styles practise their forms, they may as well discard them, because they were really getting nothing out of them. Robotic heavy vulgar moves or empty flowery moves were really not going to train one for internal health, strength and conditioning of body or combat. He reminded us that forms traditionally were much more than just a glossary of offensive and defensive fighting techniques. Contained within are also methods of strengthening, balancing, co-ordinating, internal exercises, strategies, principles and training one's force.

'On one night instructing us in combat and observing us sparring back and forth, Master Lu stopped us and began to give a lecture on the Ziranmen theory of being "no beginning or end of movement, no beginning or end of stillness and no beginning or end of changes". To demonstrate he, for the first time, started sparring with one of the taller disciples. I had seen him demonstrate beautiful forms, single applications (where I felt the pain!) and even linked combat techniques during instruction, but never had I seen him just go at it with someone else. Once again, this somewhat slim, fifty-four-year-old, average-looking man's eyes flashed with spirit and intensity and he began to shrink, expand, sink and at the same time move as if he was floating around so nimbly! Master Lu totally co-ordinated with the disciple, constantly changing hand formations, body distance and height, not only to match the disciple's attacks but also his pre-attack or post-attack. The disciple tried to attack but before he could launch anything or as he recovered after trying something,

Master Lu was there right on him! It was spectacular! A moment later he suddenly stopped and we were all spellbound. Master Lu continued the lecture, explaining he had demonstrated to show how the hands changed, footwork changed, distance changed, body height changed but his Yi [intention] stayed constant. He kept co-ordination with the opponent and never allowed him an opening. Once again he brought to life everything I had ever read or heard about Ziranmen and Wan Lai Sheng.'

'Do you think the old relationship of master–disciple has a place in the modern world, what does it mean to you, and being a teacher what do you try to convey of the tradition?'

'I believe the relationship of master–disciple definitely has a place in the modern world. Next to parents it has always been the closest type of relationship in Asia and as traditional martial arts travelled abroad so did the relationship. It's through this relationship that our precious arts are transmitted and handed down. And similar to parents, there is care, trust and a general feeling of family – a feeling of belonging and/or being part of something. So, like nurturing parents, your master knows your strengths and weaknesses and strives to build you up, physically and mentally. On the flip side, like abusive parents, there are also abusive masters, those who, through secrecy and withholding, make sure their students never outgrow or surpass them in skill.

'Also like family, this is a reciprocal relationship. On the disciple side of the equation, like a son or daughter we help with money, time and other ways of assistance, especially as the master ages. But as disciples we also do more because through us, similar to parents, masters see a continuation of their school's legacy and name, and they understand they make a difference and a mark on the world. I've seen this relationship with many other friends and their masters in various styles, most of them never having gone or trained in China. How many people actually go back to see a coach or a teacher? I go see my master every year and in recent visits he has tried to refuse my tuition fee for instruction. However, in the big picture, I see it as he is helping my life and passion for martial arts by sharing his hard-earned lifelong art with me, so the least I can do is attempt to help his life any way I can.

'Some martial arts teachers turn their passion and art into a full time occupation, which, in turn, forces them to rely on their students in order to pay for rent, bills and, in general, make a living. However, all the money, gifts, begging and waiting out in the rain is not going to make a difference so long as one's master refuses to teach him the "good stuff" and the traditional master–disciple trusting relationship is simply not present.

Master Lu Yaoqin teaching his disciple Rudy Ibarra

'I try to convey this tradition, not in a cult-like elitist and exclusive manner, but rather in a form that instils an appreciation of the art. It is very important to me to make sure that students understand that this thing we train in every day for health, self-defence and artistic expression is handed down through a long line of people to get to the student. Therefore, the students know that they are a part of a rich history and tradition and that they are the inheritors of this tradition today.'

'Can you describe Ziranmen training methods you have undergone, and the challenges of these?'

'With Master Lu Yaoqin, we worked three things every day, Neigong, Taolu [form] and Ji Ji Fa [combat]. Never before had I seen these three elements complement and supplement each other so harmoniously. There is a direct relationship between the healthful, artistic and combative aspect that I had never felt before. Not only do the theories, principles and the way in which we train them link the three, but, as mentioned, they even physically appear similar!

'There are three "outer" requirements in Ziranmen training. The first is Ruan Gong, soft and flexible skill. To be very flexible with your entire body, particularly your legs, basically to be able to go into and out of whatever position is required at that time such as being able to put your legs anywhere on the opponent. Master Lu demonstrated this by executing a "heart centre" kick to a student standing less than an arm's distance away: his knee came up and the foot popped upwards an inch from the side of his jaw and then he snapped it back down as if nothing happened. Stretching every day and relaxation techniques works this aspect.

'The second is Ying Gong, hard skill. This is the necessary ability to strike the opponent so he really feels it while having the ability to take his strikes. This is slowly developed through two-man contact drills and Pai Da Gong, which are conditioning practices where one develops external force and special skills through the use of unique equipment such as sandbags, bamboo, iron balls, iron arm rings and a wooden post. These practices are designed to strengthen the ligaments and bones for striking and are done very softly and repetitively without the use of hard force.

'About Ruan and Ying Gong, Master Lu Yaoqin says in the old days everyone had a special skill that would take hours of every day training and years to develop. In these modern times, only a basic level is required so half an hour every day on each is enough. He also commented on how certain schools mistakenly take one or the other to extremes; for example, a certain teacher who refrains from exertion or teachers of styles that overcondition parts of the body to the point of deformity.

'The third outer requirement is Qing Gong, light and agile skill. It consists of practices to work lightness, agility, co-ordination and smoothness, which includes Ziranmen's very important body method and stepping method exercises. Qing Gong is also developed with the use of forms, fighting drills and sparring. Qing Gong is so when an opponent strikes not only are you not there but you have already naturally counter-attacked. As martial artists, this of the three outer skills we want an advanced level of. If half an hour a day of Ruan Gong and Ying Gong is sufficient, Qing Gong one should work every day for the longest time of at least two hours.

'As for the challenges, I think the first of the training method challenges would be physical pain. Pain one will get from initial Ziranmen training until whatever weakness is strengthened and developed, whether it's arms, upper body, waist or legwork. For example, after more than a decade studying martial arts I had my leg basics down from the deep stance work training most Chinese styles have, but I had never felt the soreness in the lats, the upper back and the shoulders that lasted for a few months. There were days when I couldn't pick up my chopsticks. For another student who hadn't done as much stance work, his primary issue was stance work and it was killing him. Sometimes the pain involved endurance; for example, doing whatever form three or four times in a row with no break on Master Lu's count was a daily routine.

'Another challenge would be patience. Patience to do the same form, weapon, two-man set, fighting drill or Pai Da Gong [conditioning] until you derived what you were supposed to derive from it. Master Lu always set a goal for you and was looking for specific results or an acquired level of understanding and naturalness when he taught and corrected. When it comes to correcting and taking one to the next level he is relentless and never gets tired of telling and showing you the same thing. And you do the same thing until you're almost sick of it. There were many times when I thought I would never move on from a form or drill and just when I was sick of doing it and even dreaming about it in my sleep, Master Lu would say, "At a basic level you have it, but you must continue training it." Then he would start teaching me the next thing. Unlike the compliments I received in Beijing, Master Lu rarely gives them.

'Next on the list would be correcting previously trained bad habits and being receptive to them. Entire sets, fighting techniques and even certain basics like Pu Bu, had to be forgotten and relearned. Many a night Master Lu would ask me to demonstrate something previously learned and afterwards tell me to forget it and we would start new. This happened in combat, forms and Neigong; for example, in Shen Fa, discovering, studying and instilling natural instinctive motion as part of my body method, getting rid of tension and self-resistance, and allowing it to become totally natural.

'Another challenge would be our very important Neigong work. Our basic and most important is Nei Quan Shou, Inner Circling Hand. First was the initial pain of the low posture with the relaxation of the upper body. Next came the repetition of the same step and circling hand motion. And last the complete focus of intention and mind that starts off with a couple of minutes and by adding another minute every few days ends up at the eventual goal of at least one hour. The amazing thing was Master Lu would always know when I hadn't practised Nei Quan Shou. He usually would start off, "Your body seems extra tight…" or "You look very heavy today…did you practise Nei Quan Shou this morning?" Every time he was right that I hadn't.

'Of course another difficulty was language. There are five tones in Mandarin Chinese (including the neutral tone)! If your tone is off you may be saying "light" instead of "stool" or "horse" instead of "mother". My Chinese had been sufficient for basic Gongfu instruction but in Ziranmen I had to learn a completely different language of movements and theories. So besides my morning class at the university, I was studying in the afternoons and hanging out on the weekends with my Chinese friends.'

'What has been the big change in your body and mind after all this?'

'Certain physical changes happened as I trained with Master Lu. First there was the feeling of "Chen", a rooting and sinking which created a strong structure to move from. The feeling was not only in low stances, but in high stances and during movement as well. This was a direct product of our Nei Quan Shou Neigong practice, correction of the joint positions called Nei Kou [closing of the joints] typical of internal arts, proper alignment of the spine and correct postures in forms and drills. Another was the feeling of the outer "Liu He" or Six Harmonies, which means shoulder goes with the hip, elbow goes with the knee and hand goes with the foot. This was basically co-ordination in the entire body. One has to unify every single part of the body, so when one part moves, every part moves and when one part stops every part stops.

'Then there was the "Shen Fa" or body method that changed. This one is almost one of Ziranmen's trademarks. Just about every Wan Lai Sheng disciple, no matter how different they look, has incredible movement in the spine. This was the understanding of Ziranmen's Tun [contracting], Tu [expanding], Fu [floating] and Chen [sinking], which trained the body to react naturally and correctly to offensive and defensive situations and work with ones body's natural instinctive movement. It is a type of "in and out", "now you see me, now you don't" body method which basically was the ability to reach your opponent while he cannot reach you.

'Another major change was the new-found Bu Fa or footwork. This was a very important aspect of Ziranmen. As far as I've seen, only Baguazhang gives as much attention to footwork, having as many drills and patterns that work stability, agility and speed. The first Neigong Nei Quan Shou has low stepping. The first non-contact partner drill has circular stepping. The first contact partner drill has linear stepping. The first sparring drills have angular stepping and so on and so forth and all have different levels to them.

'The last major change to mention was what I derived from Ziranmen's major "Ying Gong" [hard skill] practice of Pai Da Gong or conditioning. Pai Da Gong are intermediate level practices where one develops penetrating force, works on ability to withstand strikes and other special skills through the use of unique equipment such as sandbags, iron bags, bamboo, iron balls, iron arm rings, posts and rounded blocks of wood. When practising Pai Da Gong, one simultaneously practises Neigong. Once again, as in combat, all the principles of our "Nei Quan Shou" are used during conditioning as well. Intention, breathing and rooting all are involved. These practices are done very softly and repetitively without the use of hard force and are designed to strengthen the ligaments, tendons and bones for striking. After returning from China, my longtime sparring partner and Gongfu brother, Pedro Martinez, confirmed that my body seemed heavier and harder on contact, particularly when our arms connected.

'Mentally I see Ziranmen theory and principles in everything now. I read a Taiji, Bagua, Xingyi, Ba Ji or Chang Jia classic, and I see mostly Ziranmen and how they all relate and start to become a little more similar with time. I see those arts and other martial arts and

I see Ziranmen's infinity circles (or figure eight the body makes). I look for principles instead of techniques and now understand more thoroughly the importance of Neigong and basics. Above all, the awareness and sense of mind and intention in all movement along with an applicable understanding of Yin and Yang leading to the Ziranmen principle. Movement and stillness have no beginning or end; changes have no beginning or end. Real attacks and false attacks are not fixed; they unfold naturally and spontaneously to the circumstances.'

'We know that Du Xing Wu and Grandmaster Wan had some special skills such as Qing Gong; do you think these have died out now?'

'Many things have been exaggerated and embellished upon, starting with the old Chinese martial arts novels which led to the romanticised Hong Kong Kung Fu films. As far as what is physically humanly possible, I do not think that these skills have died out. I do believe that the skills among the fantastic and unrealistic genre have always been just that. With regard to the skills that I believe do exist, the reason why they seem to be non-existent today is twofold – because of secrecy of correct instruction and lack of persistence with people taught. The fact remains that acquiring Gongfu is derived through time. Acquiring these special skills in particular add on a *lot* more time. Who walks the Bagua circle for the required time? Who stands in Xingyi's Santi for the required time? And, in Ziranmen, who does Nei Quan Shou for the essential amount of time? In the early stages of his school, Wan Lai Sheng required beginners to practise Nei Quan Shou for three years before he taught them anything else. It is a funny contradiction I have heard in some martial art circles – one needs to be smart to learn and absorb but not "too smart" to overly question or get bored quickly. Obviously the smarter the better but what this implies is perseverance. In Ziranmen, we work on light skill and I'm sure Gu Ru Zhang's lineage disciples are working Iron Palm and others are working their speciality.'

'You have researched the art in China; can you say something about your meetings with other Ziranmen experts? I am very interested having seen films of Du's grandson and he looks so relaxed but with a clear penetrating power…did you get to feel this? And what about the "push the brick over", did you see this and what does it mean?'

'In 2001, after having studied a semester of Chinese Language at Qing Hua University in Beijing, I travelled between Hunan and Fujian provinces. My goal was to research Ziranmen and its different teachers, and find a strictly traditional master who knew the complete system to study with. Du Fei Hu lives in a small rural town in Hunan. It was pretty tough getting there and they obviously received few Westerners. At the designated time, I went to his school and there waiting with him was a local government official, a reporter and a photographer. He was about five feet two inches (1.57 m) tall. We spoke about Ziranmen, his grandfather Du Xinwu, and the skills for which he was famous. He spoke of what Wan Lai Sheng had inherited as the lineage holder and what he inherited as a family member and the differences therein. He then proceeded to demonstrate his "skill" of electrical shock. He touched us all on the forearm one at time and was able to give a mild shock at will (it felt similar to static electricity). He said he was able to generate even more of a shock to an opponent. He then had his children demonstrate various basic training including walking handstands across the entire training grounds. His son also demonstrated the Ziran Quan form. As a finale, he demonstrated toppling a brick from a yard away. We continued the interview and then, as we had asked Master Lu Yaoqin, I asked if he would give me an introductory class, to which he agreed, so we set the time for the next morning.

'The first thing he showed me was his version of Nei Quan Shou, the beginner high version that was done quickly, then the advanced squatting version. Next he showed a standing post exercise where the arms are extended in front of the body with the palms facing each other to feel the Qi flow between and then other variations of it. After that he ended class. The whole lesson was about twenty minutes. I had come to see him move, research his Gongfu, and look into the possibility of studying with him. While his art seemed somewhat magical, I needed something different at that time.

'Wu Ming Hui is the headmaster of a large boarding school in Shishi, a suburb of Quanzhou city in Fujian. He had a huge office with many old pictures of himself with Grandmaster Wan in his office as well. He was a lot more formal and seemed older than Master Lu Yaoqin. He asked me to demonstrate so I once again went through the first form. Unlike Master Lu Yaoqin, he was quite polite and full of praises. He then demonstrated a small segment of Zhang San Feng Taiji Quan and once again a little of that famous Wan Lai Sheng body method came out from somewhere deep inside.

'Chen Yun Xiang is the head trainer at the Shishi school. I mention him because he would have been the one mostly instructing me had I chosen to study there. He was a very warm and friendly five feet five inches (1.65 m) tall powerhouse who exhibited somewhat of the Ying aspect of Ziranmen. During the premises tour, I had asked about the conditioning equipment I saw and with immediate joy, he proceded to demonstrate all the Ziranmen conditioning methods! These tools included wooden post, wooden dummy, iron ball, iron rings, pushing/striking cart and many others. I had heard of or seen all except the pushing/striking cart. It looked like an ancient wooden wagon and was filled with huge slabs of stone. I could not move it but he was easily able to move it with explosive "Tui-Shou" type pushes or knee and elbow strikes!

'I had a fifth Ziranmen teacher to go and see in Xiamen City, Fujian, but once I heard he was Master Lu Yaoqin's disciple, I decided not to seek him out. In summary, what I felt then after meeting many masters is that, although they all had their strengths, Master Lu Yaoqin, as a direct disciple of Wan Lai Sheng for twenty-six years, is one of the most well rounded in his knowledge with an amazing teaching method that completely harmonises the artistic, healthful and fighting aspects of Ziranmen. Once I had been studying with Master Lu, I later met and saw demonstrations from Liang Chao Qun, who was one of Wan Lai Sheng's last disciples. He currently teaches at the Wan Lai Sheng Martial Arts Association in France. I met and sat next to him at the Wan Lai Sheng Hundredth Birthday Celebration Commemoration where he demonstrated Ziranmen free flowing shadow boxing. Also as part of the commemoration, videos were released on Wan Lai Sheng's teachings and a few by Liang Chao Qun on form applications and fighting. I also met Feng Wu, who is a disciple of Master Lu Yaoqin. At the time we met, he was instructing my Gongfu brother in the mornings on basics. He is currently researching various other styles of Chinese martial arts and writes articles that are translated for the American magazine, *Kungfu Taichi*. Lastly, I had the opportunity to meet and see many other Wan Lai Sheng disciples and their students demonstrate at the Wan Lai Sheng Hundredth Birthday Celebration event.'

'Do you know anything more about Liu Bai Chuan, Grandmaster Wan's Luohan teacher? I have heard some history which indicates he was the only one known to be equal in skill to Du Xing Wu… How much of his system – inner kicking skills and so on – is now in the Ziranmen you practise?'

'Liu Bai Chuan, born in Anhui Province's Liuan County in 1870, began martial arts during childhood. Yang Cheng Yun, a senior Shaolin monk, took the then strong and confident young Liu Bai Chuan and taught him secret skills that allowed him to attain a higher level of martial art greatness, thus allowing him to pass the imperial military examination. Later, as a professional security guard escorting shipments of goods, he passed through Hong Kong. There, Liu Bai Chuan used his Luohan skills of "Zimu Yuanyang Lianhuan Tui" to defeat a known English fighter. The honourable Sun Yat Sen, who had been present, personally wrote a banner with the characters "Shangwu Jingshen" which means "Uphold Martial Spirit" in commemoration and appreciation of Liu's effort to protect Chinese pride and recognising his magnificent feat.

'His martial arts style originated from northern Shaolin Luohan and that, combined with his height and strength, made him a fearless and noble warrior. Yang Cheng Yun taught "Xiao Luohan" and "Luohan Shenda" to Liu Bai Chuan. "Luohan Shenda" includes the Internal Eight Legs, External Eight Legs, Internal Eight Hammers, External Eight Hammers, Obvious Eight Strikes and the Hidden Eight Strikes. Liu Bai Chuan learned and then mastered the essence of Luohan Kungfu and Luohan Shenda. He was extraordinarily skilful at them but excelled exceptionally at Luohan Leg Skill. His speed was said to be "fast like a typhoon and fierce like lightning" and he was known to be able to easily snap a tree branch as thick as an arm in half with his bare hands. When fighting, he could easily kick others down quickly, thus garnering the name "Number One Leg South of Yangzi".

Liu Bai Chuan with Luohan double broadswords

'Liu Bai Chuan becoming Wan Lai Sheng's teacher was a meeting of opportunity with fate. In 1928 Wan Lai Sheng led a Hebei martial arts team to Nanjing to participate in the First National Examination, where he received an outstanding score. At that time, Liu Bai Chuan was in Shanghai, but when he heard about Wan Lai Sheng's score, he quickly left for Nanjing, where he met up with Chu Min Yi, Zheng Zhuo Ping and others. They decided to go to the Gu Lou Hotel where Wan Lai Sheng was staying to challenge him to a martial arts match to determine how their skills compared. Wan Lai Sheng's master, Du Xinwu, was also there and, afraid that Wan Lai Sheng could possibly lose, he personally took up the challenge and fought Liu Bai Chuan. After the challenge, a deep friendship between them was created. Under these amicable circumstances, Wan Lai Sheng respectfully obeyed Du Xinwu's directive to also become the student of Liu Bai Chuan.

'Liu Bai Chuan not only taught Wan Lai Sheng Luohan Kungfu, he also taught him Shaolin Tongzi Gong [young boy skills] and Chinese orthopaedics. Wan Lai Sheng said that when Liu Bai Chuan learned martial arts from the senior monk, Yang Cheng Yun, he had to climb a mountain every day and go into the forest to practise "Tida, Gunfan" – kicking, punching, tumbling and turning over; and "Tengshan, Diepu" – jumping, evading, falling and pouncing. He was also required to constantly practise fighting against the senior monk, whose severity often left him covered with countless cuts and bruises. Yang Cheng Yun wanted to make sure that Liu Bai Chuan learned real Kungfu skills as opposed to skills for show ("Hua Quan Xiu Tui" – Flowery Fist and Brocade Leg), therefore he was very strict in his teachings.

'Once, while they were practising combat, Liu Bai Chuan used all his strength to attack Yang Cheng Yun so the monk retreated backwards toward a wall, then suddenly counter-attacked with a double palm strike that caused Liu Bai Chuan to fly back several feet. He accidentally hit his head on a hoisting tackle, was knocked unconscious and his head would not stop bleeding. The senior monk searched all over and found a special herbal medicine called "Quan Guo", Spring Fruit Herb, in order to cure Liu Bai Chuan's injury. After this incident, Yang Cheng Yun decided to teach Liu Bai Chuan Chinese medicinal knowledge, which kept him healthy through his senior years. Liu Bai Chuan was not only outstanding as a martial artist, but also a man of integrity and loyalty who embodied the spirit of martial arts, for which he was well respected by others. It had been these traits that originally led Yang Cheng Yun to teach Liu Bai Chuan. In addition, Yang Cheng Yun presented him a steel whip and a "Luohan Dan Jie Dao" [Single Hero Guarding Broad Sword], as a gift and exhorted him to continue to be a disciplined and honest person and to follow the rules and regulations of Shaolin. Liu Bai Chuan followed this instruction strictly all his life.

'In 1929, Wan Lai Sheng participated in the Second National Martial Arts Challenge Match held in Shanghai. He ranked amongst the top finalists and was so intent on winning, he fought very hard. Liu Bai Chuan, who was very observant, noticed this, so, together with his primary master Du Xinwu, Li Jing Lin and other senior masters, advised him on the importance of harmony in martial arts rather than participating for mere ranking and fame. Because of Liu Bai Chuan's intervention, overly fierce combat was avoided and a lifelong lesson was learned, leaving a deep impression on Wan Lai Sheng.

'In the 1930s Wan Lai Sheng was appointed Director of the National Martial Art Training School of Hunan and Liu Bai Chuan was appointed as the Senior Advisor. While there he greatly contributed in disseminating Shaolin Luohan. In 1964, at the age of ninety-four, Liu Bai Chuan passed away, leaving Wan Lai Sheng to continue his legacy. Wan Lai Sheng incorporated Liu Bai Chuan's Luohan Kungfu using Ziranmen Neigong and training methods. As part of Ziranmen, we continue to practise Xiao Luohan and the forty-eight methods of Luohan Shenda. Currently, Master Lu Yaoqin teaches these only at an intermediate to advanced level.'

A remarkable gathering of the old masters – seated from left is Yang Cheng Fu (Taijiquan), Sun Lu Tang (Xingyiquan and Baguazhang), Liu Bai Chuan (Luohan Quan), General Li (Wudang Sword) and Du Xingwu (Ziranmen)

Liu Bai Chuan, the great master of Luohan Quan

Gordon Tso

The Heritage of the Chinese Internal Arts

Song Bao Gua checking Santi posture in the temple at Pinyao

Some years ago whilst I was teaching in London's Holland Park I was approached by a rather gentle-mannered and humble Chinese gentleman who wanted to take a few lessons in Xingyiquan whilst visiting. It quickly became clear that this man already had a very good grasp of the fundamentals and principles of the internal martial arts. With his way of training diligently in whatever I taught him, and his intelligent and meaningful questions which sought to clarify subtle points which his own practice had led him towards, he was one of those people who are a joy to teach. Gordon Tso is a native of Hong Kong, a banker by profession, who has been learning martial arts with great Chinese masters for the sheer love of the art. Over the years we kept in contact, and during a recent conversation he agreed to share something of his research into the internal arts and especially his experiences on a recent visit to Shanxi Province, the birthplace of Xingyi. Although he in no way presents himself as a master – and it is indeed good to have at least one of the subjects of our book talking from the humble perspective of a long-term student – I have always admired his insights and conclusions about the purpose and benefits of practice.

'Gordon, please tell us of your background, your first contact with martial arts and indeed spiritual or religious interests growing up. Why did you begin practice?'

'Martial arts is my hobby, but also a way of life. I am very fortunate to have grown up in Hong Kong. It is a very international city, but it retains strong Chinese roots, with many immigrants old and new from China. Chinese martial arts are a fundamental part of the popular culture, but there are also many international styles of martial arts from around the world. Growing up, there were many opportunities to experiment in different martial arts. My first style was Japanese, Judo, which I started when I was about twelve years old. It is very useful to have had that experience in throwing, grappling and groundwork. Ukemi, or learning how to fall safely, is a skill I think all martial artists, and in fact everybody, should learn. After Judo, I dabbled in Taekwondo and later Shotokan Karate. Then I studied a style called Kenpo Karate which was developed from Chinese and Japanese systems. I started getting interested in the Dao De Jing with my Kenpo teacher. This work by Lao Tzu holds most of the secrets to martial arts and life and I re-read it periodically, usually with a new understanding each time.

Gordon Tso writing in his journal during training with the Song family

'My first style of Chinese martial arts was Taijiquan. I feel fortunate to have had the opportunity to study with a couple of good teachers who trace their lineage directly to two of Yang Chengfu's indoor disciples.

'The first was Master Lui Chiu Chun who studied with Dong Yinji in Hong Kong. He is a kind gentleman of the old school who started me on the Taiji path. His Taiji was soft and very smooth. His postures resembled very much those of Dong Yingji. He was more interested in the health aspects and felt the martial aspects are not useful in today's world. But I still remember that his push hands was soft as cotton on the outside but very powerful inside.

'My second Taiji teacher was Dr Yuan Shaoliang. He is my main Taiji teacher and taught me many things. He is from Beijing, where he was a doctor of traditional Chinese medicine at the prestigious Beijing Hospital of Chinese Medicine. He studied with Dr Ji Liang

Chen and Cui Yishi, another of Yang Chengfu's indoor disciples. He is a Master of both internal martial arts and Chinese medicine. I have been studying with him since 1992. His teaching is very detailed and exact. His push hands was extremely powerful and I would often get thrown all the way across a room. His skill in internal martial arts is matched only by his expertise as a doctor of Chinese medicine.'

Gordon Tso in Santi posture

'And how did you become involved in Xingyi and Bagua practice?'

'My Xingyiquan training began with Dr Yuan Shaoliang and continued with Master C. S. Tang, who is also my Baguazhang teacher. Sifu Tang is a main disciple of Ho Ho Choy, the famous Hong Kong Bagua practitioner who studied directly with Gao Yi Sheng in Tianjin. Master Tang's Bagua is amazing and very beautiful to watch, with very smooth internal energy hidden inside. His Xingyi is very powerful.

'Since visiting Shanxi, China last year with Sifu Tang and meeting Master Song Guang Hua, I developed a strong interest in Song style Xingyi and plan to study it concurrently with the Hebei style I now practise. Song style Xingyi has very robust and well-developed internal aspects and many unique external forms.

'My main forms now are Yang style Taijiquan and Xingyiquan. These two arts are quite complementary. I find Xingyi very useful for training and working the intention and for developing whole body power. Its main emphasis is searching for correct Jing power. Taiji is softer and has more emphasis on sensitivity and understanding energy. Xingyi trains the internal intention to be very strong and focused. Taiji trains energy sensitivity and conflict resolution. I find Baguazhang more complicated and perhaps at a more advanced level, with its many changes in direction and planes. I hope to understand it eventually. All three of these internal styles share common principles and are connected.'

'What motivates you to practise?'

'When I first began training, I wanted to learn how to defend myself and people around me. Later, the primary goal changed to practising for health. In recent years, the spiritual aspects have become much more important. When my friends ask me how I can have the discipline to practise daily, my answer is that although it's a hobby, it actually becomes a way of life, a fundamental part of my being. It does not require discipline. Practice feels so good that it becomes the most enjoyable part of the day. It is when I get in touch with my inner self. In fact, I have to discipline myself to *not* train the whole day. But actually, true martial artists practise the whole day even during other activities.'

'Which teachers have influenced you along the way, and can you describe some learnings with them which, looking back, were key in your development?'

'Apart from my main teachers whom I just mentioned, I would like to mention several teachers from around the world, whom I have had the fortunate opportunity to meet. They have played important parts in my present understanding of the internal systems. Sam Masich from Canada, now based in Berlin, is a very skilled push hands teacher. He pointed me in the direction of understanding energy (Dong Jing) leading to spiritual enlightenment (Shen Ming). His "clunk" position concept is great for understanding whole body power and structure naturally. Your elegant description and demonstration of the distinction of moving with and without intention has been very helpful. I also had the fortune to meet and study briefly with Master Shouyu Liang based in Vancouver, Master Rong Li, also of Vancouver, and Master Doc Fai-Wong of San Francisco.

'Among the teachers I have met in China, two stand out. The first is Cui Zhong San, grandson of Cui Yishi and Taiji brother of Master Yuan Shaoliang. The second is seventy-eight-year-old Master Song Guang Hua, nephew of Song Shirong and current lineage holder of the Song style Xingyiquan. We visited his house on the first morning of our trip to Shanxi. The four sides of the two-hundred-year-old building surround a central courtyard that looks like a perfect place for practising martial arts. My first impression was that Master Song Guang Hua looked like a gentleman and a true master. He sat and stood very straight. His demeanour was peaceful.

Master Song Guang Hua and Gordon Tso in Shanxi, China, 2009

'Master Song's bedroom and sitting room were rather basic. Obviously, he did not require any material possessions to be contented. Taking pride of place on the walls were several framed calligraphy studies. One which I particularly liked read simply "Xin Yi", literally, "heart intention". Sifu Tsang Hon Kit, who is the Song style representative in Hong Kong, told me he has learned a lot about life from Master Song Guang Hua, as much as about Xingyi.

He said Master Song Guang Hua was a real gentleman. Sifu Tsang also seemed to me a genuinely nice person; he told me that Master Song Guang Hua is not motivated by money at all. His diet is very simple. It consists of mainly vegetables, but will include an egg or some meat.'

Students practising the long spear in the Song family home

'What did you learn from Master Song?'

'I asked about the basic requirements of Santi, how to issue power (Fajin), and then it went on from there. Master Song Guang Hua answered me in great detail. His explanations were clear and easy to understand. He checked my Santi posture. He explained the fundamental requirements of Song style Santi posture and then explained clearly two fundamental concepts of Song style Xingyi. First, you need to be loose, then momentarily tensed, and then immediately loose again during a punch or strike. You want to be very loose before hitting for speed. Then you should tense your whole body momentarily during the contact. And immediately afterwards, you should be loose again so you can change. This is an important principle.

'The second important principle is that you use your waist and hip to punch, not merely your arm. These two principles, when combined properly, generate enormous penetrating "internal" power.'

'What qualities made you study with your Sifu, C. S. Tang?'

'I think it is important to find a Sifu that you admire as a person and not only for his martial arts skill. Also, he should be able to explain concepts to you, not only do them well himself.'

Gordon Tso practises with a heavy bag at the Song family home

'How has your body and mind changed through martial arts work? What do you feel about what the classics describe as "changing the tendons"…have you seen anyone either in Hong Kong or China who has unusual use or development of tendons?'

'Master C. S. Tang explains that "traditional training of martial arts is to practise not the muscle, but to train the tendon. Change the weak tendon into a strong one." Especially in internal martial arts, the emphasis is on training the tendons, and also intention [Yi] and Qi. It is not entirely on training muscles.

Master Song Guang Hua teaching Gordon Tso

'At one point during the trip to Shanxi, Master Song Guang Hua hit me with several Beng punches. The feel of an internal type of strike is totally different and I felt tremendous shock inside my body from the punches. Master Song was totally relaxed and not using muscle force at all. This was definitely the highlight of the trip for me. In the old times, masters seldom struck people, and to be hit sometimes can be considered an honour. This is because one can learn a lot of information from a strike; you can feel the quality of the power. The punch was very light, done with very little power, just to explain what he was explaining. Yet I felt power go in my body. No pain on the outside surface at all, but there was tremendous shock inside my body. I felt shocked, sort of hard to breathe; and it took a while before I recovered. And that was just a very light punch. The punch travelled only a short distance, and he was very relaxed while doing it. That evening, I reviewed the video from my camera. It showed that my body did not retract from the punch smoothly; instead it noticeably shook in waves as it retracted. This was a sign of internal Xingyi power, as opposed to external strikes which hurt primarily on the outside of the body.

Master Song Guang Hua practises Snake Form

'My body and mind have changed greatly through internal martial arts. I find I am much more sensitive to the flow of energy in my body, and in the world. I am naturally drawn nowadays to activities that increase and simultaneously calm the flow of energy and mind, and away from people or things that disrupt energy and mental processes. It is quite amazing to me that our schooling system does not teach this, which I think should be a basic skill that everybody should learn. This will be quite incredible for most people to accept, but it is possible to develop psychic powers through internal martial arts training or other related modalities like Yoga and Qigong.'

'How would you describe the stages of traditional internal martial arts practice?'

'I believe that it is useful to first train in the external arts before training in internal styles. The final goal is to be purely internal but, practically, you will probably need to rely on at least some external skills in a real fight. Some Taiji teachers nowadays de-emphasise the self-defence aspects of Taiji and teach it only as a health exercise. That is like removing the essence of the art. You will not derive the complete benefits of the art if you do not keep the martial aspects in mind when you practise. It degenerates into nothing more than a slow dance-like set of movements. The art was developed for fighting and should be practised that way even if your main interest is health. Traditionally, the different internal martial arts have different stages. For example, in Xingyi, traditionally a student will be asked to stand in the Santi posture for several months until the teacher thinks he is ready for further training. This is seldom found nowadays.'

'Generally speaking, what did you find were the big differences between Hebei and Shanxi Xingyiquan?'

'The most obvious difference is the method in which striking power is generated. Most of the Hebei Xingyiquan stylists I have seen generate force mainly by co-ordinating the timing of the arrival of the striking hand with the foot. The goal is to achieve the simultaneous movement and arrival of the various body parts so that they all add to the momentum of the strike. The speed of all the moving parts are added up. To give an analogy, the total measurable speed of a punch executed by a person on a moving car is faster than the absolute speed of a punch executed by a person standing on firm ground. The "whole body power" is mostly co-ordination in timing and momentum, less so a connection of energy inside the body. But with this co-ordination, a Hebei stylist can strike with tremendous speed and power.

'In Song style, power is generated by the whole body being connected inside. All the body parts are connected energetically internally. Power is generated in the waist and hip, connected to the ground by the legs, and travels up to the body part to be used for striking. It is more a connection of the inner forces rather than a co-ordination of timing or momentum of body parts. The entire body is connected energetically inside. At higher levels, there is also a connection between power, Qi, intention and spirit. To achieve this internal connection, you have to feel inside your body rather than be focused on the external movements and appearances. You have to feel the connection of body, power, energy [Qi], intention and spirit. When Master Song Guang Hua taught me a new move, he usually asked whether I "feel" it rather than if I understood it.

Master Song Guang Hua in the courtyard of his home

'This and many other internal aspects give rise to the distinctive flavour and appearance of Song style. It has unique internal power training and issuing techniques because the Song founders incorporated into their system their research and study of internal training manuals such as the *Neigong Si Jing*, the *Xi Sui Jing* and the *Yi Jin Jing*, plus their study in Taijiquan and Baguazhang. Therefore, arguably, Song style is a comparatively more internal style of Xingyiquan, although the differences vary with practitioners.

'Nevertheless, the styles are related and contain many similarities. For example, both styles use the Six Harmonies of Internal Martial Arts, of which the Three External Harmonies are that the hips harmonise with the shoulders, the knees harmonise with the elbows, and the feet harmonise with the hands. I will not discuss the Three Internal Harmonies here because it can be the subject of an entire book, encompassing meditation and various spiritual developments. Both styles have their merits, and neither style is superior to the other.'

'What is the standard of internal martial arts like now in Hong Kong? Has the modern age killed off the higher levels of skill or has the ability to travel and see things openly brought in a new era of research and skill?'

'The weakness of Chinese martial arts is that traditionally it is very secretive. Sometimes it was passed to very few people and often to family members only. You find that the skills get diluted from generation to generation since it was not fully transmitted or was lost. It is very hard to find a good teacher. The fact that people today are very busy and do not have the time to train as much as in the old days has also lowered standards on average. However, I think the situation is improving. I have found that teachers in Hong Kong and China in general are more open and willing to share and spread the complete arts. I have found many good teachers who have deep knowledge, with good character, and willing to teach the complete arts. Interestingly, I have found teachers who have a very deep understanding of the Chinese internal systems from around the world. They practise at a very high level and are good teachers that are skilful at explaining difficult concepts.'

'How has your Yoga and meditation work affected your internal martial arts and vice versa? In what sense can internal martial arts be a spiritual Way? At one time the masters were facing death and using the arts as a tool to help; in our time can we use them to face death, and indeed the struggles of life, or are they now about something else?'

'Ultimately all these Eastern practices work on the same thing, energy, which is called Qi in China, Ki in Japan and Prana in India. The goal of practice is to realign the flow and pattern of energy in your body and to become more sensitive to the energy in your body and in the universe around you. After years of practice in the right direction, you will begin to understand energy, your intuition will be much heightened and you will expand your psychic abilities. As your energy body becomes realigned, that will have an effect on your subtle body and, therefore, on your life. Your intentions will effortlessly manifest into reality. Your life becomes smoother as if magically. Other people think you are just a lucky person. Things will happen that appear at first to you to be unbelievable, miraculous and supernatural. But it is really not miraculous or supernatural. They are the results that come simply from learning how to align and use the higher forces of Nature. You become so in tune and aligned with the flow of the universe, nothing worries or stresses you out any more. These aspects can be quite esoteric to explain, but are actually common to higher levels of various internal martial arts, Yoga and Qigong practices. It would take a lot longer to fully explain these concepts which will probably have to be first experienced to be believed.

'When young people train in the martial arts, they usually just want to learn how to defend themselves. Later, the focus will usually change to training the body and mind, and staying healthy. Self-defence now becomes secondary. After long years of practice, some practitioners start to realise that internal martial arts can be a path to spiritual cultivation. A passage in *The Taiji Treatise*, a classical work by Wang Zong Yue, says that "From careful investigation and experience, one may gradually realise how to comprehend energy (Dong Jin). From comprehending energy, you will attain by degrees spiritual illumination (Shen Ming). Nevertheless, without an exertion of effort over time, one will not be able to suddenly have a thorough understanding of it." I was steered towards this passage by an excellent Taijiquan teacher a few years ago, and I think all internal martial arts practitioners should ponder this statement.

'One of the benefits of these practices is you become more aware of and sensitive to your body and mind, what state they are in and how energy is flowing inside you. You become aware of any stress or tension, and you can release them. Most people waste a lot of energy on unnecessary tension. Your mind becomes calmer and clearer. You then start to become more aware of energy everywhere around you and eventually might even acquire degrees of spiritual enlightenment.

'By using your sensitivity and feeling, you can also judge whether any moves in your Xingyi practice are correct by how it feels energetically in your body. You can judge and correct anything. You will be able to feel the intention [Yi] and energy [Qi] travelling through your body. This feeling can feel comfortable or not; this is how you know if it is right. In fact, taking this principle a step further, you can become so sensitive and finely tuned, you know intuitively whether any action in life is correct or not, by the way it feels energetically. You become in tune and in alignment with the energy of the world. Ultimately, you learn to sail through the currents of life effortlessly, seemingly magically to an outside observer.

'And if your actions arise out of being in tune or in alignment with the energy, they will naturally be virtuous, benevolent and righteous and built from integrity. It happens naturally, without striving, forcing or thinking because it just feels "right". Anything that is not right will disrupt your energy body. This is much more natural than doing something because you "should" or because you were taught in school or church to act that way. However, sometimes you need to listen and feel for a while to make sure the feeling is really from your heart and not from your mind. I am only just starting to discover these techniques and still have a lot to learn. I hope one day I can share them with the world in a book.

'At a more basic level, there are principles of body alignment and breathing techniques that are surprisingly similar between internal martial arts and Yoga. I find that Yoga and internal martial arts are complementary, mainly because at higher levels they focus on similar things. Spiritually, martial arts arrive at love, compassion, respect and peace through knowing extreme violence; Yoga starts from love and compassion and delves deeper. Happiness from within is one result. I have met several amazing yogis who are very spiritually developed and have demonstrated miraculous psychic abilities. Just being in their presence is an uplifting experience. To me, martial arts have been helpful in increasing the amount of Qi, while Yoga calms and aligns the Prana.'

'Often martial arts groups or teachers take the role or reality of extended family. Do you see this as a healthy factor in modern society?'

'I think martial arts teachers have the responsibility and opportunity to influence the next generation in tremendously positive ways. Martial arts can be a great help in developing character and moral values naturally in youngsters. Teachers should lead by example in how they conduct their lives.'

A Visit to the Song Family Home in Taigu, Shanxi – Excerpts from the Journal of Gordon Tso

27 August 2009

On 27 August 2009 I travelled from Hong Kong to Taigu, Shanxi, to attend the 160th Birthday Anniversary of Song Shirong and to visit the heart and birthplace of Xingyiquan.

I woke up at dawn the first morning. Looking out my hotel window, I immediately saw three men practising Xingyiquan on the street below. Then, looking around, I saw many more. I wondered to myself whether everybody in Taigu is a Xingyiquan practitioner. A big, tough-looking man in black pants had movements that are soft and oily, but very heavy. The hidden power can be felt. I observed that when releasing power, he is not only using forward arm, palm and body; but the retreating arm and body are very important. His whole body vibrated when releasing power. I started to suspect this trip might turn out to be quite useful.

The first event of the day was a brief visit to the Song family home and meeting Master Song Guang Hua, current lineage holder of the Song style. I immediately liked his bearing. He seemed like a true gentleman of the old era. He was open and approachable.

Throughout the trip, I was to witness many impromptu demonstrations and lessons on Song style Xingyiquan. At one point, a thin man was giving an impressive demonstration. His movements were very fast and had the characteristically loose, yet explosive power of Song style Xingyiquan. Another man explained to me that 'lifting pelvic floor' is done by using intention or 'Yi', not muscular strength. You tuck your tailbone and use your Dantien to do it. The lifting is a feeling and is not using strong muscular strength. The technique is identical to the 'Mula Bandha', or the 'root lock' practised in Yoga.

On the second day we were supposed to do some more sightseeing, which to me sounded a bit boring. I came here to see and learn Xingyiquan. I decided to try using Reiki energy to psychically affect the situation. When I woke up the next morning, it was raining hard, so a visit to a temple planned for that afternoon had to be cancelled because the dirt road access would be too muddy. It was to be replaced by a second visit to the Song family compound. Perhaps my mind's intentions [Yi] are taking shape [Xing]…or perhaps it is just Karma.

For Song style Xingyiquan Santi posture, here is a partial list of the requirements taught by Master Song Guang Hua:

1. Chin is tucked in slightly.

2. Head is lifted up.

3. Tailbone is scooped. This leads energy down the front leg and into the ground.

4. Chest is lifted up, but the chest is not protruded outwards. This lifting of the chest and the scooping of the tailbone create space and length in body, which is beneficial to health.

5. Back is straight.

6. Legs have both spreading apart and hugging in power.

7. Crotch is rounded.

8. Scooped tailbone leads to lifting the pelvic floor.

9. Reverse breathing is used when issuing power. When breathing in, the ribs expand. When breathing out, the Dantien expands, and Qi sinks to the Dantien.

10. Front foot turned in 15 degrees, and rear foot is turned out not more than 45 degrees.

11. Inside edge of front foot near the first toe is now on the same line as the inside edge of the heel of the rear foot. Front foot is pulled back next to the rear foot so that the heels are slightly apart.

12. Thumb of rear palm touches the body slightly.

13. Front palm, front foot and the nose are all in one line.

14. Fingers are spread, but not too wide. Fingers are slightly bent. Tiger mouth is rounded.

15. Toes claw the ground gently and arches are lifted.

16. For the front leg, the knee is bent. But the back of the front leg has strength pushing forward, and the back of the knee is tensed.

17. The distance between the front and rear foot is measured by bending the rear leg down until the knee touches the ground. The rear knee should land just behind the front foot.

18. Shoulders sink down and the two sides are balanced.

Next day, during sightseeing at a temple in Pinyao, I started getting bored again and decided to ask Master Song's eldest son Song Bao Gua some questions. He was very nice and answered all my questions with clear explanations and demonstrations. At one point, to explain a concept, he drew a diagram on the ground using a piece of rock as chalk.

On the final morning, I got up at 4:30 am to catch a flight. In the pitch dark central courtyard of the guest house, Master Song Bao Gua was in Santi stance stationary doing some 'Fajin' exercises using the lower body only, without arms. I observed for a while, and decided to try to get a last-minute lesson. Master Song gave me quite detailed instructions and explained that the power of Piquan should come naturally from a contraction first and then an extension of the body. It is not from a forced chopping downward motion without root.

Surprisingly, my taxi driver to the airport was a Xingyiquan practitioner as well. Naturally, we talked about Xingyiquan for the whole ride. At one point, he stopped the car on the side of the expressway and got out to demonstrate some moves. We ended up practising Xingyiquan on the shoulder of the expressway for over twenty minutes, with cars zooming by just a few feet away.

Thinking back, during this trip I met several Xingyiquan people who feel genuinely nice, friendly, gracious, modest, gentle and happy inside. They looked physically healthy, full of Qi, maintaining ideal body weight, despite advanced age in some. They have good postures too, not hunchbacked, like some older people. They seemed happy from deep inside. But others, like the taxi driver, were not truly happy. Internal martial arts do not automatically bring spiritual development; you have look for it, but when you know where and how to seek, you will find it. A lot of the younger practitioners I met on the trip do not yet have it. It takes time to cultivate.

The trip was very informative and useful. In three days, I learned more than several years' worth of material.

Postscript, 9 July 2012

When I first wrote the journal in 2009, little did I know that I was to be going back to Shanxi regularly to train with the Song family and eventually become an indoor disciple. The Song family has become like an extended family. Several of the people I met on that first trip have become good friends. I am also pleased to note that the instructions and impressions recorded on the first trip have proven to be mostly accurate.

Gordon Tso training with his Sifu, C. S. Tang

Paul Whitrod

Part 1: The Heritage of Chow Gar Southern Mantis

Sifu Paul Whitrod in Chow Gar Mantis posture

As a fourteen-year-old boy I met Sifu Paul Whitrod for the first time; he had just returned from living in Hong Kong with Grandmaster Ip Shui and was opening his first class teaching Chow Gar Southern Mantis Gongfu. It was held in the evening in a dark, musty basement room in a school building, where for several hours the serious-looking teacher and his three or four students would train continuously in the conditioning skills and basic exercises of this demanding and powerful system. Twelve years later I began learning Xingyiquan with him; he was a generous and hard working teacher sharing not only his whole system of Xingyiquan with me but also the Wafu Buddhist spiritual healing prayers and some of the Dit Da medical system he had learned in Hong Kong. His knowledge and skill in destroying and healing the body using vital points was excellent; several people I referred to him for healing with serious ailments had remarkable recoveries within a few sessions. When I was seriously ill he gave me several sessions of healing – including spiritual healing and prayers calling upon the power of Lord Krishna – which made a remarkable difference in my energy levels and condition.

Everyone who trains with Sifu Whitrod talks about his power. He just has more power than a person of twice his size should have, as if there are steel springs in his limbs. This is no doubt the result of his continuous daily training in the exercises of Chow Gar Mantis Gongfu, which is renowned for its explosive or shock power. But there is another side to him, and that is his character – he is really one of the most decent, honest men I have ever met in (or out of) martial arts circles. His faith in Krishna and the Vedic science taught by Shrila Prabhupada (founder of the Hare Krishna movement in the West) has inspired many people to search for spiritual meaning in their own lives, and the tangible aura of goodness and – increasingly as the years go on – of genuine human love is something that many of my friends have commented on.

The past decade has seen Sifu Whitrod spending much time in India and Thailand to study the old martial systems of those lands, and in a later chapter of this book he talks about his experience of those methods. In this present chapter we have a discussion with Paul about his memories and training with Ip Shui of Hong Kong, the late grandmaster of Chow Gar Mantis Gongfu.

'Paul, since I last interviewed you over ten years ago Grandmaster Ip Shui has sadly passed away. I know what a huge influence he has been on your training and your life. What is your memory of him now?'

'He was very skilled, very fast. He was an individual who inspired me when I was younger. I met him back in 1975 very briefly, when he came over with his daughter who was doing martial arts too. I thought then I would go and see him one day… I was about fifteen then. He passed away in 2004 and, yes, he did have a big influence on me. He made me aware of what really worked in martial arts, and what didn't work. You have to understand that when the monks came out of the Shaolin Temple they had to make a living, and sometimes the only way to do that was by demonstrating their martial arts – now, that often meant that they employed things which looked good as opposed to being effective. Still today they do it: in their shows they do back-flips and so on, it's not really for self-defence which would be boring to look at.'

'What was Grandmaster's special skill?'

'His hand speed – he was very fast. He was already seventy when I met him but he was very fast and powerful. He had his strong neck, strong ribs, and even at that age he would always ask people to punch him! Even at ninety years old he was still asking people to hit him!'

'I remember how happy he seemed even at that age…'

'Yes, he was always joking about things, having a laugh about things. Maybe that's why he lived so long. He lived until ninety-one… Grandmaster was a student of Lau Soie, who was said to be a great fighter. There is a story in Lau Soie's village about him defeating a wolf; I went to the village a couple of years ago and that's what they say. It's said that Lau Soie was already an accomplished martial artist, skilled in Monkey style and Horse style, and renowned for defeating a wolf with a kick, and then he met the monk Wong Fu Go who told him his martial arts didn't seem very good. So Lau Soie challenged him but the monk beat him. It took him some time to become a disciple but then he did and he stayed with Wong Fu Go for about four or five years. Later Lau Soie fled to Hong Kong and there he taught Grandmaster.

'According to Grandmaster his teacher had this tremendous shock power. The story is that when he started to learn he was pulled so hard that he flew across the room and hit his head on the wall. At that time Cantonese and Hakka people were not on good terms, and would not teach the others. Grandmaster was Cantonese but Lau Soie taught him anyway, and then he also looked after his teacher for two years before his death.'

'And the Wafu spiritual healing came from Lau Soi?'

'No, the Wafu came from his grandfather. He told me that his grandfather had special skills. He had lived in the Shaolin Temple and in those days you would learn that kind of skill. It is not like today, where in Shaolin the martial arts come first. Go back a hundred and fifty years and the important part was your Buddhist study and healing, and martial arts were after that. Today it is the opposite! Buddhism is not important, business is and martial arts is number one.

'So he had Siddis or special powers. Well, Grandmaster Ip Shui used to tell everyone that his grandfather could disappear. He demonstrated to everyone – he would say, "He would put a towel on the floor and spin around and he would be there, then he would be gone." But he would never show these things openly. He wanted to teach his son [Grandmaster's father] but thought his attitude was not right, so he taught his grandson who was grandmaster. But he only taught the Wafu medicine, not these other skills.

'During the Second World War there was this book – the handwriting was so perfect it was almost as if it had been printed but it was in fact handwritten with a brush. There were two parts to the book, one was Wafu spiritual healing and the other was all the Mantras for how to do all these mystical things. But during the war the Japanese raided the house and, seeing the book, they stole it. As for these Siddis, they are perfections from spiritual work. Well, as you may know, in Krishna consciousness you will be offered Siddhis, but you mustn't take them as they will only be a distraction. It is not about that, it is about trying to be devotees of Krishna.'

'Did you see Grandmaster use Wafu to cure any serious cases of illness in Hong Kong?'

'Sure. From people who had heart attacks, to people whose faces were paralysed from strokes, cancer, so many, too many to relate... He was given so many presents that he had to give many of them away. But one main present he received was a mirror which is still hanging in the school at his house in Kowloon City.'

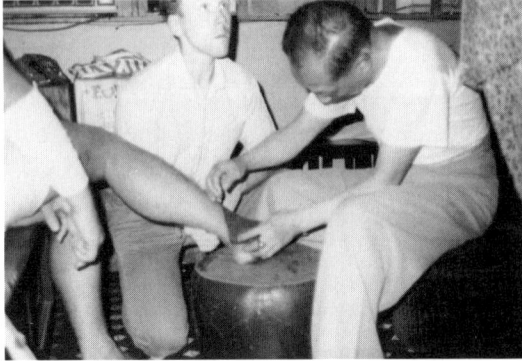

Paul Whitrod assisting Grandmaster Ip Shui, treating a patient with Dit Da herbal medicine in Hong Kong; another very old photograph

'It is quite incredible, as things like stroke paralysis are very difficult to deal with by modern medicine.'

'Yes, I watched him do this on numerous occasions. I have the forms and techniques but…it is a different time now. Really, if you are in that environment where people will come to you for that then OK…but how many people would come here for that? If someone has cancer and you offer to do Wafu then they will refuse and go to the hospital. So again it is only in my memory to practise, much like the forms of martial arts are a memory as we don't go to war any more using those things such as the old fashioned weapons.'

'What memories do you have of those times in Hong Kong?'

'Just being with Grandmaster. In those days Hong Kong seemed to be sunny and Grandmaster seemed to be more vibrant, always going through so many things day to day, going out to see his old friends and being dragged along… Just seeing him do techniques with such skill and how happy he was with doing them.

'It was thirty years ago when I first went, a long time ago. I last returned in 2008 to Lau Soie's village for Grandmaster's son's sixtieth birthday. Whatever grows must die, now is a different time, but it was good, and slowly but surely those times – all of the experiences I have had – have developed me as an individual. But the most important thing is trying to develop myself as a Krishna devotee. You may know all the martial arts in the world, but if your character is still no good then what is the point? As devotees of Krishna we must always remain humble. If you are arrogant it is because you fill yourself up with thinking you know things.'

Paul Whitrod (far left) and Grandmaster Ip Shui (far right)
sharing a meal in Hong Kong many years ago

'Can you tell us more about Grandmaster's special way of teaching?'

'I remember once in Hong Kong when Grandmaster was talking about strength not being everything. My Sifu and I were talking about certain things, about how we should practise these techniques called Chai Sau and Doi Jong. Grandmaster's son – my Sifu – was saying to me to practise Chai Sau for power, Doi Jong for double arm exercise, San Bo Jin to improve the first form, just keep doing these every day, every day... You don't have to worry about anything else, just keep doing these techniques for power. So Grandmaster came wandering over and asked what we were discussing, and his son told him. Well...Grandmaster took out his cigarette, said something and then walked off. I wondered what that was all about!

'So anyway, he came back and told me to use my strength against him. I pushed his arm and he moved to one side. I attacked him again and he moved to the other side. He looked at me and said "No strength!" So from then he started to teach me "no strength" techniques from Mantis, which is Yau Long or Swimming Dragon. And this is just one instance of many, many times when he would interact to teach something. Often he would only interact when you were prepared to ask or to relate. So, for example, if you didn't ask Grandmaster what to do if you fell on the floor, then he would never explain to you what to do. When you ask it means you are ready to know. The idea of martial art is that you will always ask the relevant question according to your ability. So if you just did lots of high kicking day after day, he might stand there and say how good it was, and if you were a stupid person you would go through life thinking how good it was doing all these kicks. Maybe one day you would wonder how to use your hands, at that point Grandmaster would show you hand techniques. So that was his subtle ability.

'When I asked him what to do when you fell on the floor he started teaching me the Poong Long Gerk [Flying Dragon Kicks]. That is why you don't see many people doing that form – they didn't ask!

'Another time I was at his place and I was doing a technique of squeezing the Fuhao [Tiger's Mouth] point by the thumb; my training partner and I were both feeling a lot of pain. So Grandmaster came over and told me to do it on him, but he just stood there with no pain! As he wandered off we were trying to figure out why he didn't feel the pain. Then he came back and showed us to do something with the other arm, put it behind your back and tense it and then you won't feel pain. He had so much knowledge.

'There was a special cigarette technique. We were in a restaurant about 1981, about eight of us around the table and I was sitting next to Grandmaster. Someone said something to him and he looked at me and pulled up his sleeve. He told me to bite his arm. Well, I tried to bite his arm but my teeth couldn't grip it, it was like biting an apple that's on a piece of string! It was so tight it just slid off. Then he took a cigarette, tore off a strip of newspaper and put it under the upright cigarette so it was hanging off the table. Then he struck the paper with his two fingers and left the cigarette still standing there!'

'What's the standard of martial arts in Hong Kong compared to before?'

'I can only say with what I have seen and been told that it has been deteriorating for the past thirty or forty years. But then again, you can't believe all the stories you hear about the great masters. Grandmaster told me about one master who was challenged and told the challenger to wait until he had gone to the toilet. Anyway, he went in the toilet and never came out! So don't think they were all so great...every Kungfu master won their fights so then who were the losers? It's like the time all those Muay Thai fighters went and fought against the Wing Chun Kungfu team in Hong Kong, all the Kungfu guys lost. Because the Thais trained really hard, and the Kungfu guys thought once a week training was OK. No, you have to train really intensively.

'Round about the 1950s things began changing in Hong Kong, lots of the Kungfu schools began closing, land became premium price, those who had big schools had their place demolished and the places became much smaller. Kungfu became associated with old fashioned things and no one wanted to do it any more. Nowadays Taekwondo is more popular than Kungfu.'

Grandmaster Ip Shui and Sifu Paul Whitrod in Hong Kong many years ago

The Martial
Traditions of Japan

John Evans Sensei

The Way of the Sword

John Evans Sensei practising with the Katana sword

Over the years I had often asked my Japanese friends about the Yamabushi, the mountain dwelling warriors who inhabited the sacred peaks of Japan and who, through intense austerities and discipline, cultivated high level skill with the sword and in the healing arts – but the reply I always received was that they rarely existed except in folklore and films. Indeed, Carmen Blacker's in-depth and poignant book about the practice of shamanism in Japan, *The Catalpa Bow* (Blacker 1999) strongly suggests that by the 1960s or 1970s such men and their mystical orders had all but died out. Imagine my surprise, therefore, to discover that living in East London was a man who had practised the authentic traditions of the Yamabushi in their homeland for many years and who held high ranking in the traditional sword arts. I happened to see an old copy of a TV documentary filmed in Japan some twenty-five years ago, showing a young Englishman meditating and chanting beneath a freezing waterfall and engaged in intensive practice with the Katana. Within an hour of seeing that film I was speaking with that man, John Evans Sensei, and without any hesitation he agreed to meet and discuss his experiences. Unassuming and friendly, and clearly someone who had worked on himself for a long period of time, here was a man who was bridging the gap between ancient wisdom and the modern world. What follows is some of our conversation during that first meeting, in which he answered several questions about practice and concerning Fudo-Myo which had been on my mind for years.

'John, can you tell me what the symbol of your school represents?'

'The symbol of our school Fudokan is Kurikara, a dragon form of Fudo – the patron of swordsmen and Gyoja [austere practitioners].'

'When did you first become involved with the practice of martial arts and meditation?'

'I started doing Yoga aged fourteen, from a book by Richard Hittleman, and at sixteen I started Taiji at an Anglican monastic community I visited after an introduction from my school chaplain. At university I practised Iyengar Yoga and Shotokan Karate. When I finished university I went back to the community to give myself a chance to reflect on what I wanted to do with my life, and I ended up staying there for five years. There was a priest in charge who had lived in India for thirty years and about twelve residents, two or three official novices and the rest of us under temporary vows for as long as we lived there. The Anchorhold in Sussex was run by an Anglican order but had its own unique mission to explore Oriental ways of helping meditation. So they invited Taiji teachers to teach regularly and they also did a daily sequence of Yoga Asanas, but not as in Hatha Yoga, more like Qigong.

'Besides my Karate training I had always been interested in Japan, especially in Zen, in Haiku and in some of the poetry coming out of America which had been influenced by Zen. When I decided to leave the community I managed to find a job teaching at a girls' high school in Tokyo for a year through a private arrangement. Two or three weeks after arriving I met someone in the Yamabushi-Shugendo-Shingon tradition, who was basically doing his own thing, a Gyoja [a Sadhaka – one following an ascetic training], who persuaded me to stop doing acupuncture and Shiatsu study, which had become my main activity in the monastery, to go back to martial arts but through the sword. This was on the edge of Tokyo, a place called Hachioji, which is very near Takaosan, a famous Yamabushi mountain. It has several waterfalls which are used for Takigyo [waterfall training]. A friend of a friend bumped into him and, knowing the kinds of things I was interested in, she told me and so I went to meet him.

'He was very intense and energetic and had amazing mental and physical abilities. He was very, very sharp in his ability to home in on where a person was in life. I recently met up with two other British people who met him around that time. All three of us were diverted onto our paths through meeting him: one is now a famous artist and the other a well-known chanting teacher. His genius is to see what each person needs. I stayed with him for five years. His name is Fushi, that is his Gyoja name and it means Child of the Wind. He doesn't call what he does Shugendo, as he doesn't have an especially high opinion of what goes by that name nowadays. Most Shugendo associations are like a mixture of a rugby club, the National Trust and a Methodist chapel. His approach to Takigyo was very systematic, with specific preparation and different levels similar to what you find in authentic Hatha Yoga. Otherwise you will just go into the falls and shriek hysterically. There was a little village in the Tanzawa mountains where the villagers would begrudgingly allow him to use an old temple close to a very good waterfall, basically because he scared the living daylights out of them! There was a local shamanic healer. As we talked to him, he started to come out with these visions, then about thirty minutes later he described the same visions again – he had forgotten he had already told us. He had obviously damaged himself mentally. He used to drink alcohol the day before he went into the falls, he didn't fast properly or prepare properly, and your blood system just can't cope in that condition. Fushi reckoned he had had a lot of small strokes and burst blood vessels…there is a lot of that.'

'So there is a lot of austere practice being done without a proper teacher or lineage, and then they damage themselves?'

'Yes…there may even be a proper lineage, but it's like a lot of martial arts schools now. Fushi didn't have a lineage. Nakamura Sensei didn't have a lineage. He was practising Toyama Ryu but that was a set of Kata, simple Kata, devised for the military by some of the Koryu [old martial schools]. I think this is a problem, just because there is a lineage doesn't mean that there is quality, and I have seen in my own case that in one generation, both in Yoga and in martial arts, the essence of something can be lost. So if fifteen generations have passed and where there is no environment for testing that art…then the fact that there is a lineage is no guarantee that something authentic or substantial is going to be taught. It will mean that if you can research properly and you have an understanding then it's possible that you can find out things. But the chances are that what you are looking at is a skeleton.'

'Did you see other teachers that you admired?'

'I didn't see anything else on the level of Nakamura Sensei or of my current Yoga teacher. I saw people who had great skill, and met some individuals who were fantastic human beings, but in terms of meeting someone who was teaching a complete system which they were fully manifesting, no. Having seen videos of Ueshiba O-Sensei [founder of Aikido] then I would say that definitely there.'

'Did you think of joining Katori Shinto Ryu?'

'I went to Katori Shinto Ryu, it was just a few years after Donn Draeger had died and Otake Sensei told me that they were not taking any foreigners at that stage, but he recommended me to their sister school at Kashima. So I took his introductory letter and studied Kashima Shinto Ryu for two years – it is a very interesting system, as is Katori Shinto Ryu. Otake Sensei [head of Katori Shinto Ryu] really had power in his hips and legs when he did Iai-Jutsu [art of drawing and cutting with the sword]. Their system is very good because the seats, stances and footwork are natural, unlike the steps used in the Iaido which are artificial. Donn Draeger says this in his book on Japanese sworsdmanship.

'Nakamura Sensei was also largely self-taught. He investigated many things himself, which is the spirit of Shugendo [which means training and testing]. He wasn't from the officer class, but a non-commissioned officer in the army, yet he was expansive in a way that I didn't see anywhere else. I met him about three years after I started training with Fushi, who regularly showed me books by Otake Sensei, Nakamura Sensei and Danzaki Sensei, who was a Muso-Shinden Ryu teacher. For me Nakamura's system was much more realistic. You have eight basic cuts and eight directions which you should be able to move freely in. There was a term he used a lot – Jiyu Jizai – which means "freely, freely". You can hear part of this in the Heart Sutra, in the beginning where it says "kanjizai". This refers to Kannon [Kwan Yin], to his ability to freely see everything without any limitations. And this is how I see Jiyu Jizai, that you freely see and freely respond without any limitation. Nakamura Sensei's nature was like that. His system was very simple, nothing extra. It took me a long time to realise this, as I was dazzled by the complexity of the Okuden [advanced] Kata of Muso Shinden Ryu, or the long complex Kata of Katori Shinto Ryu, which are performed at high speed. But I came to appreciate that the best of Nakamura's students were at least as good as those performing the complex stuff you could see.

'Well, there are systems in China comprising five movements which are considered some of the best fighting systems, so number of techniques is no indication of effectiveness. In fact it can work the other way in that it destroys or limits that freedom, too caught up in complexity.'

'Yes I am sure. And also it is the nature of the sword – if you make a full movement then the sword will take you through to the next movement. There are lots of ways in which the sword can take you through, and part of Nakamura's thesis or philosophy was the ability to use the momentum from one technique into the next.

'In contemporary Japanese martial arts there are some basic mistakes in general principles. For example, the idea that you start with unarmed arts and then go on to weapons training. But my experience with Kempo or Karate people is that the longer they have trained in those things then the more difficult it is for them to move properly with the sword. Whereas if you move with the sword first other, smaller movements come easily. You can always make a big technique smaller. Fushi showed me an old text where Aikido techniques were being trained using two Bokken, and he said that was the origin of Aiki-Jutsu, which you can see in many ways, in techniques which are based on sword movements.

'This is the problem – connecting the sword to the centre of the body so that the sword is really moving with the body. If you train in that way then you can move from one technique to the next. If you don't train in that way then it is not going to happen. I have only studied a little Bagua but my understanding is that it has very similar principles.'

'This idea of something seemingly external leading the body is similar. The sword has a weight, and just the fact of it having a weight will lead you somewhere, whereas if you try to push, it is a different feeling. Everything in the universe has this huge potential force, and if you let it go that's it. The problem is how to unbind ourselves so that we can go with that force. We normally stop the potential. It is allowing that something to take you. Is it something like that?'

'Yes, yes. It's like that. This is explained through the five elements – which Musashi used as a structure for his Book of Five Rings. The way Fushi explained it was that the relationship between the sword and body changes at each elemental level. His system was not Kata-based but based on technique. There were thirty or so sword techniques at earth level, twenty at water level, fifteen at fire and so on. So at the earth level, you ground the body, then from the body through the centre the power comes out through the sword. Then in the water level the sword starts moving and the body follows it. In the fire level they exchange around the centre, through explosive movements or switching across the centre. In air the movement is weightless. Water takes you on the surface and it can coil but air has no weight. There are many more things to discover about this but it's something like that. The techniques have a different quality at each stage requiring a different level of integration. So with the way I teach I have just made one Kata from the Waza of each of those levels, and use them as a kind of diagnostic tool. For example, there are some people who are very earthy, and very explosive, but lack fluidity. So it gives them a chance to identify and get a feeling for the qualities which they are missing.'

'When you hold out the Jien, the Chinese double-edged straight sword, it will begin to spiral, but it seems with the Katana it wants to go straight. Is that right?'

'When you hold the Katana with two hands it is basically a double spiral.' John demonstrates and his arms spiral inwards to a central point as if holding the sword. 'The way that you use the joints, well I went through a period where I had lots and lots of problems with elbows and wrists, and as I got through them I realised more and more that the movement of the limbs integrate through a combination of undulating and spiralling which eliminates stress from the joints. This is really just my own guess but since there is no such thing as a dragon – snakes exist which undulate, but dragons can undulate and also fly which gives the possibility of spiralling – I think that the idea of the dragon may have been created to describe these qualities of movement. I don't have any evidence for this but that makes sense to me.

'Complete full cutting techniques with the Katana also lead naturally to spirals. The problem is that full involvement of the body is rare. The way that the Kurikara dragon is interpreted in Tantric circles refers to the internal energy of the central channel. If the energy in the limbs is fully freed this central channel becomes accessible. This is the same with the Kundalini, the serpent power in Indian Tantra, and Kurikara actually comes from Kulika, which was one of the Naga Ragas or Snake Kings of Nepal.'

'Ahh, so there is a link there from India to Japan? I have heard that Fudo may equate to a form of Shiva?'

'Yes, Achala [the Sanskrit for Fudo] is one of the titles of Shiva. The fact that they are both warrior Yogis makes the parallels evident. I have chanted the Heart Sutra and Fudo Myo O Dharani [Mantra] for a long time but I find the Indian Sanskrit chants more complete in their use of the inner body. They have melody and a greater range of rhythmical and sound patterns. The one I use is the Ravana Stotra, which is a long song to Shiva from Ravana the Demon King, who was his great devotee.'

'Do you feel these deities are real beings or purely symbolic, or both?'

'If you read the John Blofeld [2009] book about Kwan Yin, the answer is given there when he goes back to the Taiwanese monastery and tells the monks how, thanks to their explanations, he realises that Kwan Yin is only symbolic, a complex representation of a philosophical structure. They tell him that that does not mean Kwan Yin is merely symbolic. I discovered this when I wrote "Trog" – a poetic narrative about my experiences training in Japan. I created three characters to symbolise different aspects of Trog, the main protagonist. Then I found that these characters began to have a life of their own and write their own story! The equivalent understanding that you get in the Tantric schools is in William Blake and I think he has as clear an understanding as those schools. He says the human imagination is God, and declares that "Eternity is in love with the productions of Time." If you can fully respond to an image then it can take you all the way.'

'So it is both symbolic and also more than that? I mean, you have practised a lot, John, you must have had some visions or experiences?'

'Well, yes, for example the first time I went to do the waterfall training. I was sick, I was weak, I was very scared, it was two in the morning and snowing, it was a long walk up into a very dark place. Fushi sent me further up a dark path, told me to go and pay my respects. Suddenly I came upon this great metal statue of the dragon, Kurikara [the Kami (spirit) of that waterfall]. It was as if it was alive. Definitely in my heightened state of awareness and vulnerability something communicated itself to me… I was given the strength to go through the ritual and immersion. I cannot fully explain the process of it, and I don't think it is important to try and explain it but just to be open to it.

Fudo Myo, painted by John Evans Sensei

'It is because of that experience that, two years ago, when I decided to write a book on training with the Japanese sword, I decided to use the image of Kurikara, as that was a hugely important transmission. I experienced a few things like this and looking back on such events it seems to me that you are prepared in various ways...your psyche is set for something. But if you worry about whether such things are symbolic or divine beings outside or inside, if you get into that then you will not be able to fully respond, which is what the monks were saying to Blofeld.'

'So what happened that first time in the waterfall?'

'I survived! In the winter you do the Kuji-Kiri [ritual cutting of a mandala of nine lines] a few times and then do the Heart Sutra once and that's it. It's freezing cold when the water is on the head, when it's on other parts of the body you can take it longer, but when its on the brain the body goes into a kind of panic situation as the brain tissue is non-regenerative, so the circulation gets diverted to the brain to avoid the cells dying. So you don't want to go beyond the point where the body can no longer cope and preparation of certain kinds of exercise and breathing exercises are important.'

'Did this bring about the inner heat, or make your body warmer after so much of this training?'

'Occasionally, but it wasn't consistent. Fushi would come out pink! The purpose of the waterfall training is to open the central channel. If you take it on the head or the back of the neck then it is to force the energy to go into the central channel. That means that a lot of work needs to be done before, which I hadn't done at that stage. For me it was more a kind of character building exercise for a long time, and a massage of the muscles.

'We also occasionally did the Goma-Gyo, the fire ritual; for example, when I got a new sword there was a ceremony to purify that, or to re-sanctify a statue it can be purified with a Goma ceremony.'

'And Fushi gave you a set training regime to follow?'

'Fushi gave me a daily practice to do at home and I would spend the weekends training with him. After three or four years I began visiting other schools, it was pretty much full time squeezed around twenty hours of teaching at school. I also did running and a lot of weights, which was a mistake and contributed to my back getting worse.

'The last couple of years in Japan, I had to stop training. The back problem which I had had since the age of fifteen kept getting worse, so I thought if I persisted I would eventually end up in a wheelchair.'

'Was that caused by the training?'

'Yes. I would cope with the problem for eleven months, training thirty hours a week, and then I would go into a phase where I couldn't manage any more and would end up on the floor taking painkillers for weeks. I had a basic postural problem as a child...combined with the unsupervised weight training I did as a schoolboy I had herniated a disc.'

'Were there any periods during this decade in Japan when you felt real change?'

'Yes...but the overriding feeling was always that there was something missing. I was convinced that something wasn't happening that should be happening, which was why the vulnerability in my spine was there.'

Evans Sensei in Yamabushi practice, Japan

'Did your teachers help you with this?'

'Fushi tried all kinds of treatment, and Nakamura Sensei's advice was not to do so much...which I couldn't follow. I knew that something was not connecting. I could not connect into the lower body. I had good legs, good shoulders, it was a patch up job! I was always studying anatomy books and diagrams of the energetic system to see where the muscles were, where exactly the Tanden [Dantien] was, the chakra system and so on. There were many moments when I was training in Japan which were liberating for a few seconds...there had been a couple of times in the Anglican monastery doing Taiji where I felt like I was swimming. All these experiences were momentary. For most of the time I created a body armour to overcome the back problems, yet in those special moments of breakthrough I got a glimpse of that "other thing". Or sometimes Nakamura Sensei would ask me to do a demonstration in front of all the other students, and you know there was a certain amount of resentment, or jealousy…but I just felt so at ease as if I was relaxing in his being. But this happened because of him, it wasn't mine but something I was borrowing.

'I tried lots of things. When my back gave out that last time I decided that the best thing to do would be Yoga. I had stopped sword training and returned to England. I went back to Iyengar Yoga to begin with but found I was drawn more to teachers who paid more attention to breathing than external alignment. Then I met Shandor Remete who was taking a radically different direction, and a couple of years later he began to use the title "Shadow Yoga" to describe his system. I stuck with him. He was Hungarian, his father took him out of Hungary to avoid conscription. Not only was I drawn to his approach to Yoga but his spirit reminded me of Nakamura Sensei.'

'So was he able to look at you and see what was not integrating?'

'Yes, he was working with the breathing and circular arm movements, moving in stances, using the Uddiyana, the hollowing of the abdomen during external retention of the breath, which if done correctly is the most effective way to get the internal pump going. He took me to one side after my first two classes with him and said, "I know you have been studying something, what is it?" When I told him I studied Japanese sword he said that was something he had always wanted to learn. He told me he would fix my back if I would take him to see Nakamura Sensei. He was as good as his word. We went together every year for about ten years. He pulled me back onto the sword path and gave me the necessary help so that I overcame the problem, which had blocked me so long.'

'It is interesting that you had to come out of the intensity and look at it from a completely different perspective, build yourself up and then come back to the original practice.'

'Yes. Although I would describe the process more as one of undoing than building up. Over the last ten years I am beginning to get some kind of consistent touch with that thing I am looking for. There is a long way to go but I am exploring it every day, it is communicating, and that is why I say that the lineage thing is not the most important factor in finding a real path. Yes, you have to be in contact with a real teaching but actually something has to be woken up inside you and then it gets to a certain point where you have to take it further.'

'So the key is the sincerity or purity of purpose to stick with it, the initial impetus that drove us to practise?'

'Yes, but that is not all… I have never had a problem with purity, sincerity, intensity…but those very things were the biggest obstacles. The hardest thing is to see how you are shutting out what you claim to be looking for.'

'And how was it when you picked up the sword again after a few years of the Yoga practice? It must have been different.'

'Yes it was, I almost cut my finger off! I had forgotten some things and I made lots of mistakes. You realise you are coming back to something but as a different person. My main teacher was no longer teaching, he was still there and you could go and be in his presence but beyond that it was up to me.'

'Could you tell us something about Nakamura Sensei and his background?'

'Nakamura Sensei's major insight was seeing that the eight main strokes of calligraphy were like the essential techniques of sword, the seven cuts and the thrust. That was the source of his school, the Nakamura Ryu, taking the simplicity of the Toyama Ryu syllabus, which when it was first introduced around 1920 was based on the straight vertical cut, and replacing that with Kesa Giri [the diagonal cut] and adding the basic cuts without any extra complexity. This is Batto-Do. The cutting of the targets we call Tameshi-Giri. The words Iai and Batto mean almost exactly the same thing, to draw and strike suddenly.

'If you look through the history of the sword schools which emphasised the swift drawing and immediate cutting, some of them called themselves Iai-Jutsu and some Batto-Jutsu. Kenjutsu is the art of the drawn sword.

'I have retained the essence or some of the basic principles of Fushi's system in those five Kata which I teach side by side with Nakamura Ryu, but some parts of Fushi's system are more dynamic and require different kinds of stances. If you look at Nakamura when he was demonstrating in his fifties, he spontaneously assumed different kinds of stance according to need. He had the phenomenal leg strength necessary for that.

'My main contribution is in a systematic Tanren [forging conditioning], thirty-minute Long Form using two short iron rods or the long tanrenbo [two-kilogram octagonal oak suburi bo] to give people a chance of cultivating what Nakamura Sensei had. The real demand of this form is in the gut and the legs. What Nakamura had he was not teaching: how to get that power which he had. You can see from his early picture that he already had lots of gifts naturally, and then he did Sumo and lots of other kinds of training as well as Kendo and Iaido. So I have put together a system which will systematically cultivate that.'

'Where are you trying to lead your students?'

'To give them a chance to reach the Jiyu Jizai state of Nakamura Sensei. The other area of supplementary training is with the Kumitachi – to introduce a kind of sparring which is consistent with the Japanese sword (unlike Kendo), lots of different kinds of sparring. In Nakamura's school we have six of these two-man forms. They are very simple. It's clear to me that this kind of practice alone is not enough – there are some who say that if you do the Kata enough it will come. We use a number of drills to develop sensitivity to the opponent's sword and energy. We have an exercise called Sticky Swords, a bit like pushing hands, where we have two swords up close and do circular movements. Another one is a figure of eight partner drill. These sort of exercises allow you, through the other person, to feel…to tune into the quality of the movement, to know if it is coming from the arms or from the whole body. Then using the Kendo armour we practise the techniques more spontaneously; obviously it is not cutting but you can hit realistic targets. I have had to adapt the armour a bit to use the Kesagiri as there are a couple of points on the neck which are very vulnerable, so we have extra flaps inside to protect that area.'

'I saw that you have a two-man form in which suddenly a third person attacks. Is this something you developed?'

'Yes, basically you have a rhythmic thing going between the two people and then at some point another person comes in randomly, so there is a rhythm but yet something else you have to be able to respond to.'

'What memories for you sum up the essence of your teacher's special quality or skill?'

'Fushi was talking about Nenriki, which is the magic power or mind power, he had a lot of people who came to him as they had illnesses of various kinds. One person had a very bad back, so he gave a Vajra (a small metal object which keeps energy inside) and told him to place it under his bed at night and it would cure him. Fushi asked me what I thought the healing mechanism was. I said that by taking a metal object from the metal altar where he practised, his energy would have accumulated in that object. He said, yes it does, there is that, but that is only one per cent of it. Nine per cent is the fact that the person is very superstitious and it's an object of fear so he wants to get rid of it. Ninety per cent is that it is uncomfortable having that metal thing under your bed at night, so the faster you get better... He was trying to explain to me that although there are these special powers, in the total scheme of things the mechanism by which these things work depends more on simple and straightforward things.

'With Nakamura Sensei, my wife came with me to meet him on a Saturday night where he was teaching in a big gym on the edge of Tokyo... She went in and saw an older man who was changing and putting his Hakama on and she was disappointed because she thought this must be him, clearly a person of quality yet she had expected much more but...then she suddenly felt a warmth in her back and turned around and there he was. The longer she sat next to him the warmer she got. It was a really cold room. She spoke no Japanese and he no English yet she felt completely at home and somehow they managed to chat. Many people felt this with him...'

'Is the tradition of the Yamabushi still alive?'

'There is an old Shingon monk called Yamazaki who wrote a book in the 1980s. He performed the Morning Star retreat and I think he is genuine.'

'The Marathon Monks look very special...'

'Hmm...I was watching some footage of one of them with Fushi once and he was very critical... To me it seemed like a way to use up your life force very fast, a kind of death wish, where you get to the end of it and you can say "I did it! I survived!" I don't see any merit in it at all. If somebody was doing it from an internal power, but...I saw so much of this attitude in Japan, this macho, beat yourself into the ground approach. For example, Fushi got me to teach somebody once; I was in my thirties, and this man was in his forties, a very hard but not very skilful businessman, he had come to a point in his life where he felt he was going to be a loser and he wanted to break out, he would do anything. I murdered this poor unfit man for two days doing stuff it had taken me four years to get used to! He was happy to go along with it. Then we chanted this Mantra all through the night, we had these rocks, when we started to get sleepy we hit ourselves on the head... Fushi came in at the end of the night and said we had managed to get the altar shaking slightly at one point.

'The attraction to that kind of thing is the biggest obstacle. It is looking for a simple way, to avoid going through all the stuff you have to go through. If you get some people to stay in horse stance until they cannot stand any more, some of them will benefit and some will just hurt themselves, physically, energetically, psychologically. If you are stressing yourself or taking yourself to a certain point, then it must be with a knowledge of what you are trying to cultivate with that, and if you know that then you know the point at which you should stop, or maybe just go a little bit further every now and again. If you push it on a regular basis you are going to get one of those Qi illnesses. They talk about it in the Hatha Yoga texts. To do that without nurturing yourself has no merit.'

'How would you sum up your purpose originally and now?'

'In Yoga, which is based on the Samkya philosophy, you have the Purusha and the Prakrti. The observer or soul, and the nature or the matrix. I was taught very early on by the priest in the Anglican monastery that these two parts must freely relate inside oneself. I came across the same principle in Shingon Buddhism (which had a huge influence on martial arts in Japan), in the two mandalas – the Vajra or Wisdom Mandala and the Womb or Matrix Mandala. That is what I have always understood in one way or another. A martial art is as good a medium as anything else for discovering this. This is the meaning of of Jiyu Jizai. The Jiyu is freely acting, your nature freely expressing itself and Jizai freely contemplating it.'

Evans Sensei engaged in partner sword training in Japan

Shihan Tanaka

The Way of Acupuncture

Shihan Eiichi Tanaka

In the sleepy Suffolk town of Bury St Edmunds lives a Japanese gentleman who is steeped in the ancient heritage of his homeland – namely acupuncture, Shiatsu, Buddhism and martial arts. Keeping a very low profile he has nonetheless spent the last twenty years teaching a small but dedicated group of students the arts of Hakko Ryu Jujitsu and Iaido (way of drawing and cutting with the Katana or sword), as well as treating thousands of patients using the traditional healing arts which he learned from his teacher, a Buddhist monk. I first sought him out for treatment for an ailment, and found him to have a remarkable gift for healing and a deep knowledge of both ancient and modern medical systems. His hands are highly intuitive, directly touching the problematic points and meridians after a quick visual appraisal, and his fingers – strengthened through decades of martial and sword training – have that effortless strength which proves so useful in massaging the acupressure points.

Shihan Eiichi Tanaka (Shihan is a term meaning someone who has mastered a complete system of martial art) is a fine example of a man whose training in the martial, healing and meditative Ways have become a harmonious whole. As a youth he began studying with Master Deguchi of Shitennoji Temple in Osaka, Japan, a monk of the Tendai branch of Buddhism and a renowned healer and Jujitsu expert. He later also studied with Mr Kondo, an expert in the field of meridian balancing treatment in Japan, and a man who has designed various interesting machines used to measure and transmit the flow of energy in the meridians. Now in his mid-fifties and still very close to Master Deguchi, Shihan Tanaka is a down to earth, humorous and honest man, and also very generous – he has never charged for martial arts training and when he accepted me as his student for acupuncture and Shiatsu he refused any payment. Although he had never taught his healing art as a system before, I found his teaching to be that easily understood blend of precise technical detail, reference to real-life experience, and hands on practice which makes for a holistic learning experience. The following is an interview with a treasure from the East who keeps very much in the shadows, Shihan Eiichi Tanaka.

'Shihan, please tell us how you became involved in martial arts?'

'I began practising Judo at seven years old, because my three brothers were doing it. Three days a week I would go to the local police station and train there. From ten to thirteen years old I loved sport, running ten miles in the morning and evening. But then one day I stopped, feeling I didn't need it any more. From fifteen to seventeen years old I was always missing school, gambling, fighting and being naughty. So my mother told me to go and study Hakko Ryu martial arts with Mr Deguchi, a monk at the Shittenoji Temple. He was a very soft and frank person, talking freely and naturally. So I calmed down and stopped fighting. It was easier to follow him, because to keep fighting in the street was dangerous and tiring, and slowly my thinking began to change. For martial arts study, to relax and concentrate one's centre of gravity is a very difficult work. If you are constantly aware of your centre of gravity you will not be so tense. After two or three years my teacher started teaching me Iaido along with the Jujitsu. A few years later he sent me to another Iaido master to go further with the sword, and by then I was finding it easier to focus on Tanden [Dantien, centre] and to calm down.

'Traditionally in Japan arts such as Kenjutsu and Jujitsu are considered a way of life rather than just fighting skills. If a person's mind is not straight he will want to fight, but those people don't want to study martial arts. So my teaching is to help people change their thinking, their way. For example, in some places now the army are killing people; we think it is alright, but if we do that in an English street then it's not alright! Is that correct? Anyway, to damage people is not alright. Martial arts can damage people, so even self-defence is not alright. If we see this, we can calm down and change our mind from violence to calmness. Yes, martial arts are a way of fighting! But...it uses a different way of thinking, so you can be relaxed.'

'How did training with your teacher change you?'

'My teacher was a very skilful fighter, but through training with him you calmed down. Normally people will grab a hand with aggression, for example, but with him he would just grab with no emotion. Normally if you fight you will fear, try to escape, but he was very free, no emotion...and I wanted to be like that! He is a monk and did meditation every day and found something through that. I was not a monk but I wanted that principle, that peace. When I was twenty-three years old I attained Shihan rank in Hakko Ryu, but the grade meant nothing to me. My teacher asked me if I understood what it meant, and I said yes. He told me that it was just paper, for money, but not my heart.

'This was a period of change for me. I understood that our life, your life, my life…the important point is how to help others. My teacher said that if you work in a company and are not promoted to a good division, then it is a chance to make the bad division good! He meant there is always a chance to change your life. Worry about things is nonsense! You must be able to think and sort out the problem. After training we would go and drink and talk about life. Even now he will call me from Japan and talk. This closeness with him slowly changed my life.'

'And you learned the healing arts from him?'

'Yes. My teacher is also an acupuncturist and taught me this skill. As a monk he never took money for treatment. He treated people who had had a stroke; after two or three months they would walk and the one-side paralysis was cured. I was very young and liked martial arts but my teacher told me to come every day to see him after work. The temple was a very big place with a hundred monks, and inside was my teacher's temple. It was connected to Tendai Buddhism. He gave me a book to read, then meditation, then he would do Shiatsu and acupuncture and I would observe. Every Sunday I would go to his private meeting with a group who included three Tokyo University professors, five directors of very large companies and a few students like me. They talked with each other very frankly like friends, not lecturing. We would discuss Buddhism and life problems for five or six hours. It was not martial arts but life.

'By then it was a long time since I had stopped fighting; it didn't make sense any more. My teacher came to England to make several Japanese gardens and I went with him and helped him. We discussed that maybe it was a good job, but maybe better was to help people by treating them. It could be a nice job! So I decided to work as an acupuncturist. I stayed in England after my teacher returned to Japan, and put my sons through an education here. I set up as a Shiatsu and acupuncture therapist.'

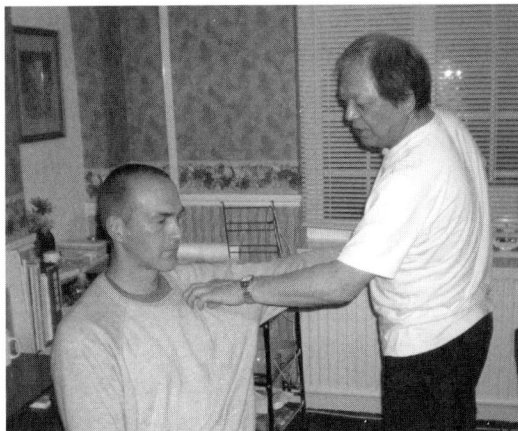

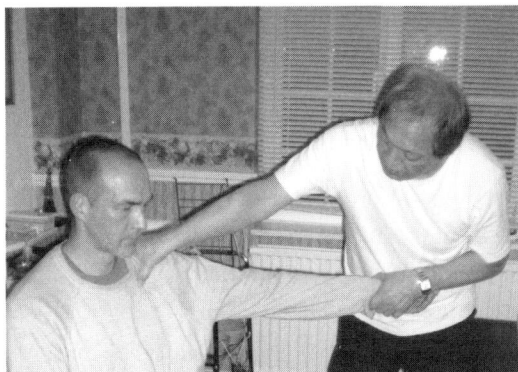

Shihan Tanaka applies treatment using acupressure massage

'Can you discuss the role of intuition in your healing? You seem to be able to instantly touch where the blocked points are just from seeing someone. How do you do this?'

'Maybe I have some sense of feeling about the person's problem, some intuition. This is a recent change, just few years, that I look and can just know what is wrong. Oh, this is hard to explain, it is the result of everything! You must have technical knowledge, like knowing exactly the flow of energy through the meridians, which direction, which lines are paired and so on. But this is just the beginning, then you must be able to have experience so that you just know the problem, which meridian line has traffic jam, how to treat best way... When I ask the patient questions I can make a basic diagnosis, when I look I can see how they stand, where is their weight, their spine and hip position; when I touch I can feel and confirm everything. We say that many diseases are caused by hormone imbalance, even though Western doctors won't agree to this. They can also be caused by injury, or blood problems, anyway we can treat many problems, if soon enough after the injury we can treat this, not a big problem, if within three years we can treat many problems.

'Sometimes for a back problem we do one treatment and it's cured, but sometimes for serious conditions we need many, many treatments. Actually what we do is not like modern Shiatsu, it's a form of acupuncture and we often use tiny pins, less than a millimetre in size. They only go into skin and don't puncture the body. If you go into the body there is a risk, so this is better. Silver is better than gold, and the metal will draw out the negative ion electricity which has collected in the damage area and causing problem, so helping stop the "traffic jam" of energy in the meridian line.

'Our history is different to the modern Shiatsu schools in the West and even many in Japan. This Way came from China long ago, and in fact a lot of the knowledge was lost in China during the Cultural Revolution and was taken back there by Japanese experts. After studying with my teacher I then studied with Mr Kondo; he had developed a different kind of pin and also a machine which can transmit something like Qi. Actually, from all of my research, and exchanging with many other therapists in Japan, I slowly developed my own understanding and found ways which work even better. In England Shiatsu is not the same as Japan; really, I have not met any here who can treat the Kyosho [empty condition] directly. Even in Japan there are only a few rare therapists with excellent skill. The chiropractors there are really excellent! They treat all the bones, all the way from the skull to the toes, not only the spine like in this country.'

'I see…now, how about your experience teaching martial arts over here?'

'I have found it very difficult to teach Jujitsu here. The technique is easy to understand, but it is very difficult for students to be able to relax and focus on Tanden [Dantien]. Only last week they asked me,

"Why are you so relaxed, how can you do that?" But this is not a one day job! It is a very difficult work. Someone grabs you, why do you tense? Feel! Don't just think of the place being grabbed, feel his whole body and your centre. A good fighter will always be aware of the whole body, the whole situation. This is important. Students here understand in the head but not the body. I told them that meditation was very good for them, even better than martial arts! For martial arts it is easy to feel change, the tension and relaxation. Concentrate on Tanden, breathing will help. Don't think one point of "me", just have eyes half closed, whole vision, good breathing… then you will naturally calm down and not be tense.

'If someone really attacks me I don't think to do anything. Punch me. Do anything. I am just feeling. To damage others is a bad thing. My martial arts are a study for life, for change, not for fighting. The meaning is – don't fight! There is a kind of method, like Aiki or Kiai, we also have breathing exercise for health… Maybe six months ago I started to have some deep change. For example, my wife has passed through serious illness, so I consider deeply how I can help, using wisdom not emotion to help. When I treated my wife from Parkinson's Disease and she regained health, the Western doctors didn't want to know how we had done it! All they wanted was to give her more drugs. But those drugs made her sicker and then I had to begin again, now I must treat her three or four times a day. So I don't know how long, maybe some years ago, I began really feeling this, that martial arts are a way to deal with life, not just fighting.'

'Shihan, what is the connection between healing and martial art?'

'When you learn acupuncture and Shiatsu you become very sensitive, feeling, receiving. Martial art is all about projecting or explosive power. From study of healing you will change your state, and be able to move on to the next level of your martial arts. This is important!

'I spent many years with my teacher. His hands were very soft, and he could take someone down without any pain. His Kenjutsu, his Iaido, was very beautiful, like his Kata. A different feeling. His character, his Way, very clear, maybe not so technically perfect form of Iaido, even though he is very high grade, but for me it had a different kind of spirit to others. Very soft. His technique just made you fall down by softness, the feeling when he touched you was very different from other teachers. Others had maybe good technique but still normal but he had…ah, it's difficult to explain!'

'We all must die. How do you view death and dying?'

'Everyone dies, you, me, maybe one hour later we don't know. But other people think it's bad if you are dying. No, that is not important, better to think how to live in good way. If my son or wife dies before me, I have to study why, make it a lesson for me to reflect on life. I told you, my teacher taught me that even though we will die, any time, but when others die around us it can make us improve our life. Not just cry with sadness, that is time lost, just worry, cannot think how to solve the problem....nonsense.

'A hundred years ago in Japan the men who did Kenjutsu, they had no thought about their life, no concern about death. Only practise, only improve skill. When they fight one wins but then one dies. This was their way. Now we cannot do it like that! But… still I have this feeling about life and death. I heard all about heaven and hell but I don't know I will go there! But I can make myself better now, so my feeling is the same, everyone will die so no need to worry. Just be the best therapist I can be, that is my thought every day. That is why martial art is a part of my life, but every day I think about these things, about life and change. Everyone will teach me by their dying, or my dying – the final teaching.'

The Martial
Traditions of India
and South East Asia

Steve Benitez

The Path of the Satria Warrior

Silat Master Steve Benitez

The martial arts of Indonesia and Malaysia, comprising several thousand different styles and systems, are collectively known as Pentjak Silat. Pentjak refers to 'skilful, artistic body movement' and Silat to 'self-defence ability'. These arts are still quite rare in the West, although their reputation for producing lightning speed and magical fighting powers has ensured that a small number of dedicated practitioners have made the long journey to seek masters who are willing to share knowledge. One such man is Steve Benitez. Born in London to Spanish parents, he began training as a small boy to try and learn how to fight against the bullies who roamed the notorious housing estate where he lived. His first main teacher was Sifu Gerry Tan of the Kuntao Mantis system, and then after some years he travelled to Holland and met Guru Ma Prem who totally revolutionised his perception of the fighting arts. A mystic and healer as well as an expert of old style Pentjak Silat, Ma taught Steve a circular, internal fighting method as well as leading him deep into the path of esoteric knowledge. (For detailed accounts of this training, and my meeting with Guru Ma, see Kozma 2003.)

My training and friendship with Steve began twenty years ago; he taught me his Silat Hasilkan Penuh (an old system of Pentjak Silat) and in more recent years the concepts and methods of a very rare and ancient Buddhist martial art passed down from monk to monk in the temples of South East Asia. Since the Buddhist Shaolin art of Luohan Quan was the first system I learned as a child it has been fascinating to see the similarities between the two methods, and it confirmed my theory that in old times monks from all over Asia – even those from different branches of Buddhism – would share knowledge of martial and healing arts along with meditative practices and philosophy.

Many students have reported strange things happening when training with Steve Benitez, and he certainly does have unusual skills which are sometimes very hard to explain to people who were not present. Once, for example, training in my front room, he was trying to teach the 'cutting hand' of Silat, where the hand cuts like a blade. Doing the motion with a sudden release of power, the big glass window which was some ten feet away and opposite him cracked cleanly down the middle at exactly the area where his hand had pointed. We were all pretty shocked, and Steve was very apologetic!

Despite being a lineage holder in Pentjak Silat and the inheritor of his Guru's complete system, Steve still has a thirst for knowledge. On a recent visit to London I took him to meet the Thai monk who I study with at the Buddhapadipa Temple, the very place where I had begun practice thirty years before with an old meditation master from Thailand. In reply to Steve's questions about practice the monk gave an hour-long discourse of startling clarity and wisdom, a little of which I can still recall exactly word for word.

'Practice can only be *now*! There is no other place or time to practise, only here and now. There is only one practice that Buddha taught for understanding Enlightenment, and that is to be aware of everything we think, feel, say and do in the moment. That is all! No need to be monk, no need even to be Buddhist…anyone can do this!'

Afterwards we were both very quiet, something about the monk's presence affecting us as much as his words. I knew from Steve's face it was what he had needed to hear, why he had come to this place where stillness and attention were prized above any material treasures. The last couple of years had seen his once highly successful martial arts school be split apart by the actions of friends and students he had once trusted. Mistakes had been made on all sides, but the pain of betrayal and misplaced trust had cloaked Steve for some time. I knew that having been placed in the role of spiritual guide at a very young age, he had had to learn the inevitable bitter lessons which such a thing brings with it.

As he shared some more of the ancient Buddhist martial art with me in the shade of the temple, I saw for the first time a lightness return to his face. Three weeks later when we met again it really looked like he had passed through the darkness, telling me excitedly of a revelation which had led to a letting go of all the negativity associated with what had happened. His face had its old glow back, which no doubt pleased the handful of loved ones and close students who had stayed by him as much as it did me. We discussed the value of forgiveness and the practicality of Lord Buddha's teachings on meditation and Vedic science, and then he told me about the beauty of the island of Kefalonia where he had recently opened a new retreat centre. His vision was of a centre where students could come from all over the world to learn the ancient ways of the Satria, the name given to warriors of ancient India and South East Asia. Having established a reputation for superlative skills in Pentjak Silat, he had now begun teaching under the banner of Satria Fighting Arts to honour the spirit of those ancient mystical warriors. At the same time he had completed two action films in Indonesia and was preparing for the epic *Dark Eden* to be produced, a film which will describe in fictionalised terms his life and training with Guru Ma. More important even than this, though, was his love for his family and close students, something which has sustained him through the trials which all must face at some point. He has three beautiful and highly gifted children with his lovely wife Laarni, whose own story in the arts we describe in the following chapter.

Technically the Satria Fighting Arts syllabus is divided into nine clear stages:

1. Ground fighting. Covers all aspects of fighting on the ground. This includes the five Ground arts of Kucing (cat), Harimau (tiger), Buaya (crocodile), Kura Kura (turtle) and the Ular (snake) as well as other non-Silat indigenous methods. These are taught in their entirety with the intention of training the body to be comfortable on the ground, in any position, and are not meant to be taught with rigid confines.

2. Upright basics. Covers all of the basic stances, fighting positions, basic blocks and strikes as well as the six basic footwork patterns or Langkah.

3. Sparring. This basic sparring will be the natural progression of fusing the first two elements – ground fighting and upright basics. This sparring is aimed to teach the student how to fight under pressure in a one-on-one situation.

4. Grappling/wrestling. This will include much of the Gerak-Gerik aspects of the Satria Fighting Arts, which means 'follow-follow' and refers to skills of yielding which produce tremendous sensitivity. This aspect of the syllabus focuses much on closing in, close range fighting and the wrestling aspects of Benjang Gulat (Sundanese wrestling) which has a combination of thirty conditioning exercises and twenty-four main techniques.

5. Advance multiple attackers sparring. By the time students begin this aspect of training they should have not only a good understanding and proficiency in the circular footwork, but also a deep understanding of how to apply the 'Web' or Sarang Laban Laban – this is the ability to draw opponents in, feint and decoy.

6. Kembangan and dances. From this point on the training can be said to become more advanced. The Kembangan (Flower Dance) is the side to the Satria Fighting Arts that brings alive and fuses all of the movement learned within the system.

7. Weaponry. Weapons form a large part of the syllabus, with both hard and soft weapons being used and integrated within the system. These include the Tongkat Pangjang (six-foot [183 cm] bamboo pole), Pisau Belati (straight knife), Krambik (curved, claw-shaped blade worn around knuckles) and the curved wavy bladed weapon called the Keris.

8. Therapies. If one has the knowledge to maim or destroy, then it's only right to have the knowledge to be able to heal and build up. This is a very important part of the philosophy of the Satria Fighting Arts.

9. Esoteric knowledge. There exist realms within Satria Fighting Arts that transcend the mere physical and it is this aspect of training that can really put the 'icing' on the cake. This of course is conditional on all of the other parts of the curriculum being truly understood and regularly practised.

As can be seen from the above, the syllabus is very comprehensive and will not only equip students to become competent in protecting themselves, but also, importantly, offer them many aspects of training that will serve to enhance all areas of their lives.

In the following interview Steve shares some of his experiences in the world of South East Asian martial arts, and stories about the teachers who have helped to shape him.

'Steve, what is the big change in your perspective and your martial practice and teaching from the interview twelve years ago?' (At that time Steve was teaching a Silat system named Hasilkan Penuh, which has since passed through various stages of evolution. He has spent much of the time since living in South East Asia and so many of his practices and teaching methods have changed due to an increased understanding of the spiritual and martial heritage of that region.)

'Since my last interview twelve years ago, martial arts have evolved tremendously. With the birth of mixed martial arts and the rise of Brazilian Jujitsu, students nowadays expect or demand that everything you teach is to be compared with those martial arts, meaning that a lot of people are looking for a "reality" based martial arts. However, what is considered reality fighting in Europe may not be reality in South East Asia, where half of my life has been spent.

'South East Asia is a "weapons" orientated culture, where Goloks and knives are still a part of everyday life. If a fight broke out in a country in South East Asia it would automatically revert to fighting with weapons and that's why a lot of my training and practice has been with this in mind, which is why I emphasis "consciousness" in martial arts a lot. What I mean by that is that the consciousness in which you are in at the time you need to defend yourself will determine what comes out of you. My practice has been a way of "Yoga" for me, a way to expand my consciousness, awareness and sensitivity to the All, to the universal consciousness rather than the "me, myself and I" concept. This focus therefore changes everything in the way I move and in the way I use the Kebangan, which is the "Flower Dance", as well as when I train with weapons or just empty-handed. Consciousness in everything you do, especially in life or death situations, is something that Guru Ma had spoken to me about nearly twenty years ago. She used to say that in all battles, the consciousness that you're in will determine life or death and that humans have a choice always. The choice to be consciously aware of the "All", or the "Our" or if you drop into the "I", and therefore being in the very "me, myself and I" wrapped in fear, most often results in disaster. You can summarise what I'm talking about as "corporate" consciousness versus "individual" consciousness. The great thing is that quantum physics has been able to prove, whether we like this or not, that every living being is connected to the All, and this has been the main change or evolution, if you want to call it that. From a purely "movement" perspective, my practice [Satria Fighting Arts] has over the years become even more fluid and circular as I come out of traditional and cultural holds or boundaries. I have found it to become more beautiful and far more effective which moves me onto my next point.

'Readers of the first *Esoteric Warriors* edition [Kozma 2010] would have known my practice as "Hasilkan Penuh", a name given to me by Guru Ma. It then evolved into Wali Songo Silat, the name of Guru Ma's lineage until, finally, my practice, evolved out of years of training, travelling and researching all the ancient warrior arts of South East Asia, became Satria Fighting Arts. Satria means warrior. The reason Guru Ma and I decided to call it "Satria" is because it is outside of title, tradition, lineage, culture, limitations and boundaries and offers a level of freedom to express itself freely in *all* the warrior arts with no limitations or expectations, but rather a completely free expression of conscious and continuous movements in motion and relaxation.'

'Please recount a few stories about meeting and trainings with the Indonesian masters which sum up what you feel is the essence of Silat.'

'With my many travels throughout South East Asia, I have had the privilege of meeting and training with some real-life warriors, and I have shared a lot of these experiences with you over the years. The late Pendekar Jumhi – who passed on in 2008 – of the village of Mahmud in West Java, with whom I trained with in the year 2006 while enduring a long fast and completing his family system, told me of a real-life experience he had. During the Japanese occupation, he along with six others in his village was taken captive and brought to a line-up to be shot. I recall him telling me the story with tears in his eyes, as one by one, the captives were shot at gunpoint and he was the last in line. He came to a point within himself of complete surrender to death as he yielded and accepted that it was his time to die. At that moment, he experienced a shift in his consciousness whereby he just knew it wasn't his time or his hour. When the

Japanese soldiers got to him eventually, they pointed the gun at him and tried pulling the trigger but the gun would not work and so they released him. This to me was another confirmation of what I had known Silat to be. Rather than just a flow of techniques or a set of movements, which all martial arts have all over the world, in times like this it becomes a state of consciousness that you look for inside yourself.

Steve Benitez in an open posture

'Another story which I'd like to share is one of Pak Rusli, from a west Sumatran village called Garegeh, just outside of Bukittinggi. He showed me a story clipping on the national newspaper which told of a huge disaster at the main bus station in Jakarta several years before. The disaster resulted in many deaths, with others severely injured or maimed, as a moving train and coach collided. What Pak Rusli told me, and again confirmed by all his family members, was that as he sat in the coach with mere seconds before the collision, he slipped into a pre-cognitive awareness state, knew the collision would take place and at that moment recited a prayer and called upon God as he slipped into a very relaxed consciousness. He said he saw the collision and everything that happened in slow motion.

He miraculously came out of the coach receiving only a scratch in his hand and a bump in his head while those around him had either died, were severely injured or maimed. The Indonesians believe that this state of consciousness is your protection always.

'In all my time of training with teachers, no one had more stories to share than Guru Ma. Most of her life was dedicated to this very thing. She was there to witness much of the suffering that her family and her people had to endure during the Second World War under the Japanese occupation of her own native land, Indonesia, before embarking on a long boat journey to Holland with her eldest son who was still a babe in her arms at the time. Her stories of all her fights, I consider both tragic and yet remarkable as this woman warrior fought for her own life and her people. She is someone who comes out of the set rules when it comes to fighting and she often used to remind me that it is all about your state of consciousness when it comes down to real self-defence and that the more one yields to its centre, its true source, its life, the more an automatic "response" and not "reaction" would manifest. She often taught that a reaction is out of the emotions of "fear" whilst a response is what is required in the moment. And that only with a heightened state of consciousness or awareness can you really perform the action that is required at that precise moment. Mothers are naturally very good at this when it comes to defending their children. When they sense danger, they automatically kick into another gear and in that moment, no thought is given to what they can or cannot do. We hear stories of mothers who pull car doors off their hinges after a crash in order to get their children out. Laarni has her own story to tell but I will let her share it with you later.

'One recent story which Guru Ma shared with me and Samantha, a close friend of mine, during a recent visit at her home in Rotterdam, was something that happened in the 1970s. Guru Ma was with her two young sons at a grocery store in Holland when the shopkeeper was held by a robber with a sharp blade to his neck. Guru Ma went into a deep trance state and managed to disarm the guy and defused the whole situation by calming everyone down, including the shopkeeper and the robber to the point that the robber even asked to become one of her students.'

Guru Ma Prem, the main teacher of Steve Benitez

'Since Guru Ma was such a huge influence in your life, please tell us some history of hers and how she teaches.'

'Guru Ma came from the island of West Java in Indonesia. She fled by boat, as most of the Javanese fled to Holland after the invasion and occupation of the Japanese regime. She came from the lineage of the Wali Songos, trained in her family style Silat from a very young age, so that, by the age of nine, she was already teaching some of her friends. She went into Samadi [a deep state of meditation] for three years where she had met her teacher, Master Mineto, an Egyptian Essene master. He opened up the esoteric teachings to her, which is why she named her school in Holland, the Sphinx Esoteric University. She has a deep connection and love for Nature and she often says that Nature is one of our greatest teachers. Many of her lectures are drawn and inspired by it and observation of Nature is a very important aspect in her teaching.

'Guru Ma knows the fighting arts for real, not the modern day "ring" arts, but real battlefield style fighting, which is why she teaches the fighting from a very real perspective and not out of forms, techniques or even a set of rules and movements. She teaches that it is best for a student to find his or her most natural, spontaneous and responsive flow of movements through one harmonious dance which we call the "Kembangan" [Flower Dance]. Within this dance, every aspect of fighting – from ground to upright, one-on-one to

multiple attackers, locks, chokes, throws, take-downs, evasion
techniques and strikes – can all be performed within the dance. It
also teaches you about your environment, your breath and your
consciousness of it; it trains your pre-cognitive awareness through
an exercises we call "listening to the wind"; helps to connect you
with Nature and the animal kingdom; and can be performed for
healing or to receive guidance on herbs and medicine. The holistic
side of our system also encompasses a number of therapies that
cover massage, cloth therapy, pressure points and trance training
called Alpha training. The Satria Fighting Arts also has its own
Yoga system known as Satria Yoga; all these subjects summarise
her complete teachings and all are very esoteric.'

Steve Benitez and his top student Alvin Guinanao

'You are a family man, Steve; please tell us how the arts have
impacted the lives of your wife and children, and students, and
share something of your philosophy of life for those struggling to
merge spiritual life and everyday life.'

'Well…many wouldn't really understand my journey fully
until they have walked my path. My wife Laarni and my children
have all been there along the way. Like most people, we have had
our smooth runs and bumpy ones too, but generally, having my
family always by my side has been a tremendous strength to me.
I've always tried to create a line in my marriage and in the way we

raise our kids that would allow us to spend lots of time together. So working together for me seemed always the best way to do just that. The world's system does exactly the opposite. It causes husbands, wives and children to be separate from each other for most parts of the day, with schooling, work and sometimes overtime at work for father, mothers or even both, just to make ends meet. I don't agree that this is the way and certainly not what a family was intended to be, and then at the end of it, your children leave you, may have no inheritance, and then you die. What a sad way to live, in fact, it is not even living! So when I got married to Laarni fourteen years ago, we decided we would always work together. That way we could spend lots of time and do many things together. So we did. The fruit of our decision is that we now get to do the things we both love to do, which is to teach the Satria Fighting Arts as well as our ventures in acting and film-making, which is something we both very much enjoy doing.

'I do many things with my family, and our children are probably some of the most travelled children around. Lots of people, including extended family, have often judged or scrutinised our decisions in many ways, but just looking how my children are all flourishing within themselves and in their own personal expressions, their creativity, their educational and social skills, has given me assurance that we've made the right decisions along the way. Our children are all naturally very creative and I've never tried to push them or mould them into something or someone that "I" want them to be or to become. I believe in letting children be who they were designed and created to be. Their greatest expression in life, their greatest works, their challenges, their success and all the things that make them unique, are already all in them. So why should I interfere?

'I think the biggest problem in our society is that children are educated in the wrong way. They are taught to get things from the outside and that there is supposed to be an order to go in life. They are taught a system and an education that teaches them that you need to go to school to get to university, and you need a degree to get a good job, and then you need to get a mortgage before you get married, then you need to have children by a certain time, and the list of programming goes on. And that's the problem in society.

There is too much programming going on. But that is for another conversation. So, going back to my family, I do feel that a huge part of my success with my students has also been through them. I know that many people watch and observe us, up close and from a distance, but to be honest with you, that really isn't and never has been my focus. I am just too busy being a dad to my kids, and a husband to my wife and love spending time with them so I bring them into everything I do with each opportunity I get.

In this series of pictures Steve Benitez demonstrates slipping the attack, elbowing downwards to the leg and taking the enemy to the ground

'Over the years of being in the public eye, there is one thing that I wish I had taken heed of from Guru Ma much earlier on though… and that is not to be too open with everyone. I am, by nature, a very open person but being too open can also bring pain. Guru Ma was always emphasising the importance of not sharing some of her "secret teachings" with students and certain people. I often struggled with this concept, because, fundamentally, I always thought that they would benefit the multitude. But, man, have I been wrong! And I learned the hard way. I was too trusting of everyone. Opened my heart to so many people, even those very close to me, but as Guru Ma had warned me on several occasions, it was inevitable that I would, at some point, learn my lesson the hard way. Life has its own ways of teaching us all a lesson, and that to me is just as spiritual as anything. The biggest thing I have learned in recent years is that you cannot share all your precious pearls with everyone and that, sometimes, what people say they want is often mixed with something else. I spent so much painstaking time to dig into myself, only to find that I really am too open, and that open comes with a price. I have always worn my heart on my sleeve and what you see is what you get. I was very trusting of everyone but now I am a lot wiser and more reserved as to whom I share certain things with. Life's events taught me about myself as well as the condition of humanity. It's also revealed to me the many truths in the teachings that Guru Ma has taught me over the years, which I have also learned to appreciate even more.'

'And so those teachings you now teach under the banner Satria Fighting Arts…what do you know about the Satria warriors of old?'

'Actually, the ancient people of Java – about three thousand years ago – had a very rich and deep culture which had been influenced by Vedic teachings. They followed a very old way of life called Kejawan, everything being devoted to God whom they called Gusti. Kejawan is really a spiritual way of life. The warriors during those times followed very strict traditions and moral behaviour. They performed many magical rituals which brought protection to the people, and these included ritual dances and what Guru Ma calls Shadow Fighting – this is all the practices of meditation, fasting, praying, going into seclusion in Nature and communicating with the invisible world and being in harmony with Nature and the elements. The warriors were walking a very noble path.

'In my school this is what I want to teach, not how to fight, but how to dance so that they can understand the spiritual path.'

Laarni Benitez

The Way of the Flower Dance

Laarni Benitez performs the Flower Dance

Laarni Benitez was born into a Filipino family and raised in England, marrying the renowned Pendekar Steve Benitez in 1996 and raising their three children – Sarah, Nathaniel and Daniel. Pentjak Silat is an ideal art for women, emphasising a fluid grace and hiding lethal combat efficiency inside beautiful dance, and beneath Laarni's gentleness and soft-spoken nature is a skill born of fourteen years of training. She has become especially adept at the system known as Satria Yoga, which contains the conditioning and yogic methods so crucial in the training of the Satria Fighting Arts system which is based on traditional Silat. As a close friend for many years I have watched her cope with the demanding role of being mother, wife and teacher whilst frequently flying around the world with her somewhat nomadic husband, always staying patient and centred and keeping true to her principles even through the darkest of times. A very kind and intelligent lady, as well as a gifted practitioner and teacher, in the following interview Laarni shares some of her experiences along the path of the Satria.

'Laarni, please tell us of your first introduction to martial arts; were you aware of Filipino traditions as you grew up? And what are your first memories of training with Steve?'

'Actually, the only traditions I learned from my culture were traditional and religious ones! None had to do with any martial arts. But my dad had learned some Filipino martial arts when he was still a young man. He didn't go into it deeply but what he did learn was enough to knock a guy out cold in self-defence. At the time, he thought he killed the guy so that he got scared when the police turned up for questioning. You can imagine the immense relief of my dad when the guy who was knocked out came back onto his feet...haha.

'But for me, my first introduction to martial arts was through the film *The Karate Kid*. After watching that film, I wanted to learn Karate. Of course, I also fell in love with Ralph Macchio who played lead role in the film. So from that moment on, I was seriously inspired to go to a few local Karate classes to watch, with the intention of joining. A friend of mine recommended me to go watch a class that she attended down at a local church hall. And so I went but was hugely disappointed and put off when I watched them trying to break bricks and just making some seriously loud noises in the process. I remember thinking to myself, "No, this isn't for me!" It was not until I got married to Steve that I learned martial arts. He was wonderful because he introduced the soft side of the art to me, the "Salutation" through the Kembangan, and the principles he would teach were often that of "softness can break any hardness". I loved it and my love and desire to learn grew even more. Steve is a wonderful teacher, very patient and very articulate in the way he teaches and speaks, and my training in the early days was more based on form with emphasis on balance, posture and alignment. Within a couple of months, I got pregnant and so my training became more internal and softer. Steve taught me deeper levels of relaxation within my Kembangan during this time, and my whole pregnancy, even the birth, was like a breeze. It was just so lovely to practise such a beautiful dance art without the pressure of combat. Those were my first memories of training with Steve in the martial arts and the introduction into it was almost as natural as life.'

'Please can you relate a few key experiences in your learning of Silat?'

'One thing does stand out. It started off with Steve and I having a one-to-one light grappling session. He told me that he wanted to toughen me up a little. I had no problems with that. Up until this point, I had not really taken my combative training seriously. Partly because, having had three children, I didn't have much time to focus and concentrate on myself and my training, but also because there was always a secret part of me that was afraid of confrontation and pain. As our grappling session got on, so did the pressure. As the pressure increased, I found myself being completely imbalanced, tossed to and fro, choked out several times and just had absolutely no grounding, not against Steve anyway. I felt the humiliation as my pride got hit and feeling sorry for myself, I cried! I laugh as I look back on it now as I realise the value of that lesson. I saw my ego rise and fall, and I also saw my weaknesses which needed strengthening. My idea of the art changed from that moment on. I hit a brick wall and I knew that emotionally, mentally, as well as physically, I had a lot of work to do if I wanted to continue in my training. That was a turning point in my learning of the Satria Fighting Arts.

'However, a more recent event took place that really opened me up to the deeper teachings of the Satrias and which has also changed my perception of life. I had received so much teaching and done a lot of training in the more inner aspects of the art, and what next took place could not have prepared me more. My family had moved out to Kefalonia in Greece as a door opened for us to set up a retreat centre there. Within about a month, Steve had to leave again for a three-week trip away. When the kids were saying goodbye to him, we both noticed our youngest son, Daniel, gave him the most heartfelt hug and cried so much as he was saying goodbye to him. We thought it was odd because Steve had gone on many trips before, some even of longer duration, and yet Daniel's hug and cry seemed to mean so much more, like he wasn't going to see his dad for a very long time. It was quite painful for Steve to leave after that and on the plane he was very quiet and contemplative as he felt an attachment to Daniel that he needed to let go of.

'About two weeks later, on 18 October 2009, I took my kids down to the beach as they wanted to play on their pool air mat. I noticed a small current so I warned them several times to stay on the beach and not to get into the water beyond knee deep. My boys were nine and eleven years old, and they were confident swimmers, or so I thought. I sat on a rock and kept my eyes on them as they were only a few feet away from me. I felt very cautious and did not feel too settled inside. My daughter and little niece were also there but were building a sand castle. Everything seemed calm and the boys were having fun playing against the waves. Within about a quarter of an hour, a thought came to me, "What if one of the boys got caught in an undercurrent and got swept into the sea, what would I do?"

'Now, whether consciously or subconsciously, I remember thinking to take my trainers off first, then my jacket and then go into the water to save them, you know the kind of things that go through your head…the what if's… Now I consider myself an OK swimmer when it comes to the swimming pool, but swimming in the sea was something I was not that good at, especially if I had no footing.

'Within a couple of minutes of that thought, I saw my two boys were thrown off the float over the waves. My older boy explained to me later that he actually jumped off as he saw his younger and much smaller brother being thrown off the float and being carried past the waves by an undercurrent which was taking him further and further out to sea. I literally saw all of this in slow motion and I could also feel myself almost moving in slow motion as I got up from the rock and did what I had previously thought I would do if such a thing did happen. I could hear my heart beat from the inside of me, and my breath had slowed down as I ran (but felt like slow motion walking) into the water, eyes transfixed on my little boy, not blinking once. It was like I got onto another zone. I called and called his name to *"Come!"* That was all I could say. I could see fear in my older boy's eyes as he looked at me, wanting to try and swim to his brother or to listen to me as I commanded him to go save himself. Somehow I knew that if he had gone to swim for him, I would be left trying to save them both, which I just knew would be a no win situation. He listened to me and fortunately had enough energy to get back to shore. But for me, all I could fix my eyes on was my little Daniel. Wave after wave came and one toppled me over, causing me to flip upside down without any control (almost reminding me of the grappling session I had with Steve many years prior). I swallowed so much salty water that I just knew that Daniel would have suffered even more. I was afraid that the strength of the waves would be too much for him and he would drown. The sea seemed so huge and I felt insignificant and powerless against it. I had underestimated its strength and its vastness.

'I got back to my feet again as quickly as I could and I inched more and more into the sea but the waves kept resisting me. I could see Daniel's head bobbing up and down in the water in the distance, as wave after wave would bring him down. With my eyes, my heart, my everything still glued on Daniel, who was about fifteen metres [50 feet] away from me (yet against the vastness and strength of the sea felt like a mile), with everything I had inside of me, I let out what I can only describe in words as a *roar!* I kept my connection with Daniel and I could feel him close to me but it was a fine line. I was not prepared to let my son go and I also knew that if I took one more step, I would have lost my footing and we both possibly could have drowned. With so many thoughts going through me, I remembered my other two children who also needed me. But deep inside of me, I knew it was not Daniel's time or mine, and yet fear tried to consume me at that moment when I envisioned before me a funeral, my whole family being there and crying, and somehow I knew that if I did lose my son, my life would have been full of remorse and regret.

'My intention to get Daniel back was very strong and absolute. Within a moment, two massive waves came and on the second wave, Daniel's hand was linked with mine. It was both grand and humbling for me, as Daniel and I held one another as we both walked back to shore. I felt like rejoicing but also deeply shaken, and I felt this deep connection with my son that I had never felt before, a connection that I felt all mothers, all souls have towards those they love. At the same time, I felt the deepest respect and connection with Mother Earth / Sea, that I also felt she had with me. It was an awesome feeling inside.'

'Wow, what an experience. Having been swept out to sea on an undercurrent as a child I can completely relate to that. What has been the hardest challenge in developing your Silat, mentally, emotionally and physically?'

'I have to think about this one because for me, my practice was not separate to my everyday life, although I often thought it was. I suppose when it comes down to the Satria Fighting Arts, no matter how hard I might try to record all the teachings and principles within the art, I just can't. The best way really is to stay open, and because the art is so intricately woven with all its beautiful and sometimes complex movements that are also highly sophisticated fighting strategies, it is not possible to say, "I have now mastered the art," simply because we are constantly changing and evolving.

'The hardest challenges emotionally and physically for me are entwined. I remember a period when Steve took the ladies aside during the Wednesday evening Kembangan [Flower Dance] class; he would take us behind closed doors and we'd go into Harimau training. In all my years of training, there was not a class more challenging than this one, mentally, emotionally and physically. "Harimau" means "tiger" in Indonesian and Harimau training forms one of the base style within the Satria Fighting Arts. It was rough and tough! And the ego of a woman is more discreet than a man's, so you can imagine the adrenaline and the emotion that went with the training. Often, women would finish the training session crying, or go deeply emotional. However, it was a vital part of the training. To learn a real jungle kind of fighting art is not often pretty, and in any kind of real fight situation, unless you can control your emotions and remain relaxed at all times, the results could be quite drastic. It was a very challenging period but it was also one of the best in terms of results. The key was to relax and you had to get into a mental state of relaxation to go through it and the only way was just to do it! I knew it was also hard for Steve to put me through the training as we were emotionally attached as husband and wife, but he'd also have to detach from me for my own personal evolution in the art.'

'So as a woman, in what ways do you feel martial arts training should be made the same or different for men or women? Can they really both train the same? What attributes do women have which can be amplified through training?'

'I can only really speak to you about my own personal experiences to answer your questions. Should men and women train the same or differently? Well, it really depends on what you're training for. The reality is that most women are often intimidated by men and to have physical contact with a male who is also a stranger can be a quite daunting experience. Personally however, I do feel that it is good for men and women to train together. I think it creates a balance within a class set-up.

'There are some things that a woman can learn from a man, and certainly aspects of a woman that a man can learn from a woman. Like the "hard and soft" or the "Yin and Yang". It's good for women to train as hard and as tough as men. Women are not as weak as they often think or are projected to be. In fact, there is so much strength in a woman that can outstand a man when it comes to the inner aspects of training called "Rasa" or "intuition" and we call this training "listening to the wind". In the right environment, women training with men develops mental, emotional and physical confidence and, to help learn some self-defence techniques, it is vital for training purposes as a man is generally bigger and weightier than a woman, and most attackers are men. Now, for men to train with women is also a very important aspect in their training because a woman has attributes like "softness" and "gentleness" that are key elements in the Kembangan.'

'Obviously Guru Ma has been a big part of your life; can you tell us of some experiences you have had with her?'

'Guru Ma is an exceptional woman with an exceptional history, and yet she is so very real, very motherly, very practical and down to earth, meticulous and doesn't seem to miss a thing. She can go in and in and in to something until there is none left of it. When I first met her, I'd already created this image of her as a "Sat Guru", as an "enlightened being", a "knower of all things" and all the things related to the simple word "Guru". So you can imagine my absolute nervousness on the day that I was coming to visit her with Steve on one of his many visits to Holland. But when I met her, she was so down to earth. Yes, she knew many things, spoke directly about things that had deeper meanings which would later manifest, but all the images that I'd erected in my head had become so tangible in that they were all true, but my perception of putting her up on a pedestal came crumbling down. She was just so lovely, like a grandmother that I wanted to hug and just listen to as she would tell many stories or give advice if needed. Her home was very well kept. It was clean and very ordered. She recycled everything. Even the pips from lemons or oranges were kept in glasses of water until she could replant them. She was big on gardening and looking after Mother Earth, and she carries a sense of responsibility towards her and encourages all her students to do so.

'She knew things over the years that she would often share but in the most gentlest and loving way to me. She often spoke to me of motherhood and often told me that I should be at home to protect the kids. I often did not fully understand what she was saying then, but over the years, have understood the importance of it. I had several dreams of her after my initial meeting, and in many of them, she would teach me movements of the Kembangan. I have the deepest respect for her as a warrior woman, a mother, a protector, a teacher and all the many things that she holds responsibility for in her life.'

'Finally, as a mother, how will you train and guide your children, and what do you hope for them as they grow older?'

'To be as natural and honest that they can be, to love and live with all their heart, to not live in fear but to fully live out their dreams and not be confined by the rules and regulations that man puts on them and really just to be themselves and accept their own individuality and just enjoy life. My hope for them is really that.'

Laarni Benitez in Harimau posture from the Satria Yoga

Simon Das

The Heritage of Pentjak Silat

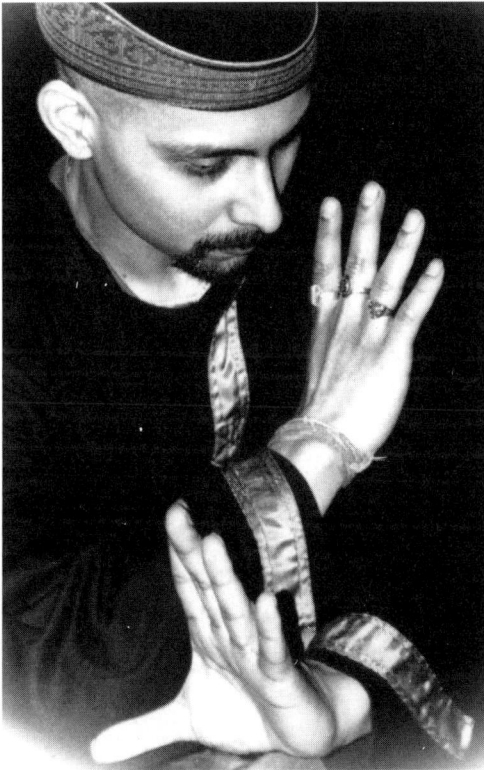

Guru Simon Das in a Pentjak Silat posture

Of all the people I have written about, it has so often been Simon Das who has piqued readers' curiosity more than anyone else, due mainly to the fact that he remains very much an 'underground' teacher. For those few who have tracked him down and convinced him to accept them as students it has not been an easy journey. He is an extremely demanding teacher, both physically and mentally, following the old way of Pentjak Silat where the student gives his heart and soul over to the Guru and the practice. The training methods of his Ksatriya Dharma (his own method based on traditional Silat) and Silat Sendeng are based around hardcore fighting drills and exercise for cultivating spiritual power. Once I was with Simon when a new student asked him somewhat doubtfully about the existence of the Ilmu, or mystical powers, which Silat is meant to develop. In reply Simon took out a very sharp knife and cut himself on the forearm so that blood ran freely. Then he closed his eyes and said a prayer, slapped his other palm on the wound and held it for a few seconds. He was in a trance. Suddenly he pulled his hand off and the arm was completely normal, no wound, and the barest of scars.

The other reason that Simon has kept a low profile is that he has fought a lot on the rough streets of his hometown, a hotbed of the racist skinhead movement which he has battled against – literally in life or death struggles – since his youth. His Silat has kept him alive, and his love and passion for the martial arts of South East Asia is very clear to all who meet him. In this conversation we discuss some of his background and the history of the Sendeng style.

'Simon, can you start by sharing your first memory of Silat?'

'My earliest memory of Silat is with Pak Rusli, he used to come to Hatfield University and teach Cimande Silat. Pak Rusli taught me some basics and a couple of Jurus [forms], but then he had to return to Malaysia. I was only thirteen years old then. Before this I had studied various martial arts such as Kungfu and Karate with the chefs at my father's restaurant; my hometown of Hatfield had a lot of racism during those times and so they needed to learn self-defence.'

'Why Silat?'

'It helped me to express myself freely and openly. It was a God-sent gift to me. The other martial arts hadn't given me real security.

I was praying a lot at that time for something to help me. I met Glen Lobo and began training with him, and then I became good friends with Abang Fazil, another Malaysian man, and I would go to his house where he would teach me many variations of arts such as Silat Sapik Kalo and certain Kelantanese arts. I began hearing from both Glen and Fazil about a London-based master named Al Rasheid Bak Eddie who was said to be very skilled. I met Bak Eddie and continued my training with him until 1997, learning Garak Ilhan, which is in fact an umbrella body for the arts coming from Bugis and Makasaris people in Indonesia. He taught me arts such as Harimau Sulawesi [tiger style], Sendeng [side body art], and Subrayan [cock fighting system]. The term Silat covers thousands of different arts. In Malaysia a lot of the arts were mixed with Chinese martial arts, known as Kuntao, due to intermarriage and the mindset of the people. There is an art called Kuntao Malacca which is said to have been developed by the monk Bodhidharma and brought from China to South East Asia, where it influenced many Silat systems such as Chimande. In Indonesia the ethnic divides are more distinct – you have the Sundanese, the Bugis and so on.'

'Are styles from different islands very distinct?'

'Yes, and this is due to the mindset of the peoples and the terrain of each place. For example, according to my research the Minankabao people are almost Zen-like, speaking in riddles and being very unpredictable. One of their fighting sayings is that "we can steal from your back pocket"! You see one thing but something else is going on, a lot of trickery and deception.

'The Javanese people on the other hand like to avoid confrontation, it is in their culture and the way they conduct themselves, they speak in circles rather than directly to avoid offence. Their arts include Perisai Diri and Seti Haiti Terrate, which are very circular and evasive methods similar to Bagua. The Bugis arts, which I focus on, come from very straightforward and simple folk: what you see is what you get, similar to Xingyi. They were seafaring merchants and pirates, businessmen, the most widely travelled of all Indonesians. They even taught the Siamese royal princes. There were Makasarese and Bugis bodyguards to the Siamese princes at various times. Even the head-hunters such as the Dyaks and the

Ibans learned from them and still have similar arts. One art, called Spring Twelve, starts from a front lead like a Western fencer, using the spear and shield and a sideways tilting motion.

'The Sendeng style which I teach and practise only contains seven techniques, seven stepping patterns and seven vital points.'

'How do you develop the courage to engage the enemy and timing in Sendeng?'

'There is a lot of mind training and drills to develop reflex, but later on comes plenty of spiritual work to have a clear mind and perception, to be in the moment, so we can respond appropriately. One example is to put on a blindfold and your teacher will attack you, softly in the beginning, and you need to sense and respond. This eventually develops lightning-fast reflexes and expands your consciousness so that you can feel your enemy's intention and react appropriately at that time. It is a very offensive art which will attack, attack, attack – there is virtually no blocking. Kuntao Malacca is very good for defence, and in my school we combine the two arts to give both impenetrable defence and unstoppable offence.

'It is an art which was used by the Bugis folk throughout history on the battlefield, helping them to consolidate their territory and to fight off foreign invaders. Our particular school goes back to a person called Longmarmant from Rial, who lived in the early 1800s and was originally from Sulawesi. Later he migrated to Jahor in southern Malaysia. He travelled to various places, teaching his art which was then called Pukulan Sendeng. It is very much a hand-based striking art with a few low kicks. One of his top students was called Haji Hammed who is our late grandmaster. Haji Hammed had inherited his own family's art of Kuntao Malacca which stems from Bodhidharma.

'In Indonesia they say this monk actually came from Sumatra and later went to China where he taught three hundred and sixty Imperial bodyguards. There was at that time a princess called Huang Li Po who was marrying the Malaysian Sultan of Malacca. She settled in Malaysia, accompanied by the three hundred and sixty bodyguards, who stayed and taught the art.

Simon Das with students, energy work at sacred stones, Wales 2008

Pak Muhammad Ariffin, Simon Das, Drdha Shivanath

'One of these lines was received by Haji Hammed, who combined it with Sendeng and another art called Pukulan Tujil Hari which is said to be the crème-de-la-crème of the fighting arts. This reputation is due to its being able to stop a fight in the first instance of engagement and the fact that it can be learned in seven days, although it may take a lifetime to master its depths. It is still a very rare and hidden art. One version of the history states that it was called a seven-day system as that was the length of time it took for the bodyguards to take princes and officials from Indonesia to Jahor in their longboats, and by the time they arrived they had learned the seven techniques and principles and were already combat ready. Another history states that certain masters of Sendeng and other arts got together and developed a method which trained the very essence of their combat knowledge. We have skills such as Iron Body, which is closely linked to the mystical training coming from the Sufi ways. Our grandmaster was a very short man, just over five foot (1.52 m) tall, but he was legendary in Jahor as his skill rendered him virtually untouchable. He had Iron Fist and Iron Body, lightning fast evasive footwork which would put him behind the enemy in an instant, and he became most famous after an incident in which he used his Iron Palm to knock down a rampaging water buffalo.'

'Can you tell me something about your own teacher?'

'My own teacher is related to Haji Hammed and became his senior student, learning from the age of fourteen. After completing the system he came to England in 1962 and studied to be an English teacher. On returning to Malaysia he joined the army and taught the special forces known as the Garakas Unit. In this period came the racial riots between the Chinese and the Malays in which my teacher unfortunately had to use his skill to survive. The communists in China funded certain groups to cause problems, and it eventually spread throughout the country. One incident concerns a hundred Silat experts who gathered under the leadership of a certain Bungali Mesalai, a deeply spiritual man who many considered to be a saint. The sultan requested this man to help the Malay people, so he initiated the Silat fighters into the Sufi path and this gave them invulnerability from blades and guns. Even now in South East Asia there are many Silat masters who have these mystical powers, but finding them is up to each person's Karma and destiny.'

Guru Simon Das in Keris posture

Drdha Shivanath

The Sacred Path of the Warrior

Drdha Shivanath shooting his bow in a Welsh forest

I pay quite a lot of attention to omens and signs when it comes to meetings with people, and I can never forget the very first time I met Drdha. It was about twenty years ago, and I had travelled with some friends who were Krishna devotees to meet a man they knew who lived in a very remote part of north Wales. They had all shared life in a temple for over a decade and told me that the man had been considered the 'mystic healer' of the group, someone with unusual abilities in the realm of subtle energies. Well…I was still a youth then and knew even less than I know now, but as soon as I met their friend Drdha I instinctively knew two things – one was that he had a strong inner power, and two, that we would be lifelong friends. Both have turned out to be right, so far. But on that first day we all sat in his altar room as he performed a healing using a peacock's feather and various Vedic Mantras, the little space vibrating with subtle energy…our backs were against the stone wall and suddenly the whole room really shook! It just happened to be the most powerful earthquake Wales had experienced for decades. I took it as a good sign, and the week just continued to get stranger from that point on. But I had connected with a man who was to be a true friend and an important spiritual elder and guide in my life.

It took me almost twenty years but I finally succeeded in convincing Drdha to teach what he had, and in recent times we have taught retreats in which his teachings have been very well received. His system of inner cultivation, based on his studies with the Yogis in the Himalayas and his years of Taijiquan practice, is very clearly structured and presented in a way that Westerners can easily assimilate. An expert craftsman and maker of traditional bows, Drdha still lives in a remote Welsh village and devotes his time to meditation, archery and other forms of cultivation. The following conversation gives a taste of his knowledge and perspective of what it means to be a warrior.

'Drdha, can you begin by telling me your definition of a warrior?'

'To be a warrior implies much more than just excelling at the arts of war and fighting. It implies more than possessing the achievements of strength and courage. Still more than the mastery of fighting with various deadly weapons. More, even, than the grand achievement of overcoming the fear of one's own death. A man may achieve all of these things, but at the same time remain undeveloped in many aspects of his character. For instance, he may still be prone to lie, or to cheat and steal… A man may achieve all of the above qualities out of a deep seated greed for wealth, honour or recognition. Maybe, he simply wants to impress and win over the hearts of women by his bravery, as was often the case in the ancient myths and histories of all the old cultures. All too often warriors are driven by the base desire for monetary profit. In this modern world whole armies of men are bought in this way. It isn't so much the power and skill the warrior has achieved that he is judged by, but the intention behind these achievements.

'Warriors of many different categories exist on earth. No doubt even those of dubious motivation, if prepared to go to battle, are still warriors.

"So what is the underlying quality a man possesses that makes him a warrior, as distinct from an ordinary man? To put it simply it is his ability for discipline. This one quality alone gives a man enough energy to confront his own personal adversity and strive for the fulfilment of his desires. Even the lowest category of warrior is far better situated than those who are the victims of lethargy, weakness and inertia – these negative qualities deprive a man of his ability to achieve. To achieve either the destruction of his obstacles or the fulfilment of his desires.

'A man without discipline will inevitably end up considering himself to be the victim of circumstances beyond his control. He will become a victim, looking for someone or something to save him from his self-created predicament, unable to find the energy within himself to tackle life's problems. What is it that discipline gives a man? It gives him the power and energy to take responsibility for his own life. It enables him to believe in himself and gives him the courage to fulfil his destiny. Response-ability is the ability to respond, to respond to the problems and challenges of life. The more discipline we possess the more power to respond we achieve. This is what sets apart the warrior from the ordinary docile man.'

'So is power essential to become a warrior?'

'Well, does power alone make a man a warrior? No, not without intelligence, awareness and focus. An archer may possess and be able to pull the most powerful bow in the world, but without focus what can he do? And without awareness how will he detect the attack of his enemy? Without intelligence his enemy will outsmart him and his days as a warrior will be short.'

'Then are there different classes of warrior as you see it?'

'Yes. The first or inferior class of warrior is, as I mentioned, motivated to fight by various self-centred desires for gain.

'The second, superior, class of warrior is best understood by recalling the chivalrous knights and warriors of old. By remembering the great heroes of the ancient stories. These men chose honour, integrity and truth as their motivation. Such men are called to action when their strong hearts and minds perceive injustice and persecution in their world... Often they themselves are in no danger, but they risk their own lives for the protection of others. The superior warrior cannot be drawn into conflict with a weaker opponent. Victory over a weaker man would mean nothing to him and would fail to awaken his will to fight. These men were not averse to rewards for their services, or the advances of beautiful women, but these were not their primary motivation. From this mentality arose the first "police forces" of the world. From the desire to protect the weak and uphold the stability of both societies and religions, for the greater good of the whole over personal considerations.

'An interesting point here is that these warriors inevitably came into conflict with each other. The warriors of different groups, countries or faiths eventually wandered into each others' territory, each believing his own version of reality was the best for the good of the world. Each firmly believing that God was on his side. That their version must be upheld at all costs. For this motivation they would heroically sacrifice their lives. These superior warriors often achieved temporary entrance into the heavenly realms above the earth, upon sacrificing their lives in this way.

'There is no rule or law that can hold a man in any of these categories. Often the lowest and most ruthless warriors learn through the harsh realities of battle and raise themselves strenuously up to the level of chivalrous heroes... All too often, too, great heroes or masters of great weapons became drunk with and blinded by their hard-earned power. Such men often reached the gates of hell in this way. The reality of battle is a far cry from the romantic version portrayed by the modern actors of Hollywood films.'

'Then is there such thing as a spiritual warrior?'

'This earth has been, and is still being, continually bathed in the blood of countless warriors, since time immemorial. Billions have died sword in hand, imbued with the spirit of the warrior. Fighting bravely, with God on their side. For surely God is impartial and on everyone's side! Trying in vain to subdue the evil forces of the world. So many great men throughout the ages have fought evil, for so long and so hard, and the evil of the world has not lessened. It has in fact grown. Then shouldn't we admit that this fight is not working? Many, if not most of these brave men, fighting for kings and leaders they never met or knew. Fighting battles that never really concerned them personally. Yet I respect them all as great heroes. What man of today would have the courage to face another, armed with swords, axes and spears, in battle to the death?

'Rarely, but occasionally, a warrior wakes up to this simple fact. He comes to understand the most significant of truths. That the enemy that confronts us in this world is merely a reflection of the real enemy, the enemy within ourselves. The evil we perceive in this world is a reflection of the evil that really still exists within our own hearts. Who am I really fighting? I am in fact doing battle with my self. This world is but a mirror in which we see ourselves, a giant mirror that reflects back to us our faults, weaknesses and failings, through the medium of those we meet and exchange energy with. It is not even possible to see a fault in another that doesn't already exist in us.

'The sages and mystics of old tell us our duty is to take response-ability for ourselves. There is no victim. No victimiser and no saviour. These are all roles we play, that we choose to identify with, in order to avoid this one truth – that the only problem with the world is us. Darkness and evil exists within all of us and if we want to eradicate it from the world we must eradicate it from within. But first we must acknowledge this fact.

'The nature of the world is duality. Heat, cold, light, dark, good and evil, etcetera, etcetera. Each of these opposite qualities are dependent upon each other for their existence. The battles for supremacy between the opposite forces of this universe are eternal and archetypal. They exist everywhere, within and without.

'If the nature of the world is dual, then our nature too is dual. As below, so above. The battle ground is the mind of man. This is the only battle ground where evil can be vanquished for ever. For then we have qualified and passed the tests of this earthly body, to evolve into finer dimensions of existence. Evil will remain on earth, for this is its eternal home. Sometimes it is weak, sometimes strong, but here it will remain to teach and to test the integrity of souls that visit earth.'

'Yes, that makes a lot of sense; it is not this world that will somehow become heaven, but our inner state. So how exactly can we use the knowledge of our dual nature to evolve?'

'It is the greatest kept secret and the easiest secret to forget that human beings, like this world, are dualistic. We are, literally, split in two. There exists within us all the dualities of the universe to some degree. But, there exists within us two opposing forces, over and above all the others. One is the dark force of greed and indulgence that wants to possess, control and enjoy all the things of this world. The other is the bright light of truth and integrity, the self-satisfied part of us that some may call our conscience. This part wants to live in harmony with the world and doesn't feel the need to possess it for our own personal gratification. This part of us is grateful, the other part is truly self-destructive. One is truth, one is illusion. The illusion can never ultimately preside over the reality of truth, but it can subdue it and cause untold suffering for substantial periods of time. This is the challenge that faces the spiritual warrior: to identify these two forces within the world, then within himself. To identify and hunt down the real enemy and subdue him. Whilst understanding that this enemy within can not be killed, or permanently eradicated as long as he lives on earth.

'No man is born a warrior, let alone a spiritual warrior. We must learn to become one. The path of the inferior warrior is well rewarded in this world, but the path of the internal warrior is a thankless task, unappreciated and un-rewarded in this world. But once this truth is revealed to the warrior, how can he go back and fight an illusionary enemy? He has no choice but to go forward. This is a battle that doesn't end until the body dies; the internal warrior should prepare himself to fight to his last breath. Finally, at the time of his parting with planet earth, when the enemy is subdued, he voluntarily steps out of his body, in full awareness. Stepping upon the very head of this enemy, as he climbs into an invisible golden chariot, which then ascends to the subtle realms of the highest heaven. Face to face with his true nature and the nature of this world, he then sees the face of God. His challenge has been accomplished, and victory is his to be enjoyed – for a while!'

'Can you tell us about archery as a way of cultivation, and why it has always been an important part of the warrior's training?'

'Yes. The practice of archery in the older cultures was an integral part of a warrior's training, both for the defence of the country and for his personal development. In the ancient Vedic culture archery was considered the most refined of the warrior's skills. Kings and princes were obliged to become expert archers and the priestly class of Brahmins were allowed to develop skill with the bow, although they were restricted from the use of other weapons. Even the great Lord Rama chose the bow as his weapon of choice.

Drdha in the Himalayan Mountains

'The path of the warrior would demand that the aspirant complete many types of training with and without various types of weapons. Both internal and external disciplines were taught. In the more evolved cultures this included various types of meditative practices alongside deadly weapons training. That is a combination you will not find in the modern warriors and armies of the world today. This type of training was designed to develop all-round, powerful individuals who were developed in all aspects of their personality, although they were capable of exhibiting fierce fighting skills when necessary.

'They were also very culturally refined and conversant with the threefold harmonies of life, these being the inner harmony of the body and mind, or harmony of the self; harmony between man and Nature; and social harmony, harmony between man and the society in which he lived. The warrior's path became a vehicle for the development of awareness, whilst affording the ordinary members of society a peaceful and stable social situation, free from the fear of aggression of neighbouring tribes or countries, as well as from the aggression of disturbed and undisciplined individuals within society. Enforcement of rules in protection of the natural environment is of course in everyone's interests and this too was part of their role within society. This gave everyone the maximum possibility for self-development, freed as much as possible from fear and stress. This is very different from the present idea that a warrior is a heartless, insensitive killing machine, trained only for warfare and fighting.'

'What qualities does archery develop?'

'The practice of archery will develop many attributes within a man. There is one quality, however, that it develops above all others and that is the quality of focus. For internal and external, material and spiritual success, the development of focus is both integral and essential. It complements and aids all other areas of development. For personal development and meditation it is maybe even the key to success or failure.

'To fully appreciate the value of focus we must ask ourselves the question: what is focus? Focus is a type of concentrated awareness. To go even deeper, we can ask ourselves another question. What in fact is life? This is a very difficult question to answer, because life is so many things to so many people. There is, however, one thing that life is, that no one will disagree with. Life is an experience and it is an experience that we all experience through the medium of awareness. What are we other than sparks of individual awareness, experiencing the variety of life? Awareness is an intrinsic part of us and the intrinsic nature of existence. It is fundamental to everything. Our life is simply what we are aware of at any given moment in time. What we are aware of is always a choice: we have the choice where to focus our awareness at every moment, we therefore have the choice to change our lives by deciding where to put our awareness. Control of our awareness is therefore dependent on our ability to focus. So you can see the importance of focus. We all have the ability to focus, but some have it more than others and those who have developed it more are the ones more able to adjust their lives to their liking, simply by altering their focus.

'Other than the North Star, it is said that change is the only constant in this universe. The nature of this world is that it is effervescing and flickering. Things are always moving and our point of focus is always moving. Mostly, for the average man, it is moving as if it had a will of its own, except for when he has work to do and he must concentrate upon a task. During periods of concentration we are applying a type of focus, but not a focus that can stop the flickering of our internal and external awareness.

'Contemplation is a similar thing; it is a type of focusing. But not full pinpoint focusing. In Sanskrit, the spiritual-based language of the ancient Vedas of India, the closest translation of focus, for the type of focusing used in internal practices, is Dharana. Dharana interestingly also means "to hold". In terms of focus, it literally means to hold your awareness still, to hold an image within your mind, or within your vision, totally still. We can of course all do this for short periods, some more than others, but the problem is to sustain it. Lucky for us though, that the internal apparatus we possess that performs this act can be quickly developed. It is similar to a muscle, in that it develops and grows stronger through constant use. The more we focus the more able to focus we become. For many this ability to sustain their focus comes naturally, but for many more this must be learned. There are many tried and tested methods to strengthen our focus. All that is required is the desire to do so, along with some patience and determination...

'The type of focus needed to be a successful archer is the ability to hold the target within one's gaze. According to the ancient sages, whatever we focus on at the time of death will decide where we take our next birth. In archery, whatever we focus on when the arrow is released from the bow, decides where the arrow will hit. In Taiji, the ancient Chinese art of internal energy cultivation, they say "energy follows the mind". This is true, but when the eyes are open the mind follows the eyes. What we look at in this world is very important. Human beings are predominantly visually oriented. This may not always be the case, but it is the general rule.

'Total focus is the end result and not the starting point of the process of shooting. We arrive at a state of focused attention by the alignment of all the various physical, mental, emotional and spiritual parts that make up the "totality of our being". Anything else will only be a partial focus. Yes, it is possible to hit a target by focusing our gaze upon it, with our mind elsewhere and our body posture out of alignment, but it is unlikely and would be down to luck. The archer is looking for consistency and continuity of his practice and this requires not just whole body and mind focus but, as mentioned earlier, the focusing of the "totality of ourselves". Then success is guaranteed.'

'What do the myths of old teach us about archery?'

'There are many stories and myths about legendary, mystical bows that the common man is unable to string and draw. Usually, only the hero of the story can string the bow and shoot it. Then some great prize or success in battle was guaranteed. Often these bows were given to man by the gods, or made by gods or beings from other worlds, signifying that the bow was to be used for the attainment of a spiritual, rather than an ordinary goal. The bow of a warrior is a powerful bow. It is not the bow of the sportsman, target or flight archer. A weak bow can be drawn with ease using arm power alone, the draw can be held with ease while aim is taken and the arrow carefully aligned with the target. This is similar to shooting a rifle; it doesn't engage the totality of our being. Yes, our eyes will be co-ordinated with our fingers, but the body itself is not fully engaged and the mind too will be only partially engaged.

'A warrior is always pushed to achieve the peak of his potential; he is trying to achieve the impossible. He wants to gain access to the true power that he knows to be his birthright because he feels it deep within himself. He is convinced that he is a powerful spiritual being, as opposed to a weak domesticated version of a human being. For this reason he chooses a powerful bow with no sights or aids to drawing, pulling or aiming and relies only on his total alignment and focus to hit his mark. Nothing less would be satisfying to his integrity. The way of the modern sportsman archer is to rely on the "totality of his equipment", to invest in a bow made of the latest modern energy-saving designs and materials, with as many shooting aids as possible, or as many as he feels he needs, strapped to his bow. These men lack awareness and understanding as to their true, powerful nature and potential. They may achieve success in competitions and practice grounds, with the help of their modern bows, but this does not help them on the battle ground of life. They will have failed to connect the totality of themselves, and their true potential as men will be, unfortunately, unfulfilled.

Drdha teaching archery to Arjuna Das, Wales Retreat, 2008

'This is one of the new tasks of the modern warrior, to avoid the temptation of the short-lived gains offered to them by this technology-based, materialistic culture. All the equipment and gadgets this modern world has to offer come with the promise of making our lives easier by saving time and energy. Before accepting them, though, maybe we should ask ourselves: what inner potential will this machine take from me if I accept it? Am I really getting a "good deal"?'

'What does the arrow represent as well as being a weapon?'

'In archery the arrow represents the energy released from the bow when it is shot. Energy follows the mind and the mind follows the eyes and the arrow hits what the eyes are focused on. But is this the full picture? What, or who, is guiding the eyes? *Desire is the root of all action.* First we must have the *desire* to hit the target. We can also ask ourselves, what are the motivating factors behind this desire? Why do I desire to hit this target? This *desire* will have somehow arrived in our *mind* as a result of the information gained through the medium of our *senses*. The *mind*, which is closely linked with our desire, will then use this information to makes various calculations and decisions when to shoot. We then engage our *intent* and the *will* follows through. The brain then engages the body and under the extreme muscular tension of the draw everything comes together and focuses on the target. The arrow is released.

'The idea is to try to appreciate all of the various parts of ourselves that we engage and pull together when we perform any action. How can we focus the "totality of ourselves" if we are unaware of these inner processes? Such self-awareness can only be achieved through a meditative process. Some form of meditation must accompany the "way of the bow". Otherwise it is simply archery. Some may question the necessity of being able to recognise and align all of these subtle forces. They may say, it all happens automatically! Maybe these people pick up their bows automatically as well? Maybe they do everything automatically or maybe they act when, like machines, the world pushes their buttons? The process of automation is, however, more suitable for mass production of "things" than the production of spiritual warriors. The warriors follow the path of awareness, not the path of automation. These two paths are totally opposed to one and other.'

'Drdha, you have made many bows and I know this is often a long arduous task. Can you say something about the esoteric meaning behind the bow?'

'Well, we can take a look at the bow itself and how it can be used as a vehicle for self-development, as well as just a weapon. Whatever exists outside of us must also exist inside of us. This is the mystic vision acquired through meditative practice. As above, so below. The warrior must become one with his weapons – and the material his weapon is made of... These weapons become extensions of him and allies on the path to his ultimate freedom. Like the cutting edge possessed of a sharp sword, the warrior must similarly develop the "edge of discrimination", or the "edge of sharp intelligence", within himself, to become effective in this world. The tough quality of steel imbibes its toughness into his body, making him resilient in his struggle and battles. If, though, he relies solely upon his sword's edge, he will externalise his edge at the expense of his internal edge. This would be to lose more than he gains by practice of the sword. Instead he must use his sword to develop and hone his inner edge.

'Applying this same method of reasoning to the bow we can ask: what qualities does the bow possess that it can help to enhance our inner development? The secret to the understanding of the esoteric energies of the bow lies in understanding the true nature of tension. *Tension is the root of creation.* Desire is the root of tension, and tension lies at the root of action. Action precedes creation. Without tension this material plane of existence would not exist. It is created by and held together by tension. Every atom, every particle and every cell is held together by tension, as the various particles and cells are also held together in groups. This is the nature of this world. Even the planets are held in their orbits through tension, as per the desire of the Creator.

'If all the tension were removed from an object or being, it would no longer exist in this world. It is desire that creates tension; too much tension is a sure sign of too many desires. For the spiritual warrior he must reduce his desires to a minimum; energy can not flow efficiently through a tense body. When the desires are minimised, it is then a matter of equally distributing the remaining stress/tension in a balanced way. When we move our bodies or parts of our bodies, the brain is simply sending energy signals to the various muscles and tendons to tense. Through the systematic use of tension all our movements within the body are carried out, and all desires are achieved.

'We now come back to the bow. A bow is a length of wood or composite materials, such as bamboo and animal horn, capable of being bent and held by a string in a state of high tension. As the string is pulled the bow is further tensed. This stretches, or expands, the back of the bow and simultaneously compresses the belly. One of the main points in making an efficient bow is that the belly and the back of the bow must perfectly complement each other in their ability to be expanded and compressed. It is this use, or play of tension against compression, that enables both, the bow and this human body, to move. Also, integral to the make up of a bow is its upper and lower limb. One points to heaven, the other to earth. These two limbs must be perfectly matched for the bow to function efficiently.

'All the material that comprises the mass of the bow serves a purpose, there is no redundant wood or horn. This would serve only to make the bow slow, clumsy and inefficient. I could keep going but the idea is to explain how to make comparisons between our own body and the body of the bow; to see how, through the understanding of efficient energy generation and transmission to the arrow in archery, those same rules relate to the same processes within the human body. We are continually shooting the arrows of desire at targets in this world. Wouldn't it be good if we could repeatedly hit our mark?

'So to sum up in answer to your questions: the interplay of the opposing forces of expansion and contraction is fundamental to the production of energy and movement; this correlates to strikes and blows in the martial arts world! It is this interplay that the Yin–Yang symbol represents. The interplay of light and dark is secondary to that of expansion and contraction, or compression. There is always tension between the opposing forces of the world, except for the all too brief moments of total balance. If total balance was the only state to exist, all activity in this world would stop and this world would no longer serve its function. The bow simply replicates the working of all life forms.

'When we breathe in we expand our energy, when we breathe out we contract our energy. This process keeps us alive. The universe itself is contracting and expanding, enabling itself to exist. To understand this one point is to master the cultivation and manipulation of energy. When the bow is drawn and released, this same process is repeated, both within our body and within the bow. More importantly, however, it is happening within our internal energy body and our awareness. To focus on a pinpoint is to contract our awareness. To relax that focus is to expand it again... If the whole process is completed successfully then the arrow will fly towards its mark.

'What other activity provides us with such an exacting opportunity to put our balance and alignment to the test? Not to mention our ability to focus the "totality of ourselves" and be shown by the placement of the arrow how close we really are to achieving this? In many of the warrior practices we can be tricked into believing we are better or more advanced than we really are. It is much harder to put them to the real-life test. The bow and arrow, however, don't lie.'

Pak Muhammad Ariffin

Heritage of the Indonesian Warriors

Pak Muhammad Ariffin, Silat Master

I was introduced to Pak Muhammad Ariffin by the Silat fighter Simon Das, after having heard about him for a couple of years from various people. He had been variously described as a 'wandering Dervish Chimande master' and 'a miraculous spiritual healer', and I heard reports from people I trusted that he had a special energy. He could channel electricity and had cured cancer, and he conditioned students' arms and shins by virtually fracturing the bones and then making them harder with special herbs and massage. Naturally I was curious about him! My first impression of this softly spoken man was of a very intense, quietly powerful individual, bearing the aura of the old school Silat fighters I had encountered in Indonesia. I found out that though standing little more than five foot (1.52 m) tall he had fingers like steel and a strong inner force, but we had little time together so there was still a lot I had yet to ask him about his practice.

Our second meeting happened when he travelled half a day across country, at the request of my brother, to give me treatment during a period of serious illness. He spent a day and a night working with me, doing traditional blood cupping, massage and spiritual healing. During that and subsequent meetings I confirmed for myself that he was indeed quite a unique person – he wore the lightest of clothes in bitter mid-winter weather and somehow his body stayed remarkably warm, he slept three hours a night if at all, sometimes fasted for days on end, and spent his life travelling from place to place to perform healing for all manner of ailments, often for very little money. He had good success with stroke patients, often helping them to walk again after one or two treatments, and I heard many reports that there were verified cases of cancer remission amongst his patients. My brother, Arjuna Das, apprenticed to him as a healer and, along with Simon Das, told me countless first hand reports of people being cured of serious and chronic disease.

Pak made it clear to me that he prefers teaching and practising healing rather than fighting, even though he is quite clearly a fighter with dangerous skills. He is also a lineage holder of the rare Girang Cimande 'Upper Mountain' system. This is the 'mother system' of the many branches of Cimande, with its emphasis mostly on the spiritual aspects. In this case the mountain is that which looks over the sacred Cimande River, where a saintly practitioner once dwelled and sanctified the area. Taking its practices from an observation of Nature, the movement of the river water, sacred prayer and esoteric methods, Girang Chimande is a system aiming towards total freedom from form and the gaining of spiritual power. It is, like almost all Pentjak Silat I have encountered, a total way of life involving practices which deal with all aspects of the student's nature. In the following conversation Pak Muhammad Ariffin answered some of my questions about his life and practice.

'Pak, I have heard that your family has a long tradition of healing and Silat, can you please explain more about this?'

'Sure. I was raised by my grandmother until the age of four, and she was a traditional healer and midwife, she had much compassion and skill and so everyone loved her – then I met my parents, but my whole childhood I was beaten by my family. It was so bad I went up to the roof and prayed to God, asking why my life was so bad. Always I was told just be patient. Then aged about fifteen, sixteen, I started to feel I had some power in my body, some knowledge, I would demonstrate to people how I could make fire in my body, or break wood and things like that. I had the power but as I was so small I felt shy and embarrassed and didn't often show those things. I went to Chimande Village, where many of my family lived, and learned Silat there. When I was twenty-five I was able to really go deeper into Silat, and from then I have understood it. My grandfather was a bone setter, and my great-great-grandfather was a healer so this is our family tradition. We are descendents of the Wali Songo spiritual warriors, the great saints of Indonesia.'

'I see...and what about your system of Silat, what does it specialise in?'

'My system is the Girang Cimande system and in this system we hunt for the attacker's arms or legs, to attack his punch or kick, disable him so he cannot attack. This attack can be breaking his fingers, his arm, his elbow, his shoulder...anywhere. Our arms we develop very, very strong, it takes many years and we must massage and use special Balur ointment. My teacher's name is Hajih Umiati, and it was he who explained that when I attained a deep level in Silat it should be used for healing, not fighting. At that stage you must be very humble to everyone. Actually I have only two or three students for the fighting art, mostly I like to teach people healing and to help people with my healing knowledge.'

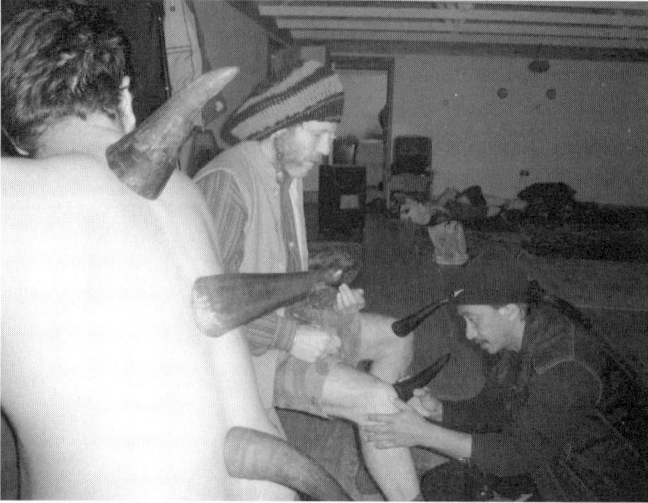

Pak applying blood cupping with buffalo horns

'How was this system created, is it based on older Silat arts?'

'Actually, this Girang Cimande has influenced many, many styles in Indonesia, it is very old. It comes from spiritual exercises, meditation, breathing exercises to build spiritual power and stop you being tired; this one we call "Isim Silat". We always practised breathing and meditation in the jungle, in Nature, in the rivers or under waterfalls or on the rocks. You must experience that you and Nature are unified, this is part of our training.'

'You mentioned the spiritual aspects; what exactly does this mean? What does the student need to do to be ready for these kinds of practices?'

'If you take Silat as a spiritual path there are some requirements – first, you must bow to the teacher and follow him, second, you must be humble to all people, not proud, give them love, and third, you must be close to God, Allah, by prayer and fasting. The more you fast and cut down sleep, the more God will give you internal power for both healing and fighting. I don't know sometimes how to heal people, but when I am close to God with meditation, prayer, fasting, then I feel I have a lot of inner energy and people are healed. We have special training Thursday nights, 2 or 3am, many angels come and can transmit inner power and make you heavy in Silat. Deep breathing and prayer can make you full of internal power.'

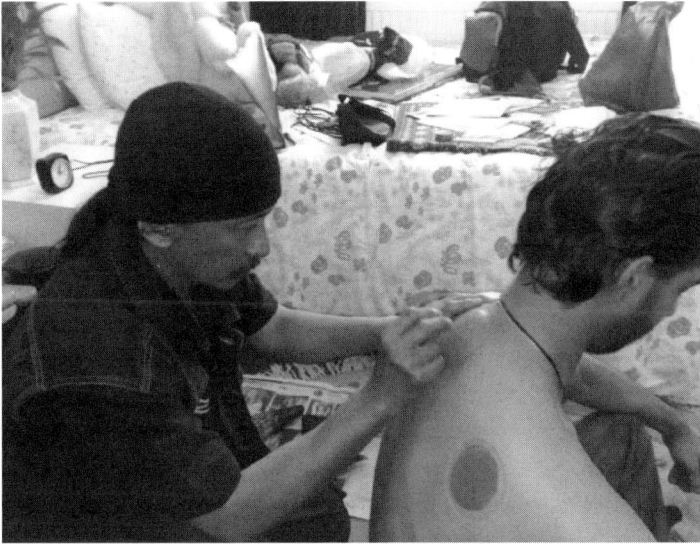

After removing the horns, stale blood comes to the surface

'What about the technical side of the Cimande, do you have certain forms and fighting exercises which you do?'

'Yes, we have thirty-three jurus, short forms, these are for fighting hand or against knife, these open up all the energy centres and condition the whole body. We start training sitting on the earth cross-legged and facing the partner, then drill the movements. These have sitting, standing, dodging and then all kinds of weapons, including many kinds of bladed weapon. Also, the Langkah is very important, this is the stepping patterns to move freely against many attackers.'

'So you use the Kris [wavy bladed sword]?'

'Yes. The Kris is a magical weapon, it can possess inner power or can lose it if you don't live a good life.'

'Who were your teachers in Silat?'

'I studied ten years with Haji Dumyati from Cimande Village. We are from the Cloud Tiger, my grandfather learned from the tiger and you could see him on the rock with the tiger. I had no nails but from that I had powerful claws. We had practices where we would sit underwater in the river for hours reciting the name of God in our hearts, and then real inner power comes.'

Pak with his students in London

'In your healing system do you have anything similar to the concept of meridian lines? I know you work a lot with spiritual healing, can you explain what this is?'

'Yes. Our healing system uses lines of energy similar to the meridians in acupuncture, but we use our fingers instead of needles. From the toes we can diagnose the head, neck, blood pressure and all the organs. Whatever God made is the best, so we use buffalo horns for blood cupping, to bring out the poison blood. If people have poison, or black magic, or serious illness, the cupping will take away the stagnant and poison blood and allow the good blood to flow where it was stuck. I am working any time people need me, often I have to attend people's houses where they have demons or black magic stuck there, I do some prayers and help them like that. This is the Way I learned from the Wali Songo, it doesn't matter the religion of the people. God gave us this healing and this Silat to protect us; it all comes from God. When you face a knife you must have complete faith in God, this is what will protect you!'

*Pak attacks the incoming punch and immediately
follows up with the same arm striking the head*

Gerry Tan

The Way of Kuntao Mantis

Master Gerry Tan of Kuntao Silat

I had heard of Sifu Gerry Tan twenty years ago through his old student Steve Benitez, with stories of six-hour-long training sessions, fearsome full contact sparring where the student's only protection was a crash helmet, and about Gerry's Kuntao, whose trademark skill was ferociously aggressive attacking combinations with extremely fast hands. He taught on the roughest council estates in north west London, training a small group of devoted students who had entered and won all the fighting tournaments they could find.

Meeting Gerry in his small north London home, a place full of the memories of decades of teaching and training, I found a humble and quietly spoken gentleman. The past years had presented him with severe trials, but he had used his skills to survive several life or death struggles. He is sixty years old, but when he stands up to perform his Kuntao Mantis there is a sudden explosion of movement and then hands moving extremely fast with that trademark aggression of the southern Chinese fighting arts. The following interview reveals some of Master Gerry Tan's experiences and memories along the path of the traditional Chinese martial arts as interpreted in South East Asia.

'Gerry, please tell us how you became involved in martial arts.'

'I was born in Medan, Sumatra; it was a place full of good martial artists. When I was five years old my parents took me to a Judo club run by my dad's friend. I did well there, attaining Shodan grade, but then I met a friend who was doing Kuntao. I tried to throw him but he evaded me each time, it was like I was fighting empty air. So I began doing Kuntao, and it was very hard, really hard training. In 1963 the government closed down all Chinese martial arts teaching. Silat and Judo were still taught publicly, but all the Chinese arts went underground. Our group met in a hidden location and it was done very secretly, and during that period three of the original group dropped out, leaving only five of us. Our teacher we called Ah-Pek, or elder uncle, and his lineage came from Chukung, connected with a famous Kuntao exponent in Jakarta called Lubangteng.

'In the pre-1963 Kuntao there were no forms, just eighteen combinations or methods which could be strung together, and their unique nature is that these combinations are very, very fast and can be used simultaneously for attack and defence. Ah-Pek's philosophy of fighting was that it is better to make someone busy than for him to make you busy! If you are in defensive mode you will have a problem countering your enemy, if you attack he will be busy trying to stop you.

'He also taught me that speed is the most important attribute of all, in any sport, and especially fighting, but equally important is alignment and co-ordination. If your alignment is wrong then all of your energy will leak out and your strikes will lack power, if it is correct then your whole body will be co-ordinated as one and your power will be explosive.

'Around this time I also met another teacher, a master of Northern Mantis Gongfu, who we called Ummauldi. In this Mantis system we have lots of forms – ten lines of Tam Tui, or spring legs, which is the foundation of martial arts training, teaching you how to move your legs very fast, shift your body and kick quickly. This method was spread by the famous Ching Woo school from China, founded by Huo Yuen Jia. It builds up leg strength and strong basics, this is vital to have.'

'And how are the Mantis techniques applied in real fighting?'

'In terms of using the Mantis methods to fight, my teacher was clear that we have to analyse every technique, strip it down to its essence, find out what it is for, its strength and weakness, before we can really use it. Look at this technique, Opening the Door, as an example: it's a quick entry and strike but can be used with fingers, palm, Phoenix-Eye Fist, claw and so on. In this way one technique becomes countless applications.

'Although there are dozens of forms in traditional Preying Mantis systems, our one – which is close to the Mei Hua Plum Blossom style of Mantis – has been stripped down to eight forms, the classical weapons plus all of the ways of researching the combative applications.'

'How did Kuntao develop when it left China?'

'Kuntao was developed over the past two hundred years by the Chinese who faced persecution and troubles in Indonesia, where they are essentially second class citizens. It is an art which is taught individually to each student according to their body type. It is purely from south China with no influence from Silat. If facing a knife attacker our speed and power will stop them, and I also had to fight against the chain which is a very dangerous weapon. These eighteen combinations will cover any kind of attack. It is so difficult to spar due to the nature of the attacks, so we use crash helmets as protection.'

'What memories do you have of your teacher?'

'My teacher was old and very skinny, but so skilled. I remember one night three hoodlums tried to rob him, but he moved so fast that in a moment they were all taken down. He was a very eccentric person, he didn't speak much, just wearing these khaki shorts and flip flops, but so many people respected him due to his speed and power. There were other famous fighters around then as well. One was an enforcer for the Triads, a very violent man, but when the troubles happened he came out and protected the Chinese community with great skill. Also Lobanteng of Kuntao was very famous.

'Go Chaikim, a famed Kuntao Silat exponent, came from Kweetung; he resided in Java during the Dutch occupation and combined the Chinese arts with the Silat to found Kweetung Silat. In the Silat community the Wali Songo were very famous: they were eight brothers who all had high spiritual attainment and had strong links with the Indonesian royalty. The most skilful exponent I knew during that time was a Buddhist monk in a temple, everyone wanted to learn from him but he rarely took students. His name was Sek Koh Sum,[1] incredibly skilled with Shaolin Iron Palm, and later he went to Singapore and took one or two students. His grand-student Donny Siew used to live in England and has left a few disciples here, but they are still very underground and keep the knowledge to themselves.

'My Mantis teacher also had high skill with Iron Palm. Once we saw him hit a melon, it looked like he barely touched it and nothing appeared to have happened to it. But when we cut it open all the flesh inside was mashed up! We could not ask questions, this was the old way, so it wasn't until later that we realised that we had seen a demonstration of Iron Palm. There was the inner circle and the outer circle of students, and we had to listen diligently to our seniors when they discussed the arts. We didn't dare to ask questions! Later when we were older we were able to spar with the seniors and then you really learned by getting hit! Afterwards you think to yourself why you got hit, and then try again and attempt to overcome their techniques next time. You must spar all the time with more experienced people, you will learn so much. We always had bruises and injuries, we had no protection at all. There were no tournaments, only challenges from one school to another.'

'Do you focus much on weapons training?'

'My favourite weapon at the time was the fan, it is so compact and made with iron ribs so it's very practical. Nowadays it's hard to find these real metal fans. I also love the pole, it's a bit flexible and can express the explosive, whipping power. Weaponry is good, the classical methods teach us a lot, but you cannot use them on the street nowadays so it's better to drill your hand techniques more. Train the flow of your energy, forward energy, co-ordination of the body.'

'What kinds of trained force does Mantis develop?'

'In Mantis we have five kinds of energy or force – hard and soft, open and hidden, and slippery force. Hard energy is full force, physical power. This travels from the pumping of the Achilles tendon up to hip, waist, ribs, armpit, elbow to hand. Soft energy includes all the slapping and parrying type actions. Open energy is one where you control how hard you want it to be, and hidden energy is short distance power. Slippery force is deceptive, swaying and tricky use of power, it is very soft.'

'I see. How about the classical posture we see Mantis fighters using with the hooked hands? How is this applied?'

'The classical Mantis hooking hand posture has three main uses – to block, strike or to hit a vital point which we call dien hsueh. I teach all the students the vital points, but it takes very good timing, conditioning and accuracy. The real reason to teach them is so they can avoid hitting the points in sparring. You need to fight with intention but not bad intent, you must have control when you spar as bad accidents can happen if you don't.'

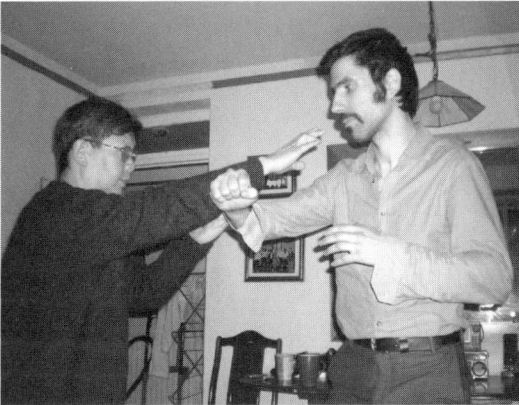

Master Gerry Tan shows form and application of Kuntao

'Can you please describe the internal aspects of your arts?'

'When I came to London in the 1970s I only taught Kuntao to my senior students, the others I taught Mantis to. When we learn external arts we need to go to internal at a certain stage to balance us out. I teach three types of Qigong. One from Mantis is Iron Shirt, another is I Jing Jing [the tendon changing exercise]. The third is a standing Qigong method, holding the ball, where we gather the energy. We also have Daoist meditation practices for the circulation of energy, aligning the Dantien, Huiyin and Taihui points; we can do this standing, seated and lying down. As a traditional Chinese man I keep the old ways alive in my teaching. Fighting is only a small part of what we do, we also have healing practices including acupressure massage, Dit Da [fall-hit] medicine for injuries, Tui-Na massage and cupping. I also love calligraphy because it helps the breathing, the steadiness of hand and the softness of touch as the rice paper is so thin. We also do lion dancing and drumming, a very important part of the culture.'

Master Gerry Tan applies simultaneous strike to arm and leg kick

Master Gerry Tan with Mantis grab and take-down technique

'Can you recall any of your healing work which has helped serious ailments?'

'Well…I will tell you of one experience using our healing methods, helping a man I knew who had severe cancer. It was almost in the bones, very bad case. It was my first attempt at this kind of disease, and along with a student named Delroy I channelled my Qi into his groin area. A while later this man's wife rang me, thanking me for the improvement in his condition, at last he could sleep easily and the pain was much reduced. His cancer blood marker had gone from 5.6 down to 2.4. He is able to enjoy his life! We attacked it from outside in. I channelled my Qi for two hours but afterwards felt very drained, and soon after came down with a hyperactive thyroid condition. Even now I am easily getting dizzy and tired. So healing can bring problems…'

'What is your view on martial morality, as a teacher?'

'We need to teach students how to respect their parents and other people. This is Adat [Indonesian term for conduct and manners]. Back home we used to have this respect for parents and teachers, to do good and so on. But you never know what problems are waiting around the corner. You need to teach students at an early stage how to contribute time to the community. Everyone has their own spiritual Way, you cannot force this on others. I am from a Daoist family, and I still enjoy listening to the old Daoist music and emptying my mind, it's good if you can achieve even five minutes of inner calm.'

Master Gerry Tan with students, young Steve Benitez front row centre

'What are you memories of teaching Steven Benitez and other students?'

'When I think back to the old days when I was teaching my students, I have very fond memories of that group. Steve Benitez was one of the small group of very talented ones, obsessed with training, who would hold their Horse stances for hours on end. In those days we got disqualified from all the tournaments we entered due to excessive contact, but we had no idea how else to fight! Later when full contact became popular we entered and won the British Championships. Nowadays few people want to train hard, they are too busy making money and other things. And here we are, still training in the same small room after all these years, just a few dedicated close students. Now I am sixty years old, and I still love to share the arts with them.

Note

1. In 2005 I met the top student in Penang of the late monk Sek Koh Sum, named Png Chye Khim. His Iron Palm skill was superb; when he hit the big hanging bag filled with stones it simply folded in two, hit the wall of the school, causing the ceiling to shake. Although the hands of Sek Koh Sum's students look somewhat disfigured they seem to have no problems with the joints into old age. One of Sek Koh Sum's other top students recently had his hands X-rayed and the doctors said the bone quality was that of a young man. It is possible the strong herbs they use before and after training keep the bones healthy despite externally appearing disfigured, however, these kind of practices must always be approached with extreme caution and I do not recommend them or consider them necessary for attainment of striking power.

Pedro Villalobos

The Sacred Path of Muay Thai Sangha

Kruu Pedro Villalobos in Northern Thailand

When I first began teaching Baguazhang in the northern Thai city of Chiangmai I heard from several students about another foreigner who was running a school there. He was by all accounts an expert in Muay Thai Boran, the old style of Thai Boxing, and was recognised as highly skilled even by the native champions of the art. I kept hearing the name Pedro Villalobos as someone who had been tested by the Thai boxers and proved his worth as a fighter, and also as a quite unique teacher with a very Buddhist-oriented approach to martial arts. This had led to his founding the Muay Thai Sangha system.

I discovered some time later, when I was faced with a problem involving Thai magic, that he was also a very kind man who immediately offered whatever help he could provide. He not only has excellent martial arts skills but also a great sincerity which has kept him going through difficult times and endless challenges along the path of cultivation. In the following interview we discussed the many aspects of his martial arts study and teaching, and the values which he holds close to his heart.

'Pedro, please tell me how you came to study martial arts in the first place, and something of your youth, which led you towards a spiritual path.'

'The main reason to study martial arts was because in high school, a group of kids used to get together to abuse the younger students. I was among the younger kids and I was afraid to go to school. That is why I decided to practise martial arts and learn how to defend myself. Those days were perhaps one of the greatest lessons that until today are alive in my heart. Because of those lessons I came to understand how important it is to respect others regardless of how much power, size or experience we may have. It was an early lesson in life, teaching me for what was coming ahead. There were no spiritual signals, or at least that I was aware of, except learning the basis of self-respect.'

'What are the outstanding memories of your travels through the Muay Thai camps of Thailand and your fighting career?'

'That was perhaps another great stage of my martial arts life. On my travels around Thailand I have learned some of the basic concepts that we share today in our school. I will say that the two most valuable lessons that I learned from the Thais was to always be humble towards everyone regardless of whether you are a champion fighter or just a beginner inside or outside of the martial arts school. They are incredibly humble people even with two hundred professional fights...! Beautiful.

'The second lesson that called my attention was the determination in their training. Hard and continuous training, overcoming tiredness and pain. It truly is a great skill if we want to surpass the frontiers of our own mind. To achieve this, it is necessary to have responsibility for yourself so you cannot be distracted by other things. I always tell students that there is not secret training to become the best you can be except inner awareness flowing with what is there and never giving up.

'I consider myself lucky to have learned from different champion masters around Thailand. Thai people are very open with their teachings and they accept students easily as long they are not bullies. Many times when I was training in the countryside Thai trainers give me food and shelter for free because they saw that I didn't have much money to buy it. I ask myself many times why the masters would take care of me if I didn't have anything to give them... Later on, I came to understand that the masters saw something that I was not aware of at that time, that was "to be determined to train over any circumstances..." They like that!'

'What is the purpose of ring fighting in Muay Thai? Is it really just for money or to test one's skill?'

'In recent years in Thailand the direction of Muay Thai has changed and now ring fighting and business are becoming the most important aspects in the art. A few masters are still outside this "fashion money disease" but it is very rare to meet them unless you are recommended by other special teachers or you can recognise them.

'I also can't deny that for a while I was in the fighting business. I see fighting as another experience in the process of learning. Each person has a different reason to fight and their actions end up in a different result – some become champions, some become teachers and some stop after the first fight. Perhaps my personal experience about fighting can help someone to understand the reason why he is fighting or why he wishes to fight. I've always been a kind of person that doesn't like to fight or hurt others. I went to fight professionally because I was aware of my fear and anger in street confrontations with others. I thought that I would like to know more about these emotions that were living inside me, and that is why I went to fight...to confront my own fears. Many fighters have watched my fights and have told me that I didn't want to win the fight, rather to spend time at the ring hanging out with the opponent. It is true that I had no desire to win, but rather to gain experience about my emotions under pressure and understand the strongest opponent of all...my ego. The result of the fight was not important; to be champion was not important, all that kind of stuff. I came to the conclusion that it comes from the ego mind. This kind of fighting path can be dangerous if it is done without a teacher. As soon as fear and ego are understood, fighting should stop. If the fighter cannot stop that means that he has become addicted and that can end up in a destructive path for the body and for the spirit. My best advice is to be aware of the result of our actions and to have a spiritual constructive goal so we don't get lost inside our ego.'

'How did you discover the old styles of Muay Thai?'

'Since an early age I always had two deep interests in life, spirituality and martial arts. At an early age I started with Judo, then when I was a teenager and the problems in the school started I went to learn kick boxing; it was also in my younger days that I went to visit some of the different esoteric schools that existed in Spain at that time, among them Krisnamurti, Ounspensky and Gurdgieff, Mormons and Jehovah's Witness. I learned the philosophies of many schools and religions until I moved to Atlanta. In the United States I continued my martial arts training for seven years and I forgot spirituality. After seven years I had a big car accident; because it was not my fault, they gave me some money and I went to train in Thailand for a year. When I returned to the USA, I opened a Muay Thai and Krabi Krabong school for two years while I was travelling to Thailand one month per year. Many students came and soon the school became well known in Atlanta.

'One day I was tired of professional fighting; I felt an emptiness in my heart that was telling me that there was something else and that I should continue my path in Asia. Three months later I left everything behind and I went to Thailand where I became a monk for a few months. Every martial arts friend and school partner in Atlanta became very angry with me. They didn't understand why I was leaving. At that moment I didn't have any answer to give them.

Kruu (teacher) Pedro Villalobos shows technique from kneeling position

'After finishing my Buddhist monkhood in Thailand I want to study a spiritual style of Muay Thai because I was tired of rankings and prize fighting. I searched all around Thailand but I failed to find a spiritual Muay Thai martial arts teacher or style. I found really good teachers and I studied with them but they were all focused on fighting or on preserving the fighting heritage of the nation. Disappointed, I decided to open a school in Chiang Mai, Thailand, to blend all the spiritual teachings with the concepts of ancient Muay Thai styles, following just my soul.

'Sometimes it was hard when people laughed in my face, especially when I was doing my best to promote spiritual aspects inside Muay Thai. It's their culture, so when a foreigner teaches Muay in Thailand… A few times they came for a challenge. I fought with them at the entrance of the school, with Thais and even with foreigners. I just took them to the ground and choked them out. When they stood up they could not believe what had happened… Some were very angry, they told me they would show me again! And again… I took them down and choked them one more time. They left and never came back. I knew that soon, the next person would show up at the door of the school and again would do the same thing. These experiences taught me a lot about my ego. I understood later on that when someone laughs at you you have a choice to fight with him or invite him as your teacher for today. When I understood that I laughed at myself a lot about how silly the mind can be…

'During that period I didn't know what to do to continue the inner growth…so I became isolated in the school and started to clear out or reject many teachings that I was taught in the previous twenty years of martial arts practice that I didn't understand. I entered a strange way of life in which many hours of prayers, a few hours of sleep, followed by long sessions of meditation and seven hours of hard training was my routine for five long years. On the full, new, waxing and waning moon days I used to go to caves to visit old monks and hermits all around the north of Thailand. Their teachings were hard and strict but contained many great concepts.

'I will say that Muay Sangha was designed with the only skills that I understood, based in balance, centre line theory and timing, all rounded by a deep spiritual philosophy.'

'I see. And what then drove you to travel to other countries to seek further teachings?'

'Years afterwards, in meditation practice, I kept asking the spirit teacher how I should continue my martial arts path. The answer came, telling me that I should travel in the four directions to better understand the concepts of different martial arts. The four directions were: in the East go to Cambodia, in the South go to Indonesia, in the West to India and in the North to China. It took me three years to travel the four directions, recompiling the "key concepts" of each martial arts style from each country. The core of Muay Sangha style is still the spiritual development of the human being.'

'What were the skills of these teachers which made you devote so much time to studying with them?'

'For a long time I did not have any dealings with any martial arts teacher. I do feel respect and gratefulness towards them for teaching me their vision about fighting. It's been a long time since I departed from the Thai martial arts. I guess I reached a point at which I saw the end of their styles as they did not understand the spiritual practice within the martial arts. And that is when I went to study other disciplines and continue developing my inner self with martial arts training. As I said earlier, I am not looking for winning anything except inner freedom.

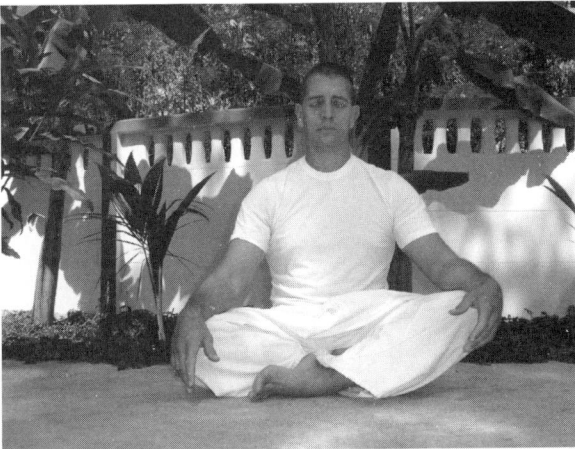

Kruu Pedro meditating at his school in Chiangmai, Thailand

Kruu Pedro faces an attacker in guard stance

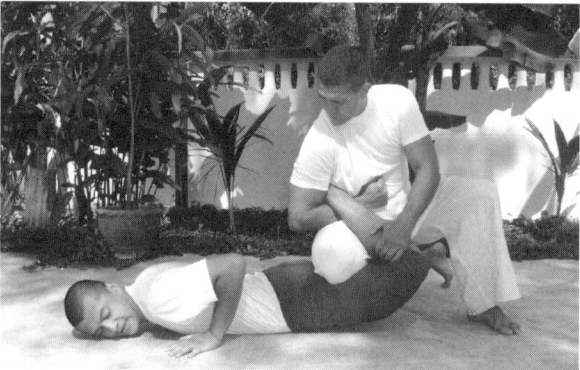

Kruu Pedro shows defence and counter against round kick

'Martial arts are one of the many ways to understand the body and the mind that we possess for an uncertain number of years. Other styles of martial arts share different concepts of movement. Some of those concepts are absorbed according to my vision about fighting – efficient, direct, economic, practical and healthy movements.

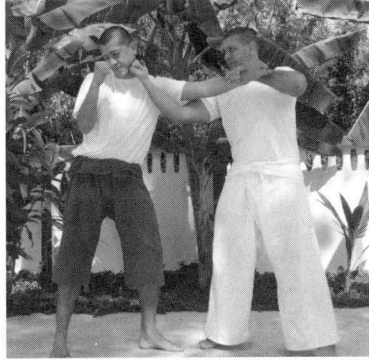

Fighting combination shown by Kruu Pedro

'I did have proof to myself that meditation is the most important task in everyday life. Meditation helps to calm the mind so we can consciously observe the result of our actions. With more practice we will be able to see when our actions are happening and even before they are happening. Seeing and understanding the source of our actions is the first step to end suffering. Meditation is a tool that can help us to understand ourselves better.'

'How do you relate the concept or being of God with the teaching of Emptiness in Buddhism?'

'Talk about God is very delicate. I would like to refer to Him as "The Beginning". The Beginning was there since I opened my eyes, I see him everywhere…in the water, in the fire, in the birds, in the war and in the misery. I see him in everything. For me, He is the universe and all things inside the universe are part of Him. I am very grateful to be part of the universe – to be part of Him, as I consider to be born an opportunity to refine my soul.

'I am grateful to be happy and to be sad; without duality we will not be able to learn about ourselves. To learn, we need to be born many lifetimes and be aware enough to absorb all the life lessons, or to have a spiritual teacher. Buddha was one of the great teachers. His teachings, the Dharma, taught us that, in order to learn, first we need to be aware of our own actions. If we want to be aware, our mind should be trained to be empty – in silence.'

'And how does one align such a violent practice as martial arts with the peaceful way of Buddha?'

'Violence and peace are judgements that exist only in the frontiers of our mind. According to our actions we will have our consequences. If we become involved in constructive actions, they will affect our soul and spirit in a different way than if we do destructive actions. The intentions of our actions are also an important aspect in the chain of Karma. The intention of the Muay Sangha school is to reach inner freedom, even if the actions of fighting are judged as violent. The actions of our school may appear the same as other fighting schools yet our intentions are very different.

'Fighting creates destructive Karma but also, if it is done with awareness, it brings to the student, for a short period of time, a higher level of conscious energy… If this energy is used properly, it can bring the student to a different level of consciousness in a short period of time. Be careful with this, please, as it is the same as it is as if we were walking on the edge of a cliff. Without guidance it can be a destructive path for the student and for the teacher.'

'Please tell me something about your travels in Indonesia, Cambodia, China and India, and why you set out to learn these ancient arts. Can you relate some stories about the teachers you met?'

'As I see it, every human being is special in his own way. Every brother or sister, they have many skills within. Some practise enough to recognise these skills within; for some it is not their time yet. I lived in Thailand for many years and I have travelled all around Asia visiting very amazing people with very amazing skills, but let me share with you that those people are not different from you. How important is it that your neighbour can fly if we are in jail?

'I will not describe how amazing these teachers are, rather how amazing you can become if you truly realise with what kind of gifts you were born. To understand your possibilities, it is necessary to be brave enough to analyse the programmes that since your childhood have been implanted in your brain. Question yourself if the concepts of modern society meet your goals of spiritual growth. If not, I will share with you some other ideas that perhaps can help you in the path.

'To travel the four corners of the world living in contact with your heart, not thinking of the future, rather observing each moment day by day, breathing the ancient knowledge of different cultures and listening the different opinions about life, is important.

'It is not "the more rich the one that has more", rather "the one that needs less". It is an illusion of society that the concept of having more is better. If we all learn to have less, we will have time to cultivate our inner qualities and to learn and experience different cultures and ways of life. These experiences perhaps can give you a different view to understand the actual state in which society lives.

'Breathe in brother and listen who is inside… Open your wings and get ready for the trip of your life. And if you cannot now, don't worry and project a wish to the universe. One day, you may become ready and the universe will provide you with that opportunity.'

'Thank you, those are wise words. What have you learned from teaching and running your school?'

'The greatest lesson was to understand that putting effort into training the people who come to learn can make our own path clearer.'

'What do you hope to accomplish in the future regarding teaching?'

'I am already here!'

'And for your own personal development?'

'Nothing personal, rather to serve brothers and sisters for the good of all.'

'What is the role of a true teacher?'

'To surpass the role of being a true teacher.'

'And that of a true student?'

'To be humble and grateful towards the teacher because he is the one who shares his experiences with him. To respectfully listen carefully and to not disbelieve or believe the teacher, rather to experience the teachings for himself and learn from his own experiences. And…not to forget that all of us have been born with the greatest teacher inside.'

Kruu Pedro enjoys the nature of Northern Thailand as the sun rises

Paul Whitrod

Part 2: The Heritage of the Vedic Warriors

Sifu Paul Whitrod practises Krabi Krabong in Thailand

In the last chapter of Part One, on Chinese martial traditions, Paul Whitrod discussed his training in the art of Chow Gar Southern Mantis Gongfu. He is, however, also an expert in the arts of Thailand and India, having achieved master rank under the tuition of lineage masters of those countries. His long study in the ancient culture of the Vedas gave him an interest in Indian Kalari, the art some consider to be the root of all Asian fighting systems, and then the Thai systems which are of course renowned as some of the most practical and brutal methods of combat. We continue this discussion with Master Paul Whitrod as he shares his experiences along the path of the Vedic warriors.

'Paul, what inspired you to learn Indian martial arts?'

'I had studied Chinese martial arts for a long time, and then around 1991 I met some individuals who practised Indian martial arts. We trained with each other for some time and they suggested I go to India and have a look. In 1999 I went over there.'

'India is quite a different environment to China or Hong Kong; was it difficult for you to study there?'

'No, not really, I am used to that type of atmosphere so it never really shocked me. I think that if you live by the means of the culture that you are in without trying to impose your own then you can live quite comfortably. It's when you start to put your own values on to theirs that you cannot live comfortably. It is very important, and that's why I was comfortable throughout my studies.

'I met several teachers, actually all of their martial arts have roots back to Tamil Nadu. One was Sathidananda, and after meeting him and his family I slowly but surely discovered more of the village arts as I went along. I avoided the more commercial schools, not because they were not any good…just sometimes you need to see a little more than what is put in front of you. The people I initially swapped knowledge with in England were taught by Mathavan, but I heard that he died around 1994. These were all southern styles, Erikan Kalari – most of the film footage you can see on YouTube is of the northern styles, but Tekkan and Erikan are very rarely seen. The footwork is different, you have fixed footsteps, meaning forms where one leg is stationary, you have circling forms, square, triangle, many different ways of moving your feet. Some are based on the square, on Pancha or the number five, on star shape, crouching then jumping up…according to the situation. Northern styles on the other hand have lots more stretching and deeper movement, more like Yoga techniques, and with the southern styles you focus a lot on locking and grappling methods. Basically in Tekkan Kalari you have sixty-four Adi Tarda, which are the sixty-four blocking and attacking techniques to respond to different attacks. Then there are sixty-four locks, sixteen types of footwork and eight positions of the body – so you could be on your front, your back, your side, on one knee, on both knees. From barehand you then move to the wooden weapons such as the short stick, Kuruvadi, similar to the Arnis stick, then the Neduvadi, which is the long stick about nose height. Then you go on to other weapons such as the mace, the sword and shield and so on.'

'And are the techniques or symbolism of the art related to the ancient Vedic texts like the Shrimad Bhagavatam?'

'These arts go back to the Sage Agustia, who learned from Lord Shiva. So Agustia is the patron saint of martial arts and also medicine, which is known as Marmasiliksalayam, a form of South Indian medicine which is similar to Ayurveda. In northern Kalari they say that Parusarama is the founder of their style. Now, according to the Mahabarata [India's epic sacred book], Parusarama vowed never to teach the warrior class martial arts again, he only taught the Brahmins or priestly class. That's why in the northern Kalari you have lots of stretching, salutations and Brahmin prayers.'

'There is a story about Kana, a warrior who wanted to learn martial arts from Parusarama, but Parusarama had vowed never to teach the warriors again after kicking them out of India and chasing them twenty-one times around the globe. They had abused the knowledge. So Kana, who was on the side of Duryodana in the struggle against the Pandavas, approached him to learn martial arts but disguised as a Brahmin. So Parusarama began teaching him military warfare, battlefield tactics, strategy and so on.

'The story goes that one day his teacher was telling him about warfare, and Kana got bitten by an insect. He was hearing about tactics that he could use to defeat Arjuna [the head of the Pandavas]… Now, if he was a Brahmin or priest he would have shown fear and pain, as that class were so sensitive and soft. But being a warrior and oblivious to pain he withstood the pain of the bite in order to hear his teacher. But his teacher looked and saw the insect biting him, giving away his disguise. Then the teacher cursed Kana, saying that during the time he needed the knowledge he would not be able to remember it. So later, during the war, at the point when he needed the tactics it left his body and he could not recall anything!'

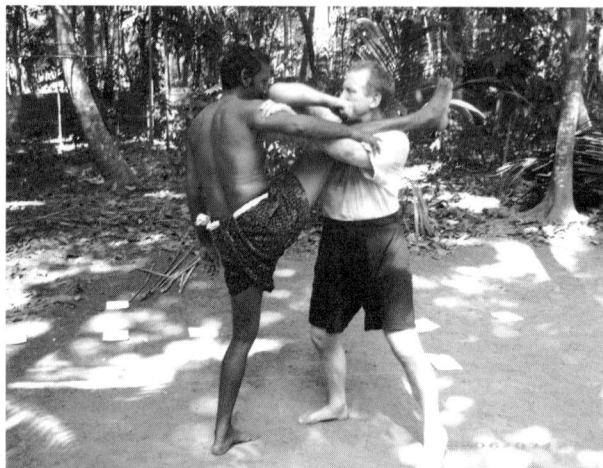

Master Paul Whitrod training Kalari in India

'So do you consider that the northern Kalari styles have lost some martial effectiveness and become more of a Yoga?'

'It's hard to say. One should adhere to the truth in martial arts, and there are lots of martial arts around the world which are more for show and not for fighting. This happens if people don't use the style in fighting for some time, it becomes more for demonstration. Until about thirty years ago in India martial arts was never demonstrated in public, as martial warfare was secret and not for demonstration. With the northern arts I don't know the extent to which they keep that side of things hidden or what's been lost, it's hard to say.'

'Are the southern arts still widespread?'

'Yes, but it is difficult to find as most of the masters keep it in their families. All the people I have learned from – Satchidananda, Master Mradavan Asan, Suresh Asan – they are all from family styles and it was handed down by their fathers. None of them have really taught any outsiders. Also, in India today not many people are interested in learning, same as everywhere.

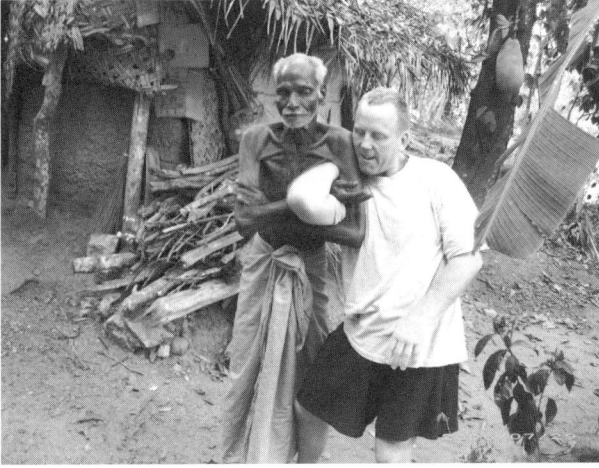

Master Paul Whitrod learning from his Kalari Guru in India

'They are all healers as well. Satchidananda's medicine is quite powerful, a lot of good injury treatments. They have cured many people with problems associated with martial arts, just like in China you have the martial arts and the Dit Da, the fall and hit medicine, side by side. They also do Chowtitirimul, massaging with the foot from Marma point to another Marma point. They do a form of acupressure, but never pressing and holding the point but rather circling massage. They consider it's not good to put a needle in the body unless you are really sick. Even in China today there is a theory now that putting needles in the head is not so good.'

'What impressed you about the skill of the Indian masters?'

'The locking techniques, head locks, that's one of the most interesting things. Very similar to what you might see in Jujitsu now. Some of these skills are very ancient. What we now assume is traditional is not always traditional, it's actually fairly modern, and what we think is modern is actually traditional! For example, Brazilian Jujitsu techniques go back hundreds of years, whereas some of the Chinese forms you see only go back fifty or a hundred years.'

'So from what you have seen do you now think that martial arts have their root in India and spread out all over Asia from there?'

'Some of the people in India emphasise that that is the case. My view is that if it is or is not isn't important, but the important thing is if it is effective or not! Sure, certainly many of the skills you see in Malaysia or Indonesia have their roots in India, that is very clear. But that's not to say that they didn't evolve over time as well. If you train hard and are sincere then you will evolve, that is very important. There is a distinct flavour according to the region. In Indian arts you have the Pranayam or breathing teachings, and some of the exercises where you breathe with two people facing each other, for energy development. Then they have some hard exercises like the hard Heigong [Qigong] from Chinese arts. I was astonished, because some of that was very similar to what Grandmaster Ip Shui taught me long before in Hong Kong! So here I am in India twenty or thirty years later doing almost exactly what Grandmaster showed me.'

'Did you see anyone in India who had genuine Siddhi or spiritual powers?'

'I have heard there are, but I never met anyone there who had a Siddhi, and if I did I am sure I would not be so impressed because of my belief in Hare Krishna. These days Siddhis are very hard to perform! I heard of some people who had but they were not willing to show it. India now has changed; before people were living on the land and trained in martial arts. Now there are a lot of taxes and so on and people don't have time to train. Those who can survive and train are being paid huge sums of money to learn, it has become like a tourist attraction – so you can go there for a couple of weeks, do a bit of sightseeing and then do a bit of Kalari! You pay a lot of money – and that's a shame as the art was never meant to be taught like that.'

'How did you come to study Thai martial arts?'

'Around 1999 I went to Thailand to do some medicine courses, massage and foot massage, at a place called Wat Po. Then I came across Krabi Krabong and I wanted to learn it, it is the Thai martial art and based on the positions of great Indian characters like Rama and Sita from the Ramayana. Weapons include the double swords, single sword, sword and shield, the Nahl, which is like a long stick with a sword in the end which they used to use on elephant back, spear, and the Maisok which looks like the Japanese Tonfa. There are empty-hand skills against weapons, the barehand art is Muay Boraan [ancient boxing]. There are similarities again with the Tamil systems, but the Thai arts may have been a little influenced by Chinese martial arts. For example, in Satchinandanas art there is an uppercut movement which is identical to a technique found in Muay Boraan. In Thai style you have Hanuman Jumps Up, which is an elbow to the top of the head, and you have exactly the same technique in southern Kalari. But, hey, martial arts is martial arts, it is not about culture! First comes the martial arts and then when it develops in a certain country they add other aspects. In Muay Boraan you have a toe kick, and exactly the same toe kick is found in Aditada Southern Kalari.

'In Thailand these guys are tough, they have had about thirty or forty fights by the time they are ten years old, and a hundred fights by the age of sixteen!'

'It is obvious that in ancient times people travelled all across Asia exchanging skills and knowledge...'

'Yes, sure, before the sea levels were low and the landmasses were closer and you could walk from India to Indonesia.'

'Yes...have you seen those satellite photos taken of the underwater bridge between India and Sri Lanka? This was made by Hanuman or Lord Ram...?'

'It was made by all the devotees of Lord Ram. The story was that Rama called the Sea God, but he wouldn't come, until eventually he did come, he said he was sorry and offered a gift. Ram asked that the stones floated on water to the island of Sri Lanka, so all the devotees piled stones on there until they reached Sri Lanka! Obviously we have to be careful but...these are not myths, they are actual events which happened. I am a great believer in the Vedas.'

'Yes, maybe the context is different to what we imagine in modern times. For example, didn't the atom bomb in the Vedas come from a Mantra rather than a mechanical bomb?'

'It was a proper bomb but from Mantra. The chap who brought out knowledge of the modern atom bomb is on film saying that "I have unleashed a power not seen since the days of the great wars of India." Even Srila Prabhupada says that Hitler had the atom bomb,

and if Srila Prabhupada said that, then it's final. Now, where did
Adolf Hitler get all this information from? One of the things which
the Nazis did was to get people from India to decipher the Vedas.
He rejected anyone who had been educated in England, as they
would be contaminated with Western thought. Now, the nuclear
bombs of today are fire bombs, but those of the past were done by
Mantra since those men had done great Tapeshwar [austerities].
The highest weapon was the Brama Astra which was able to destroy
the universe; it was let off by one person called Ashutama. During
the Mahabarata war, knowing he had lost he released his arrow to
destroy the entire war. But like most of these weapons they could
be pushed out and pulled back, but he didn't have the knowledge
to bring it back. At that time Krishna intervened and stopped the
weapon, and he summoned Ashutama. Ashutama had been born
with a jewel on his forehead. Then, for that sin he had done, Krishna
plucked the jewel, and he was told "Until the end of Kali Yuga [the
present age of quarrel] you will be walking the earth"…so he is still
walking the earth with this hole in his head which is festering and
getting bigger and bigger as the Kali Yuga progresses.'

'Hmm, that is a big lesson for those who have created and use
the weapon nowadays…'

'Yes, of course. I was reading what Shrila Prabhupada was
saying and he was talking about all the holes we have made in the
earth. Just like the space in our bodies is kept afloat by air, so too
the earth is kept afloat by its inner force or inner air. So if we keep
doing that then all kinds of things will happen, earthquakes and so
on…and if Shrila Prabhupada says it then it is a hundred per cent
true. Many things he said people think, oh no, it cannot be…but it
is true.'

'Actually, a lot of things he said are now becoming true…'

'Yes. For example, he said that in the future we would be taxed
so much by governments that we would not be able to live in the
cities eventually. And now it is happening! You have to remember
that a spiritual master knows past, present and future. But his main
thing is to promote Krishna consciousness, not to try and foretell
the future for everyone because then you get a different kind of
follower. You should follow him for getting out of this world and
going back to Godhead, to Sri Krishna.'

'Yes. OK, if we return for a moment to the Thai systems, how do they test their skills in terms of weapons and blades…generally how do you work against a live blade without risking death?'

'Well, you know the only time you can test it is when there is a war! Now there are no wars with swords and shields so there is no testing. You can only play with the weapon and see what works. I will give you an example…in India I trained with a live blade against the Guru, and we had sharp knives, and on two or three occasions I cut my hands. There is a risk but you are not going to kill each other! You go to within an inch close. With a wooden knife you would go in and do things…with a real blade there is hesitation and that is what you have to overcome. In the school here we have live blades and if people feel they want to do it then they can. We use the wooden ones, but when we use live blades there is a lot of hesitation as there is fear of the blade, that point coming at you… How far you want to go is up to you.'

'How about your own development of force over the years? You have studied Bagua and Xingyi along with the other arts, do you see things in terms of progressively moving from obvious force, to hidden force to mysterious force?'

'Well, I think you have to change as you get older because your body changes. The idea with martial arts was that you developed a more relaxed power, you cannot be tense. For my own personal development I take a leaf out of everything. It is all an experience. Do you need to learn every martial art? No, but you need to know what is important for your own development. If you have to go outside of your system, then maybe that is needed…

'My personal change is in my approach to a lot of things. How to move the body, how to use the art to defend myself, that is what is important for me. As for the type of power I have, I leave it to the people I train with to tell you that! But to be able to use your power and strength to overcome someone who is twice as big, then you need to develop technique and skill as well as force.

'Basics should always be there as they are your foundation. I spend a lot of time now doing grappling and locking; especially as you get older this is vital in order to subdue and control a person. Body mechanics as well, how to manipulate his centre by pulling, pushing and so on, and as you get older your energy level is very different to a young person so you need more skill. Some people ask if high kicks are effective – well, of course they are, but it depends on your ability, it has nothing to do with whether they are high or low. Martial arts is about self-defence, this is very important to me.'

'How do you advise people who are struggling with the fear of death? What is the relevance of martial or spiritual work to facing our inevitable death?'

'Well, that is to do with the spiritual life. Martial arts is a discipline of the body, but if you are able to have some spiritual life and understand yourself as being a soul it is more important. If you understand that you are a soul then you are not so bewildered by your coming death. You know the verse in Bhagavadgita: As the embodied soul passes from youth to old age to death, the sober person is not bewildered by such change. It is just like you have your clothes, then they wear out, so you take another body. At this very moment our body is wearing out, at this very moment we are reincarnating ourselves. You have a different body to fifteen years ago, but you are still with this body. The ultimate change is when this body is totally useless and death comes.

'Martial arts can only discipline the body. All martial arts begin with some form of salutation, some form of respect sequence, so with this you can start asking yourself questions and those questions will be relevant for your stage. You have to change and learn. If you are still thinking the same way as seven years ago then you have not learned! For us this is our opportunity, here in this human form, to enquire, and that's why martial arts starts with salutation.'

'What are your plans for the future?'

'I have just returned from India and Thailand where I visited the Gurus. I would like to see myself develop further in Krishna consciousness, have a farm where I can grow organic vegetables… I love training and exercise but it is not everything. I will always be training and teaching people, that I love. My plan for the future? Hmmm…let Krishna decide, fight for Krishna!'

Paul Whitrod practising Krabi Krabong weapons in Thailand

APPENDIX

Some Stories of the Masters

Here are a few stories I have heard from friends over the years about different masters and adepts.

The Great Daoist Master Lio Pei Zhong

Born in 1883 in Shandong Province, Lio Pei Zhong was recognised at a young age by certain special marks on his body and thus entered the Imperial Palace at the age of nine. There he learned astrology, geomancy, Feng Shui, meditation and Taijquan. The Empress Mother appointed him as her astrologer when he was aged only fifteen, and he held the position for four years. It was then that Lio Dao Ran ordered him to leave the palace and go to Kun Lun Shan. Carrying only a very simple bag and a sword from his family he spent one year walking to Kun Lun.

Once there Lio Pei Zhong stayed for several years, learning from three very special teachers. The first was Lao Tze, the second was Hong Jwing Shi Ju (Original Ancestor) and the third was Lu Dong Bin, one of the famous Eight Daoist Immortals. After some years the three teachers told him that he needed to leave and help people. So he then returned to China, and hearing that the revolutionary hero Dr Sun Yat Sen was in the jail of Jing Wen (the emperor's brother), he rescued him. That was why when Sun was dying he ordered Chiang Kai Shek to treat the Daoist master as a National Teacher.

When the Guomingtang fled to Taiwan Chiang invited Lio to go, so he moved there and set up two temples to begin training and helping people. It was there, at Yang Ming Mountain just outside of Taipei City, that Chen Yuen San began training with the Daoist as a young boy. He would visit him a few times a year and spend time with the master.

Grandmaster Lio developed a theory called Dao-Gong, which posits ten systems which permeate the universe. These systems emit ten energies, five long wave (low frequency) and five short wave (high frequency), the Tien Gan. Then there are also twelve systems on earth, six long and six short wave, the Di-Jir. It is due to these functions that all life systems are formed. The Jing-Qi-Shen (essence, energy, spirit) comes from the effect between the Tien Gan and the Di-Jir. Human beings should practise to enable Yin–Yang inside the body to be balanced, and Qi can be enhanced by Yin–Yang harmony. We can absorb energy from the Sun, Stars, Moon, Water, Wind and Earth.

I heard that Grandmaster Lio had many special abilities. He could appear to people in dreams to give teachings and would make 'unusual things happen'. For example, once the old Daoist was walking through a train station lobby with a student when a brash young man bumped heavily into him and walked off without saying anything. The old Daoist walked around him in a circle and then left to go and sit in a nearby tea shop. The young hooligan, meanwhile, was unable to leave the circle of energy and began to panic. A policeman came over and asked him if by any chance he had offended an old man, and told him that unless he apologised he would not get free. Finally the young man called his apologies and Grandmaster Lio released the energy, giving the hooligan an unforgettable lesson in good manners and treating the elderly with respect!

Whilst in his eighties Lio Pei Zhong married and had a child, and finally passed away in his nineties leaving his teachings with his disciples in Taiwan.

Sun Lu Tang

Sun became famous for two things – first was his incredibly fast walking and footwork,[1] even when he was in his old age, and the second was that he had written extremely deep books on the martial arts of Bagua, Xingyi and Taijiquan, effectively promoting a theory of these three styles being the 'internal' or Neiji boxing systems as opposed to the external arts of Shaolin. Sun's favourite technique was Xingyi's tiger form, a double Piquan to the chest done in a loose pouncing type of action. He correctly worked out the date of his death a year before it happened, and died in a peaceful and conscious manner, apparently by sitting still in meditation and then simply leaving. His son also had skill, and when his students in the park asked him how he was so powerful he told them that by doing standing 'hold the ball' Qigong they too could achieve the same skill. However, his training at home involved using a very heavy steel pole, which he didn't mention to people.

Shang Yunxiang

This rather short and powerfully built man was a real expert in using Xingyiquan to fight with. He walked miles a day barefoot doing the Beng Quan or Crushing Fist form. In his old age he lost his sight but continued to teach. He would sit in one room and shout out to the students training next door. 'No! That is not correct!' or 'Good!' When students asked him how he knew without being able to see he replied that the sound was enough to tell. If the five fists were done badly the sound would be long and dull, if done well it would be a sudden clap like thunder!

The Fruit Monk

This Pure Land Buddhist monk was born in China and then moved to Taiwan, spending decades living in a cave which he shared with a tiger and eating nothing but fruit. He rarely spoke but what he did say was profound.

When asked how to find enlightenment he said, 'Are you honest?'

When asked how to be successful he replied, 'Are you honest?'

At his death there were many strange phenomena, and at his funeral service hundreds of people saw strange lights in the sky which were photographed from many different angles.

This phenomenon of light is often associated with great spiritual beings and Buddhist monks. The famous Xu Yun or Empty Cloud of the last century, who died aged one hundred and twenty years, once did a ritual and a light shone for seven continuous days from a stupa (a Buddhist dome-shaped structure which contains sacred objects and relics), witnessed by the thousands of people attending.

These photos show some of the strange lights photographed at the Fruit Monk's funeral in Taiwan

Note

1. Shihan Tanaka told me of his Buddhist brother in Japan who had spent two weeks walking with one of the elder Marathon Monks on Mount Hiei near Kyoto. He said that the old monk was unbelievably fast, more amazing because the six-hour non-stop walk was up and down very steep and tortuous mountain tracks mostly in pitch black and mist. His conclusion was that it would be impossible for normal people to do this without a spiritual power moving them; it was far more than just a great athletic feat of endurance. This reminds me of another story which I heard from a monk who went to stay in Samye Ling Buddhist Monastery in Scotland. The first night he was there he was woken by a very strange sound which went on for ages; curious, he went out only to see the head monk Lama Yeshe moving very fast in front of a stack of bricks in almost pitch black. The next morning the monk was surprised to see a perfectly made brick wall where the bricks had been.

Bibliography and Information

Blacker, Carmen (1999) *The Catalpa Bow: A Study of Shamanistic Practices in Japan*. London: Routledge.

Blofeld, John (2009) *Bodhisattva of Compassion: The Mystical Tradition of Kuan Yin*. (Shambhala Classics.) Boston, MA: Shambhala Publications.

Cheong Cheng Leong and Draeger, Donn (1977) *Phoenix-Eye Fist*. New York: Weatherhill.

Evans, John Maki (1992) *Trog*. San Francisco, CA: Saru Press International.

Evans, John Maki (2010) *KuriKara: The Sword and the Serpent*. Berkeley, CA: Blue Snake Books.

Jinghan, He (2009) *Bagua Quan Foundation Training*. London: Singing Dragon.

Kozma, Alex (2003) *Beyond the Mysterious Gate*. Taipei: Line of Intent Books. (Out of print)

Kozma, Alex (2005) *A Single Perfect Note on the Bamboo Flute*. Taipei: Line of Intent Books.

Kozma, Alex (2010) *Esoteric Warriors*. London: Paul H. Crompton.

Wei, Lindsey (2013) *The Valley Spirit: A Female Story of Daoist Cultivation*. London: Singing Dragon.

Whitrod, Paul (1986) *Chow Gar Praying Mantis Kung Fu*. London: Paul H. Crompton.

For details of instructional internal martial arts films by the author please contact: retreats108@gmail.com

Teachings by Dr Serge Augier: www.sergeaugier.com

Chow Gar Mantis UK Headquarters in London with Master Paul Whitrod: www.paulwhitrod.com

Muay Sangha Fighting Arts in Thailand with Kruu Pedro: www.ancientmuaythai.com

For other masters in this book contact the author: retreats108@gmail.com